IMAGES
of America

HISTORIC MEXICO

Town of Mexico

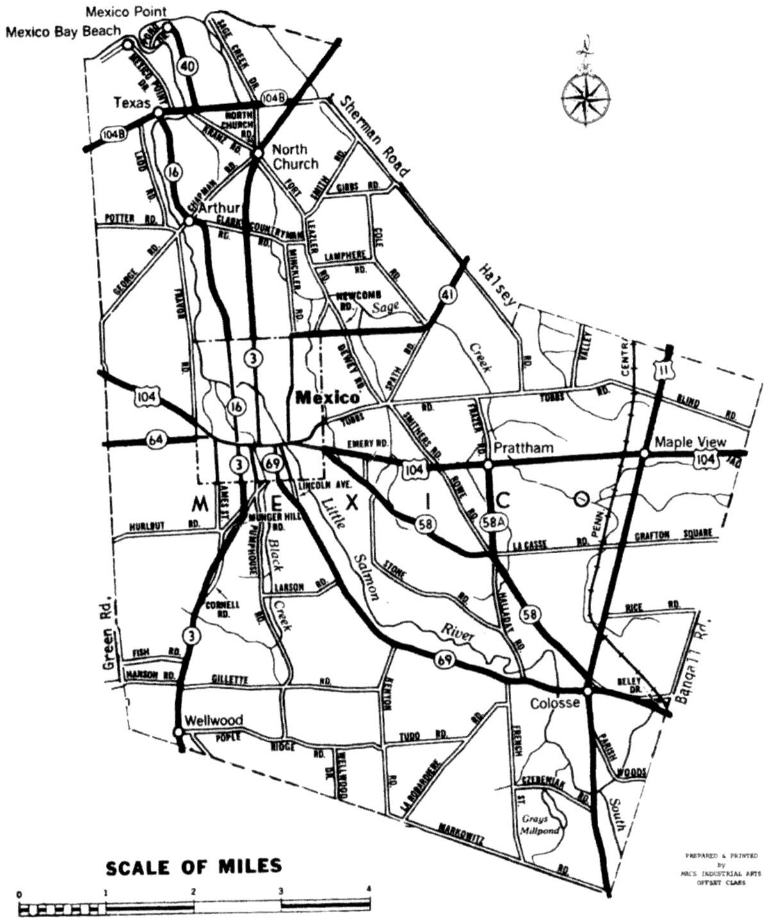

This map of the town of Mexico was prepared and printed by the Mexico Academy and Central School industrial arts offset class for the Mexico Historical Society.

On the cover: The soil in Oswego County is excellent for raising strawberries. Many farmers put in large fields of the plants. The women and children picked the ripe fruit to be shipped by team to cities. (Courtesy of the Mexico Historical Society.)

IMAGES
of America

HISTORIC MEXICO

Bonnie Shumway

ARCADIA
PUBLISHING

ISBN 978-0-7385-6593-4

Published by Arcadia Publishing
Charleston, South Carolina

Printed in the United States of America

Library of Congress Control Number: 2009921711

For all general information, please contact Arcadia Publishing:
Telephone 843-853-2070
Fax 843-853-0044
E-mail sales@arcadiapublishing.com
For customer service and orders:
Toll-Free 1-888-313-2665

Visit us on the Internet at www.arcadiapublishing.com

This book is dedicated to the members of Mexico Historical Society, who collect, preserve, and share the history of Mexico.

CONTENTS

ACKNOWLEDGMENTS

Many people helped to get this book ready for publication. A special thanks goes to Main Charles Vaughn for doing the scanning of all the pictures and to Marcia DeLong for doing all the typing. Proofreading was done by Allie and John Proud, Marilyn and Charles Marks, and Sue Vaughn. Also helping were Madelyn Schmidt, Edith Marsden, and Sandra Scott. Unless otherwise noted, all pictures are from the collection of the Mexico Historical Society.

Introduction

The residents of Mexico are often asked, "How did Mexico get its name?" The name was used for this area three times. In 1792, the land commissioners were directed by the State of New York to lay out more towns in the center of the state as the population began to move farther west. They formed a town from Oswego County south through what are today Onondaga and Cortland Counties and named it Mexico. Onondaga and Cortland Counties detached in 1794 to make individual counties, leaving only three or four settlers in the north section of the township, and the organization was dissolved. In 1794, George Scriba, a land speculator, bought a large tract of land and used the name Mexico. The patent included Oswego County east of the Oswego River, across the north shore of Oneida Lake, north following Black River, and a large portion of Jefferson County. The third time the name was used was by Benjamin Wright, the surveyor of Scriba patent, in 1795. He reported to Scriba that township No. 20 (Mexico) had the best soil and water in the patent. Perhaps Scriba and Wright just used the commissioner's name, or maybe they heard the name elsewhere and decided it was a fine name for the new township. In 1796, there were two Mexicos—the surveyed large Scriba patent and the 20th town within it. There are still two Mexicos today—the town of Mexico and the village of Mexico.

A second question residents are asked is "Why is Mexico called the mother of towns?" Taking into consideration the first Mexico of 1792 and the second Mexico of 1796, there are 84 daughter towns, as a whole or in part, that can claim Mexico as their mother.

There were very few settlers here in 1796. More families began to come in the early 1800s, and settlements began to organize with cabins, a church, a school, and a general store. There was a sawmill and later a cheese plant, a blacksmith, a mill (in Mexico), and a tavern. Colosse was the first settlement and later Prattham (which disappeared through the years), Maple View, Texas (first called Vera Cruz), and of course the village of Mexico. The latter was a self-contained settlement with the pioneers raising their own food and making their own clothes. What they could not get for themselves came from traveling salesmen, a cobbler, or a seamstress. They saw their neighbors at church or holidays and special events, such as a wedding or a birth where the women acted as midwives for one another if the doctor could not get there in time.

The purpose of this book is to share with all those interested in Mexico how the people lived and played from about 1900 to 1939. There are a few pictures before and a few after, but for the most part, the reader will see how the town and village looked 100 years ago. A chapter on churches was important. It was one of the first considerations for the pioneers, especially the women. They brought the love of their church with them and wanted a church in their new community for themselves and the children. The men agreed and put up a building after homes were built and the land cleared.

They also knew the importance of an education. The boys needed as much as they could get, and the girls needed to read and write, although any math past multiplication and division was thought to be too much for a girl's delicate brain. The boys had work to do on the farms from the first of March to the end of the harvest season in October, so school for them was divided into summer school and winter school, the boys attending the latter.

Everyone loved the companionship and fun of a community event. They crowded the streets for a Memorial Day or Fourth of July parade, and a special day always had several events planned so the community enjoyed a whole day of fellowship. A few pictures in the book show this. Sometimes it was an unplanned day, like a Sunday at the lake when 100 people would gather for a picnic or a ball game or to just sit quietly in the shade. On the east side of Mexico Point, the Twice Told Hotel was the most popular for that kind of a day. On the west side, the Mexico Point Inn did not have a large field for play, but it was host for an elegant dinner for a group or organization, as well as individuals.

Mexico is just far enough inland from Lake Ontario for the northwest winds to blow clouds full of moisture and drop snow on the town. It does not get as much as the foothills, but one chapter is about snow and dealing with it in days gone by.

An effort was made not to use pictures that have been seen in other publications but unusual ones like ones of the inside of the Presbyterian church after the ceiling fell in or the 1932 girls' basketball team. There are many old houses in Mexico, and a few were chosen for the book because of their outstanding architecture or because of the people who lived in them. These are found in the sixth chapter and show a few of the interesting people of the community in days gone by. There are many more houses to tell about and many more people who have contributed much to the community to be told another time. For more information on any of the photographs, contact the Mexico Historical Society. The purpose of the book is not to tell the complete history of Mexico but to show life from a different era. It is hoped that readers enjoy it.

One

AROUND TOWN

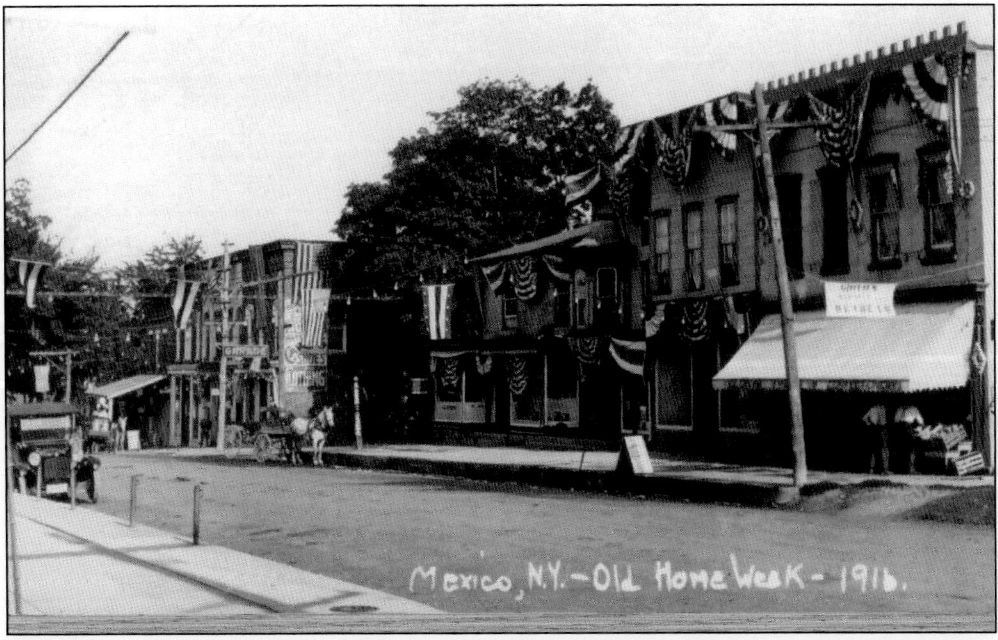

The whole village became involved in the old home week celebration in 1916. There were 130 people on committees. Activities included church reunions, ball games, a grand reception with music and singing, an automobile ride to the lake for visitors, a parade, a concert, a formal ball at Washington Hall, and other events. Hundreds of people came to participate and share memories. (Courtesy of the Barry Haynes collection.)

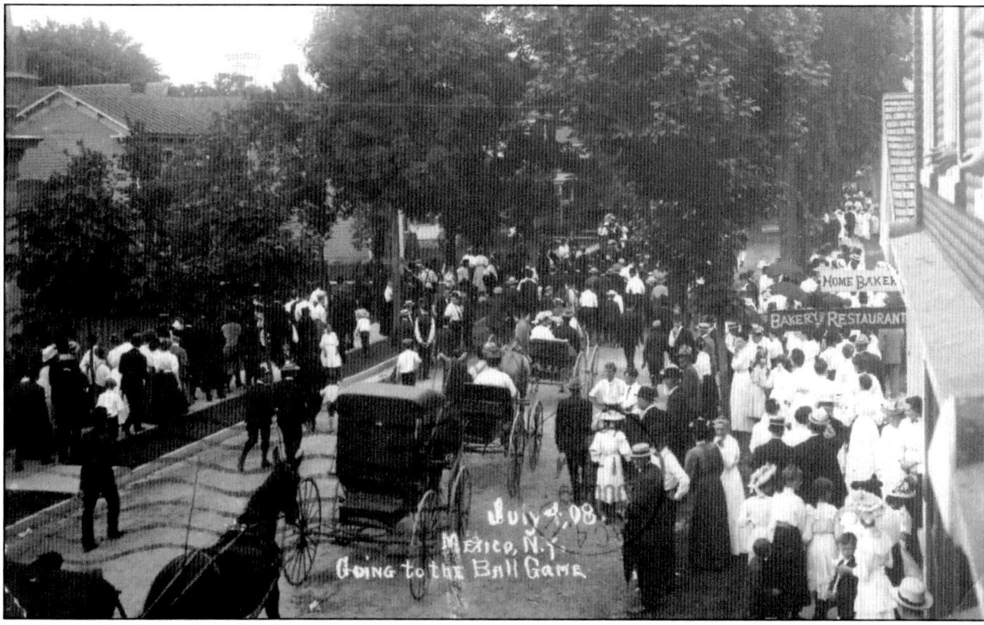

In the early days, the whole community took time off from daily work to celebrate the glorious Fourth of July. Firemen planned a day of celebration that always included music by the local band, oratories, and games like sack races or climbing a greased pole. The finale was fireworks or a huge bonfire. In 1908, the crowd moves down South Jefferson Street to a ball game. (Author's collection.)

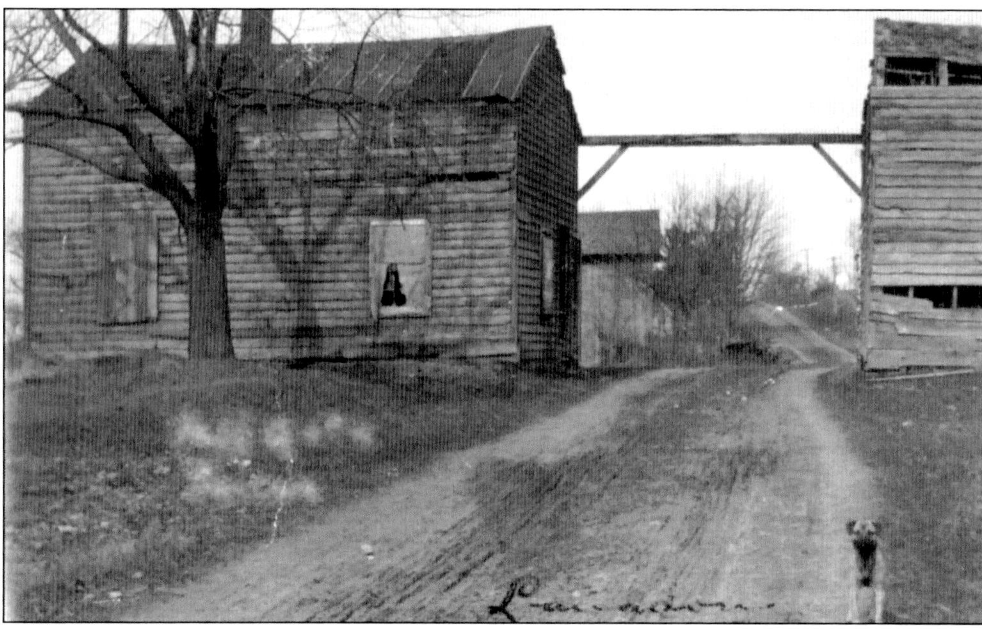

Under this picture is written, "One of Oswego County's great landmarks which burned in the fall of '05 [1905]." The Rome Oswego Plank Road Company was organized in 1847 with Mexico's James S. Chandler as president. The company built the plank road through Scriba, New Haven, Mexico, and Williamstown. This tollhouse stood west of the town of Mexico on Hughes Road near George Road. (Author's collection.)

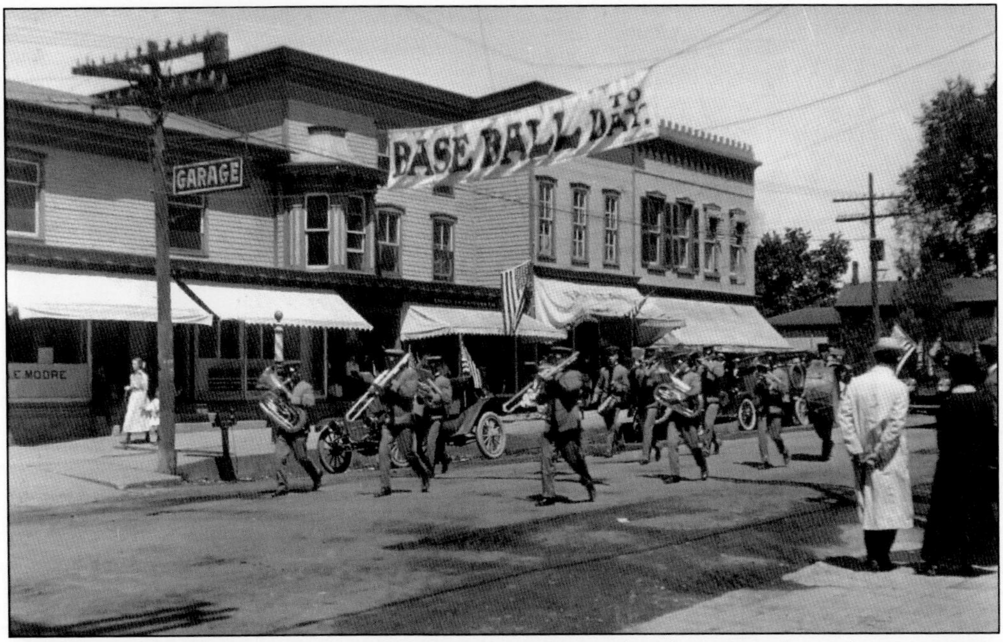

F. J. Smith organized the Mexico Chamber of Commerce band in 1919, shown here marching down Main Street. Glen Smith, his son, became director in 1925, and the name was changed to the Mexico Merchants band. There are some members of the community who remember the Thursday night street concerts of the 1920s and 1930s. Mexico has had a band to lead parades since the Colosse band was organized in 1873 (Courtesy of the Barry Haynes collection.)

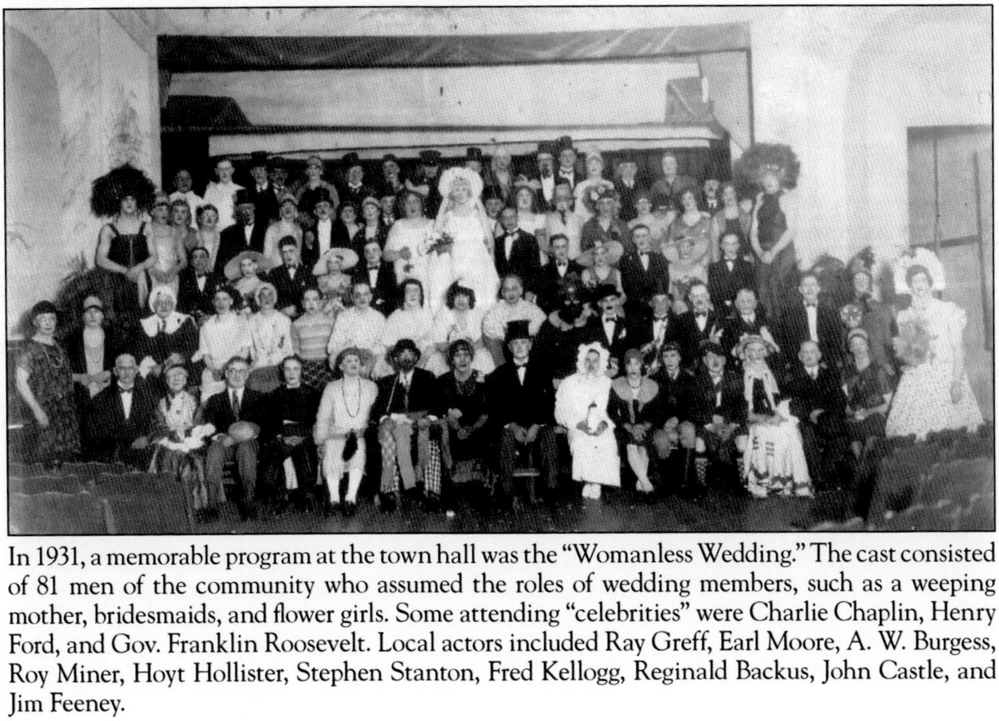

In 1931, a memorable program at the town hall was the "Womanless Wedding." The cast consisted of 81 men of the community who assumed the roles of wedding members, such as a weeping mother, bridesmaids, and flower girls. Some attending "celebrities" were Charlie Chaplin, Henry Ford, and Gov. Franklin Roosevelt. Local actors included Ray Greff, Earl Moore, A. W. Burgess, Roy Miner, Hoyt Hollister, Stephen Stanton, Fred Kellogg, Reginald Backus, John Castle, and Jim Feeney.

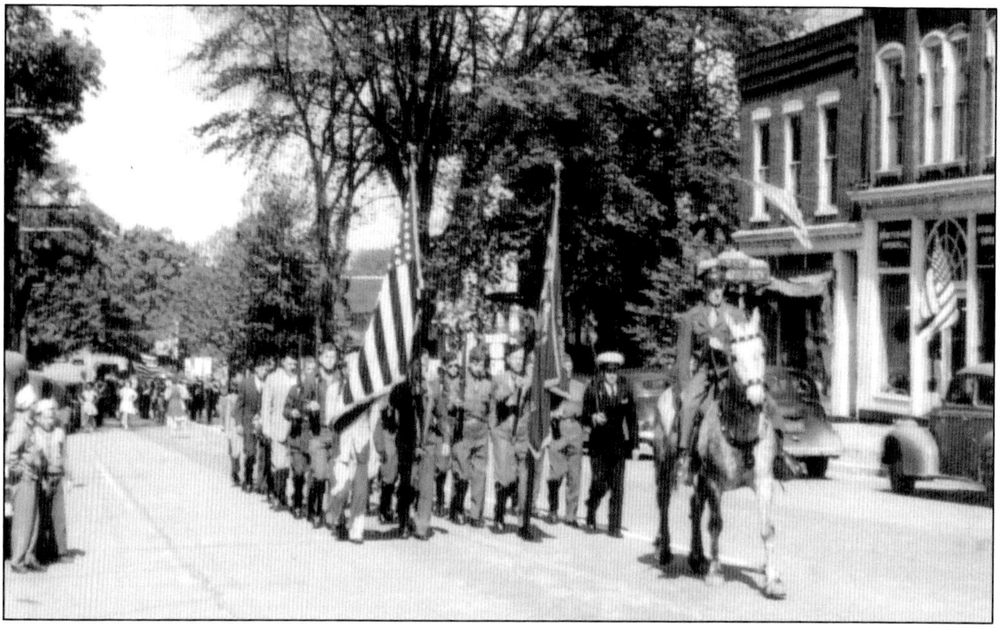

Bill Preman, a World War II veteran, was the marshal for the Mexico Memorial Day parade for many years before his death in March 1977. The year he died, the parade was led by his horse with an empty saddle and boots turned backward in honor of the fallen soldier. The parade was first organized by Civil War veterans and continues today under the direction of the Veterans of Foreign Wars (VFW).

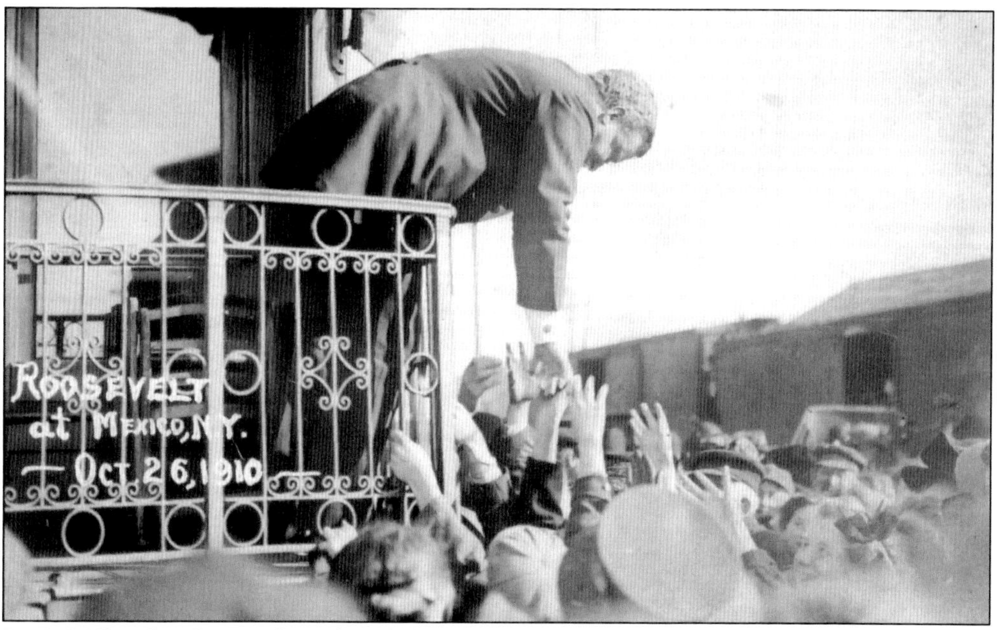

In 1910, Theodore Roosevelt's political philosophy brought him into conflict with the Republican Party's conservative leadership. When he did not get support from Pres. William Howard Taft, he went to the people with a tour of Upstate New York. He traveled by railroad from Oswego to Watertown and through Mexico on October 26, presenting the policy of the Progressive Party. Roosevelt was the presidential candidate for the Bull Moose Party in 1912.

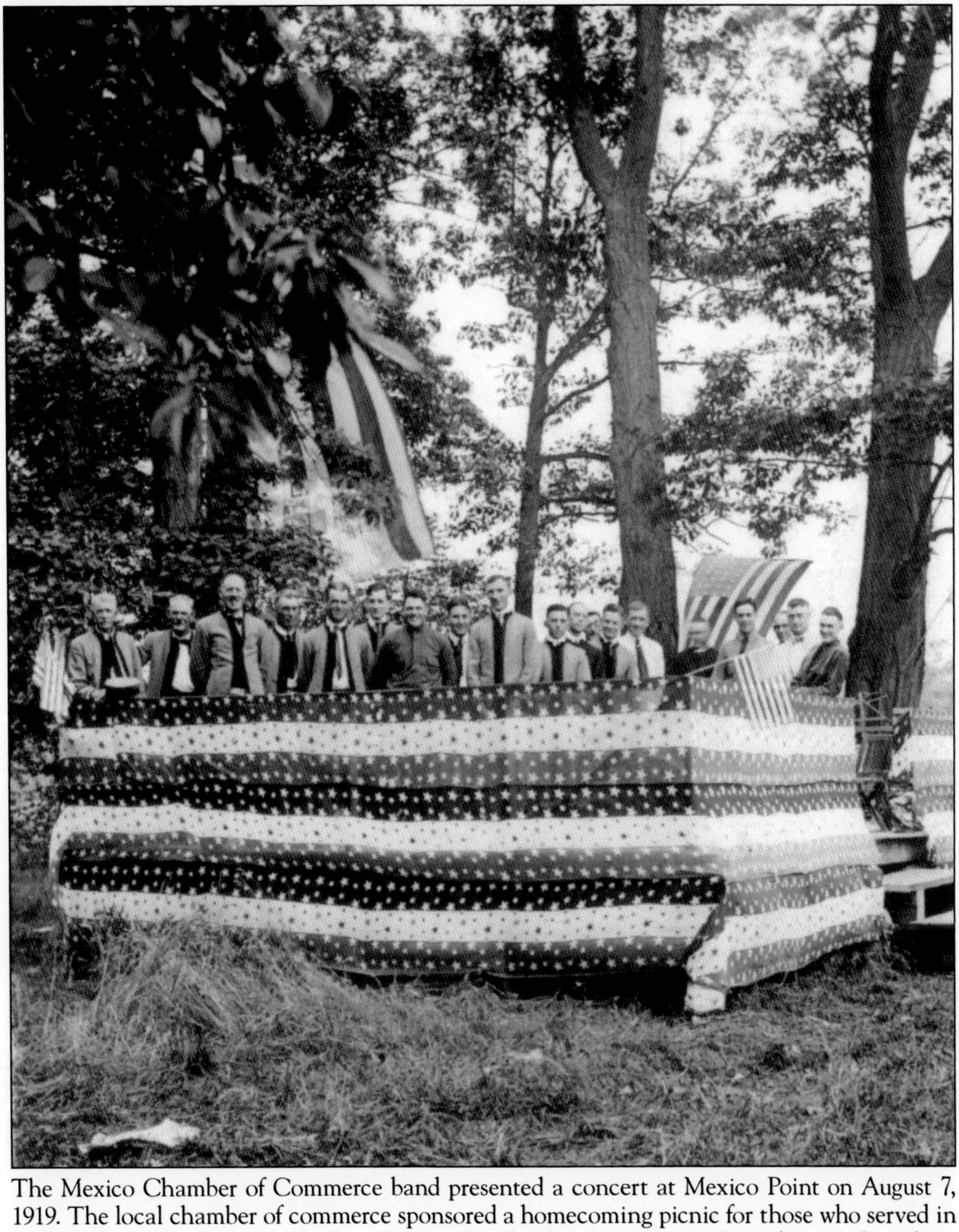

The Mexico Chamber of Commerce band presented a concert at Mexico Point on August 7, 1919. The local chamber of commerce sponsored a homecoming picnic for those who served in World War I. The guest speaker was Roosevelt, who flew in a Curtiss Canadian airplane from Watertown and landed in Ramsey's Field. The trip lasted 50 minutes. He was then driven to the grove at the Twice Told Hotel at the lake. He spoke of being enthused about the future of the American Legion and the return of the servicemen of whom it would be composed. He said, "Before the war we heard talk from fellows who wanted to get what the country owed them. During the war they put something into the country. The service men now have stock in this country. They are interested in its future and how it is to be run. First, last, and always, America for all Americans." The local newspaper reported that a crowd of 12,000 to 15,000 attended the event. (Courtesy of the Barry Haynes collection.)

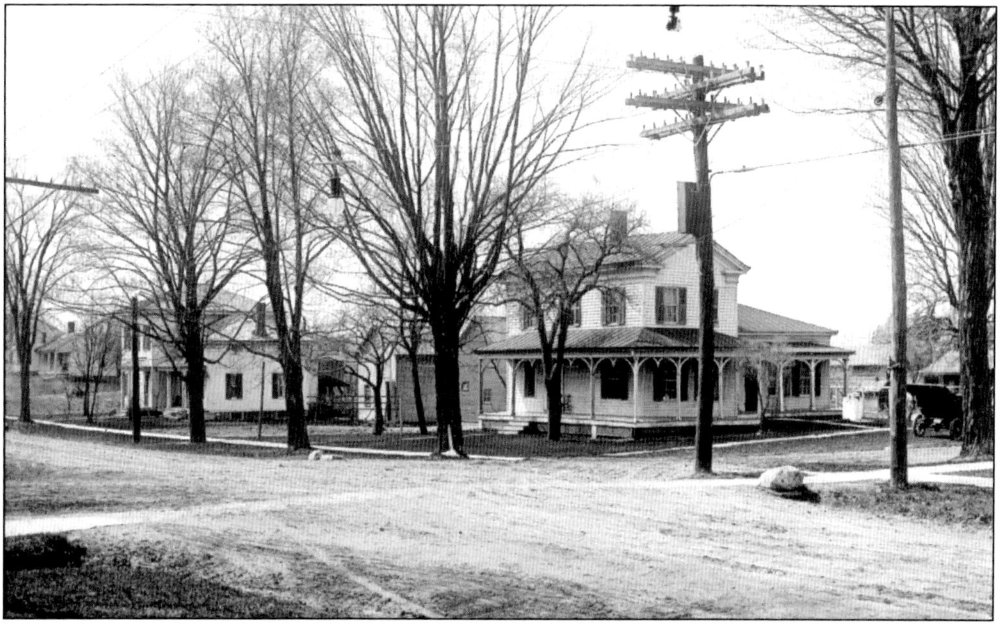

The corner of Main Street and Mill Street (Academy Street) is shown around 1910. The village encouraged home owners to replace sidewalks with cement or flagstone walks for many years, and the walk in the foreground shows that the owners had complied. The lovely home became a paint store in the 1940s and was last used as a Century 21 Real Estate office until its demise, which made room for McDonald's in the 1990s. (Author's collection.)

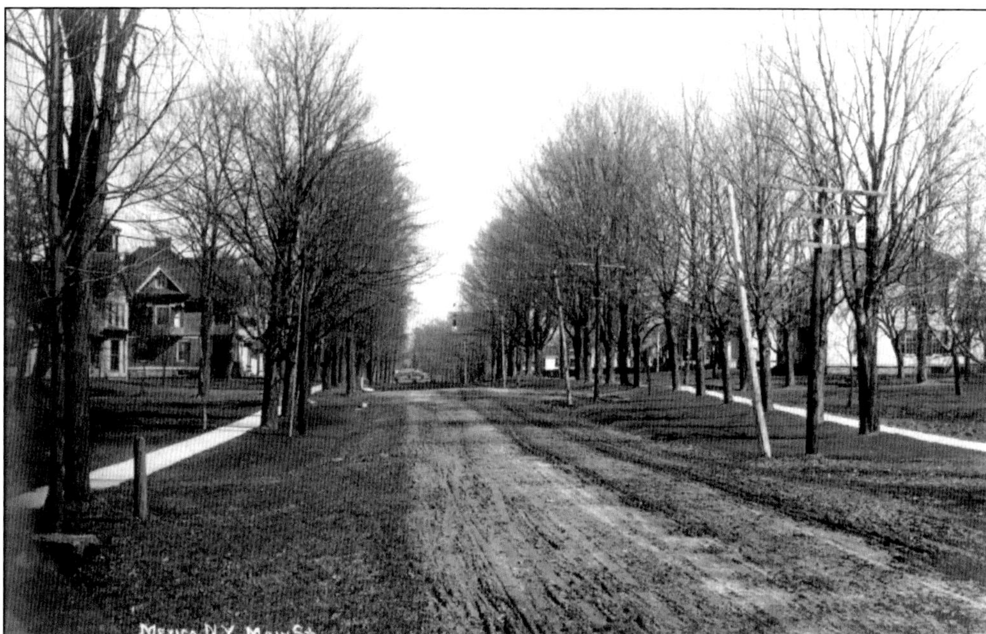

Main Street was hardly more than a path at the beginning of the 1900s. This photograph is looking east with a streetlight at the intersection of Main Street and Norman Avenue hanging in the middle of the picture. The trees were planted between the new sidewalks and the dirt streets as homes were built. (Author's collection.)

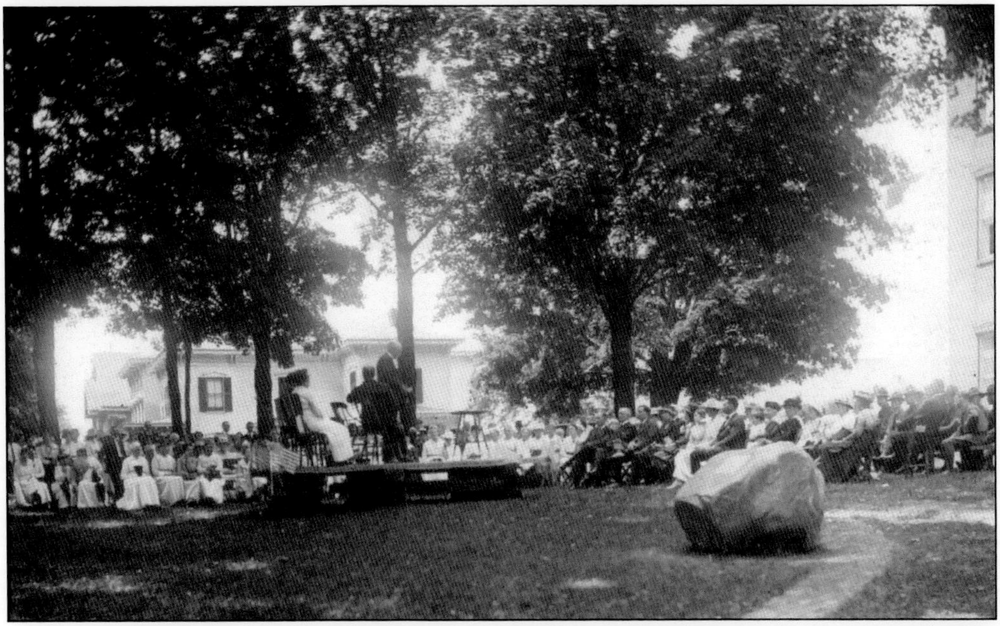

Dedication ceremonies were held when a large boulder was placed on the academy grounds after World War I. A plaque on the stone honors Lt. Donald Stone and Lt. Gurley Davis, two men who lost their lives during the war. Stone served in the French Ambulance Corps and in the Lafayette Escadrille. He was shot down in 1918. Davis died of pneumonia in a Brest hospital in 1918. (Author's collection.)

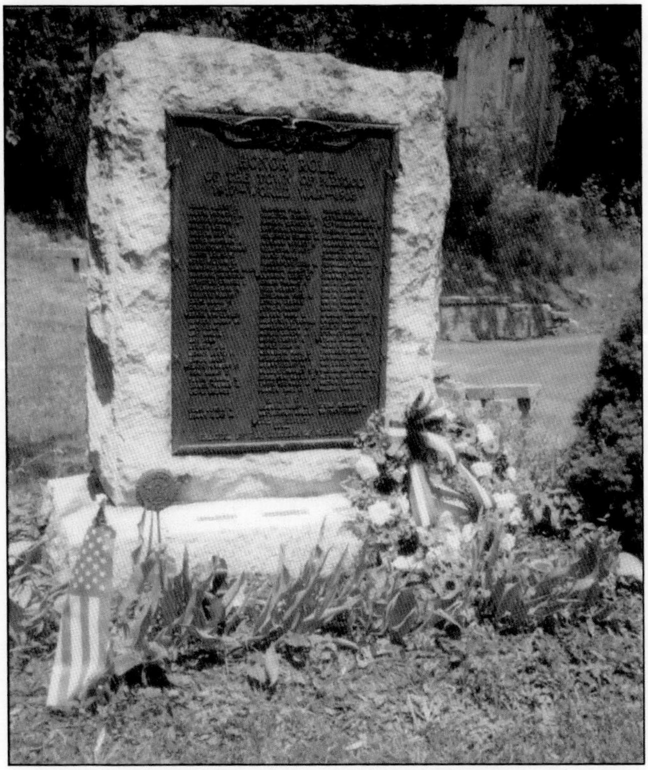

The veterans of World War I organized the Stone Davis Post of the American Legion and were issued their charter in 1920. The post auxiliary raised money for a monument to honor the young men who went into the service of their country during the war. The veterans' monument was placed on school grounds, east of Black Creek, and bears the names of 92 veterans, including 6 who made the supreme sacrifice.

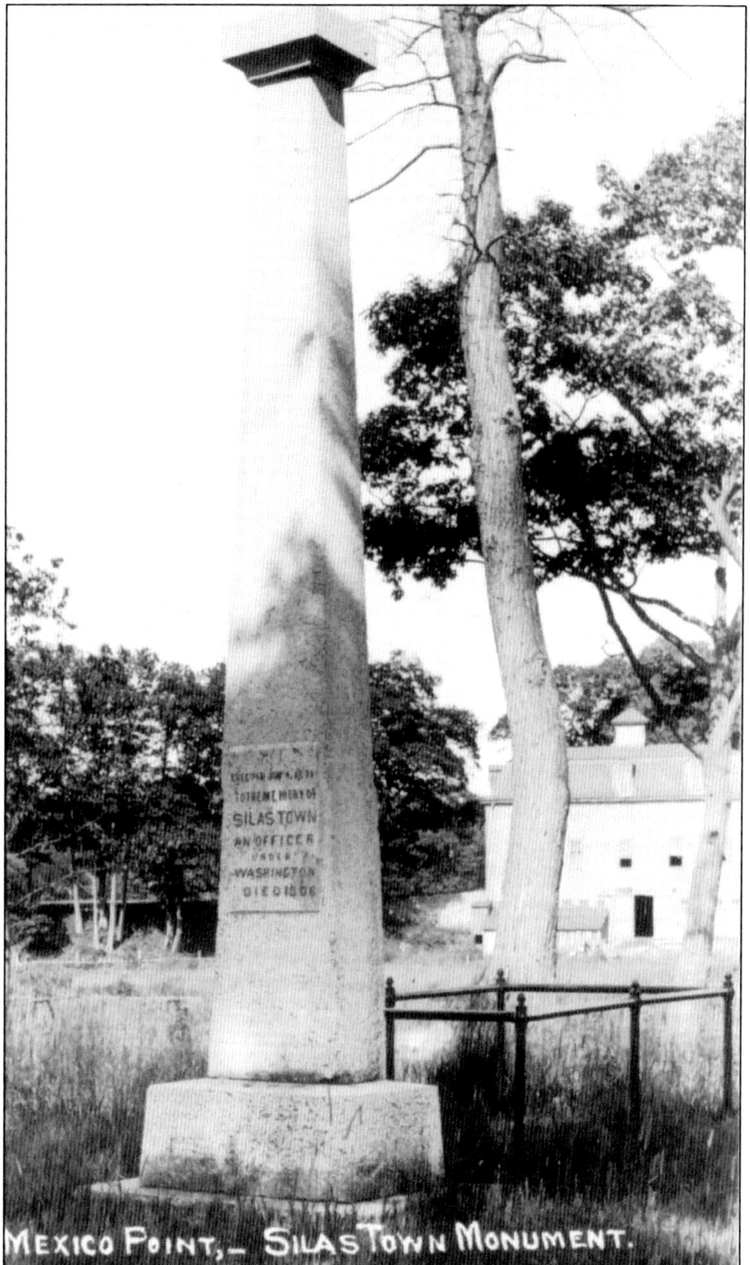

A monument was erected on July 4, 1871, on a small island at Mexico Point to commemorate the burial place of Silas Town, a revolutionary soldier and government spy who aided George Washington. In 1777, Town learned that Col. Barry St. Leger was going to invade New York by way of Lake Ontario. Town reached Mexico Point before St. Leger, concealed himself in the underbrush, and heard the plans for getting to Fort Stanwix. Town was able to report to the commander at Fort Stanwix to allow time for the troops to prepare for the attack, and the invading troops retreated. Town returned to Mexico after the war and lived a solitary life along the shores of Lake Ontario. He died in 1806 but was neglected until 1871 when a monument was erected. (Author's collection.)

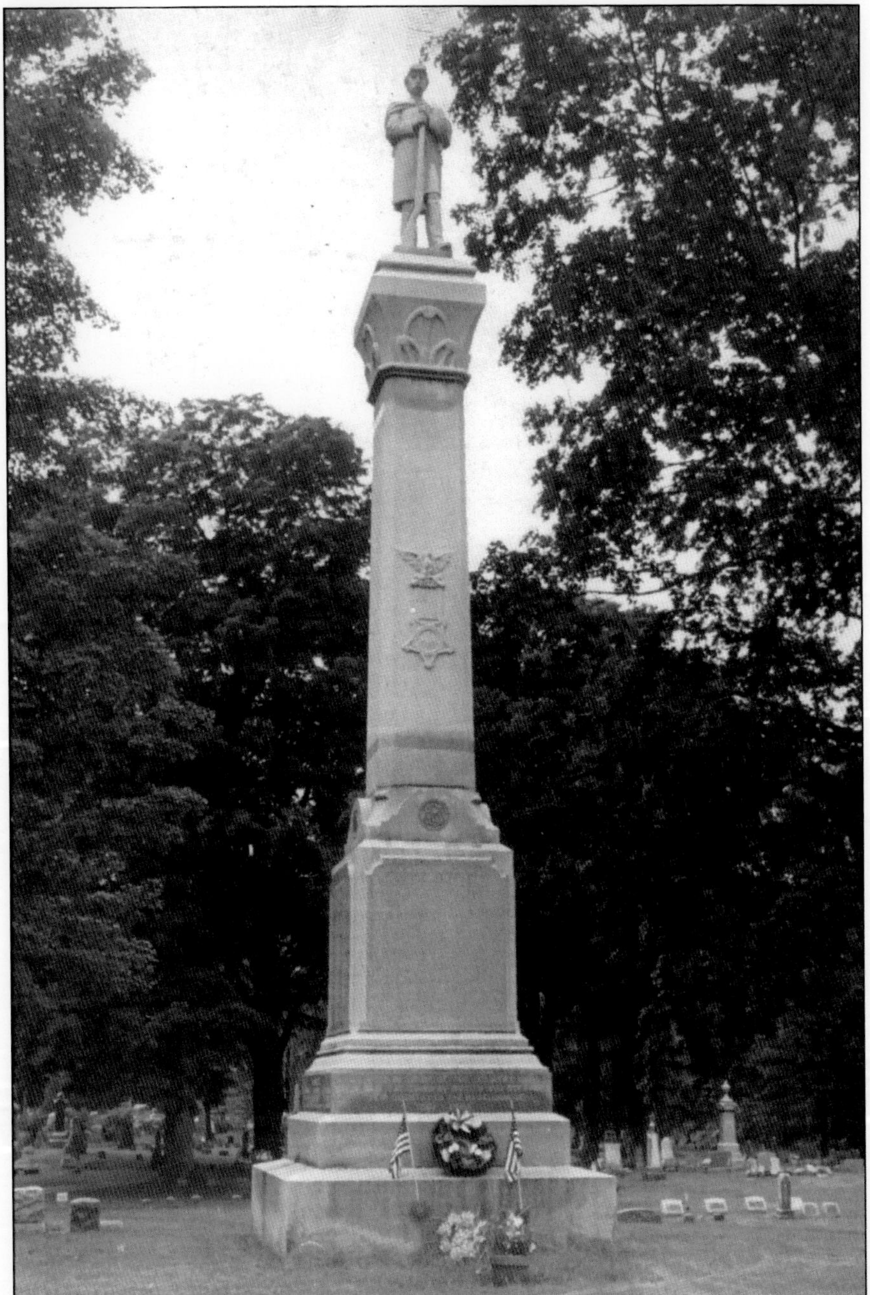

As early as 1865, the people of Mexico began to think of a memorial for the Civil War veterans. The idea was discussed every few years, but it was not until 1888 when final action was taken. The committee decided on a 34-foot-tall granite monument surmounted by a private soldier standing at rest. The monument arrived in 1889. There had been heavy rains, and by early July, the roads were deep mud, and the wagons had extreme difficulty moving the monument from the train station to the cemetery. A Miller wagon was brought over and stood the test. Built to carry 5 tons, yet 10 tons were loaded, it got to the cemetery safely. Memorial Day services have been held at the monument since it was erected.

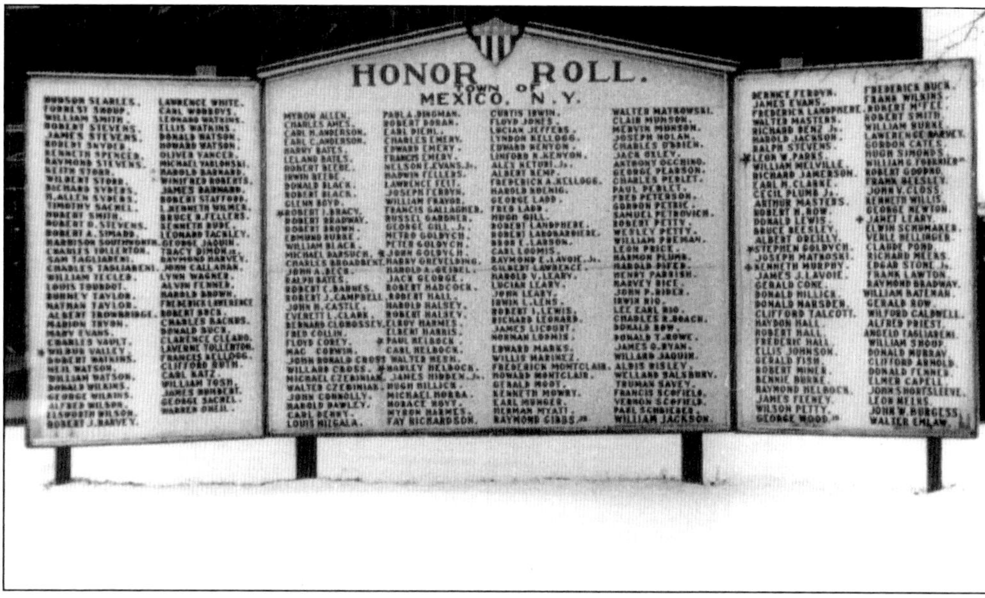

The names of Mexico residents in the service during World War II were listed on a large honor roll placed on Main Street. A red cross was placed in front of the names of those who entered the service to work with the Red Cross, including Kenneth Murphy, Janet Leary, Harold Barnard, Winifred Roberts. A gold star was placed by Robert Bracy, John Goldych, Stephen Goldych, Leon Parks, Paul Helbock, and Wilber Valley, who were killed in action.

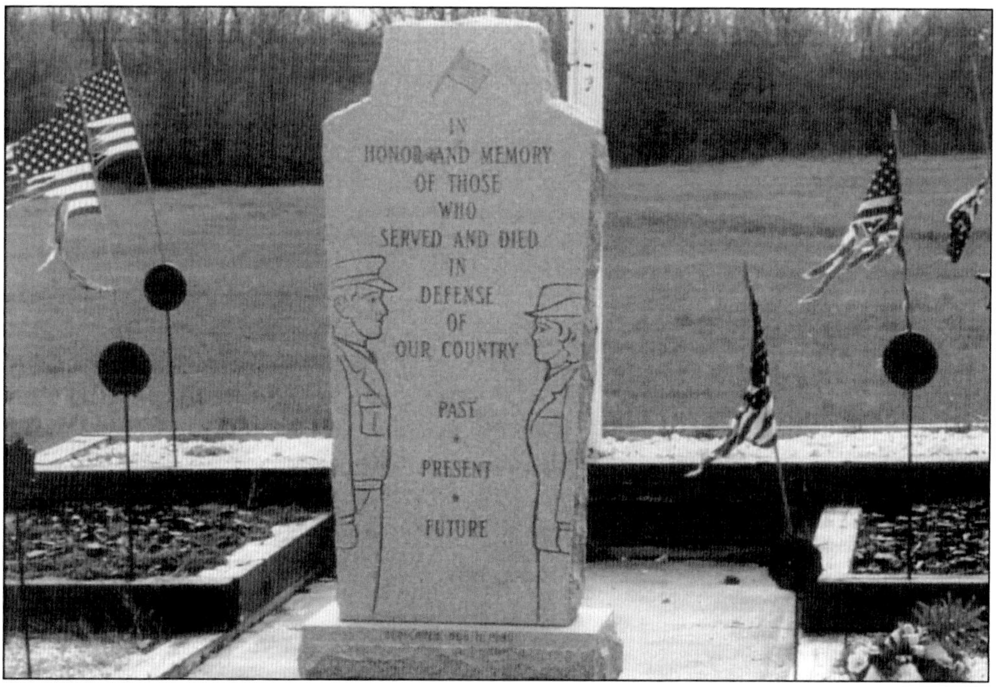

After World War II, the VFW and the American Legion considered a third memorial to the men and women who had served in that war. However, the Korean and Vietnam Wars ensued. In 1989, the VFW commissioned a monument that recognized all veterans. The stone was placed on the VFW Field on State Route 3 north of the village.

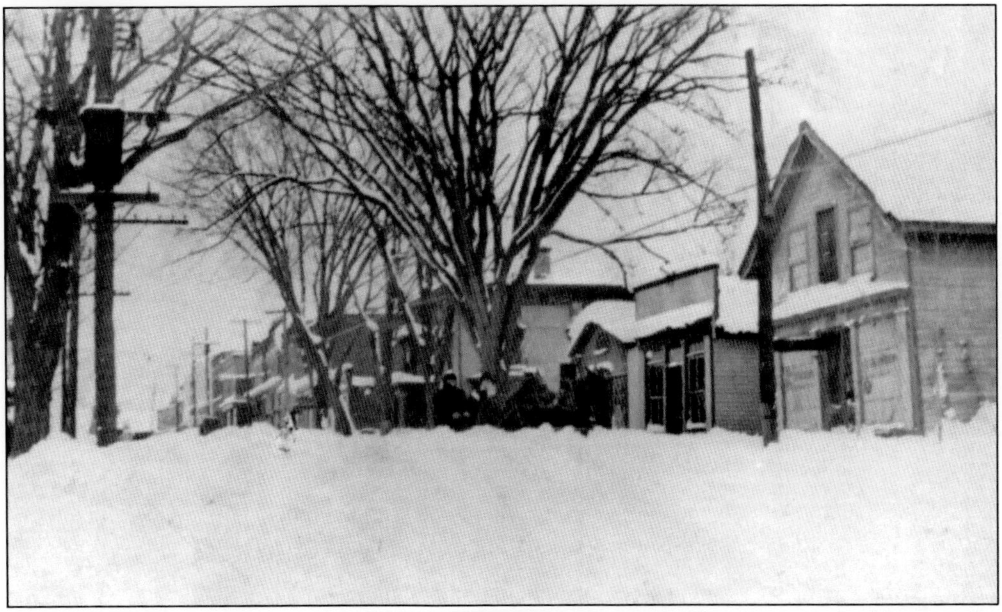

These shops were old business buildings on Main Street in 1907. The two-story building on the right was gone by 1910. The middle business was the shoe shop of Joseph Tagliareni from 1922 to 1967. The building on the left was a gift and antique shop for a few years. Local churches often used the building for rummage sales. The Mowry Law Office now stands on the site. (Courtesy of the John Castle collection.)

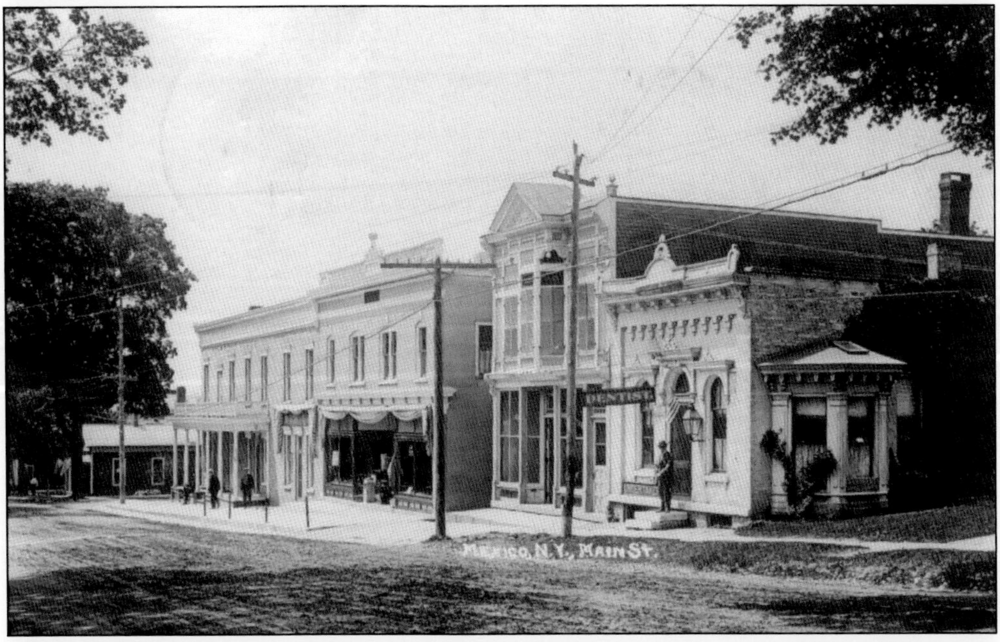

These attractive buildings were used by thriving businesses in the early 1900s, adding much beauty to Main Street. The large building on the left was the popular Boyd House. The one with the large windows was a furniture store and then later a five-and-dime. Next was the post office with a nice apartment above. The pretty little building on the right was a dentist's office and later an insurance office. (Author's collection.)

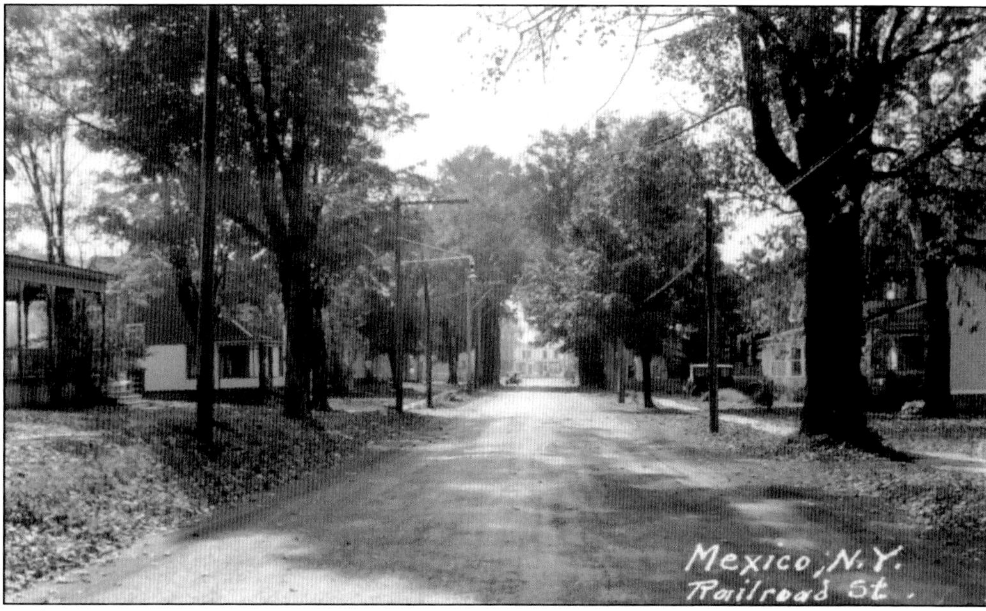

Railroad Street was first named Center Street and is now known as Scenic Avenue. This view is looking south toward Main Street. The Hotchkiss Restaurant and Tourist Home on Main Street is framed by the trees at the end of the unpaved road. The west end of Fayette Street can be seen in the center of the picture. (Courtesy of the John Castle collection.)

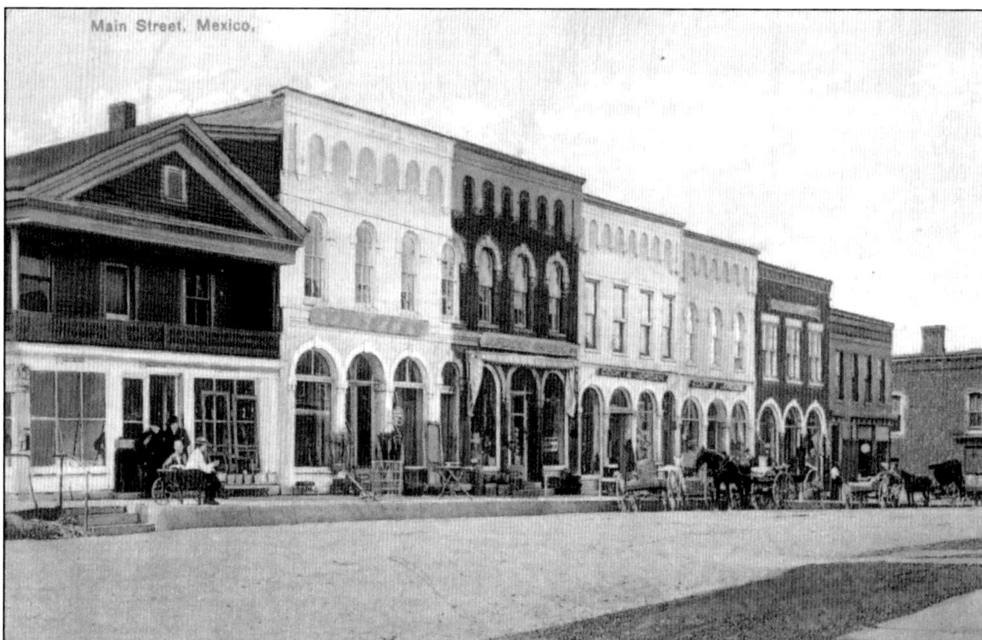

This scene shows the stores on the south side of Main Street from Church Street to South Jefferson Street in the early 1900s. The merchants put some of their goods on the sidewalk to show them off and get the customers to come in for more. The two buildings in the middle of the block housed the business of Cook and Jordan, which later became S. J. Ramsey's dry goods store. (Author's collection.)

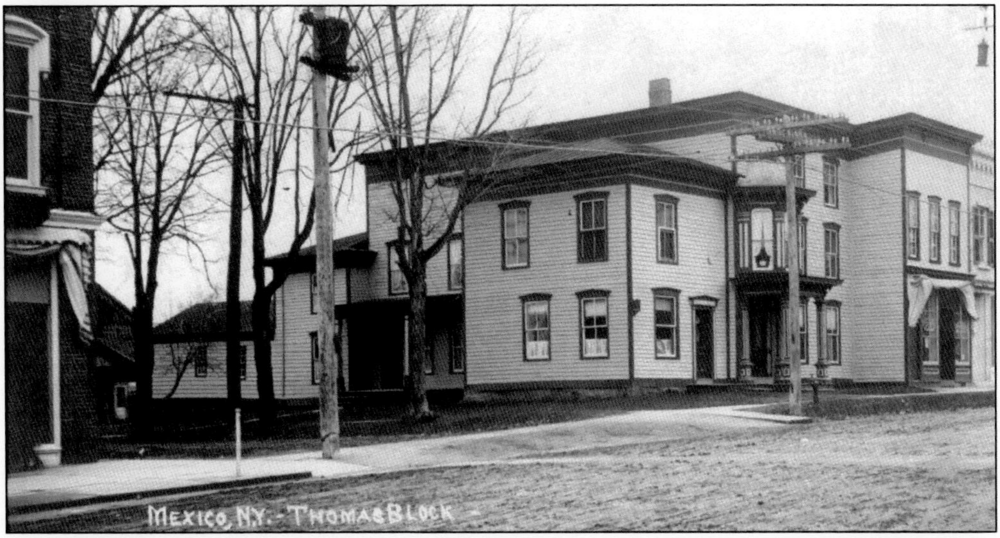

This block of Main Street in 1900 is unrecognizable today. The telephone pole on the left marks the northwest corner of Main and North Jefferson Streets. The building partially shown on the far right was Giovo's. The building in the middle later was extended west to the sidewalk and was a jewelry store and barbershop before 1910. (Author's collection.)

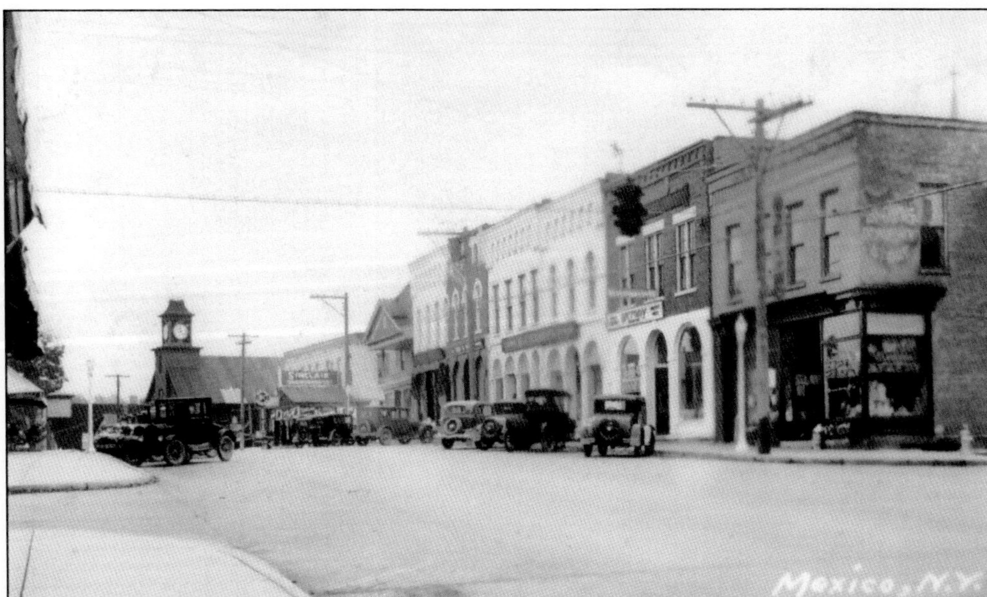

By the 1920s, Main Street had changed. It was paved, and diagonally parked cars replaced the parallel-parked horse and buggies. A stoplight in the center of the road hangs where a streetlight once hung. Just to the right of the town hall is the Mexico House with the small Sinclair station in front of it. (Author's collection.)

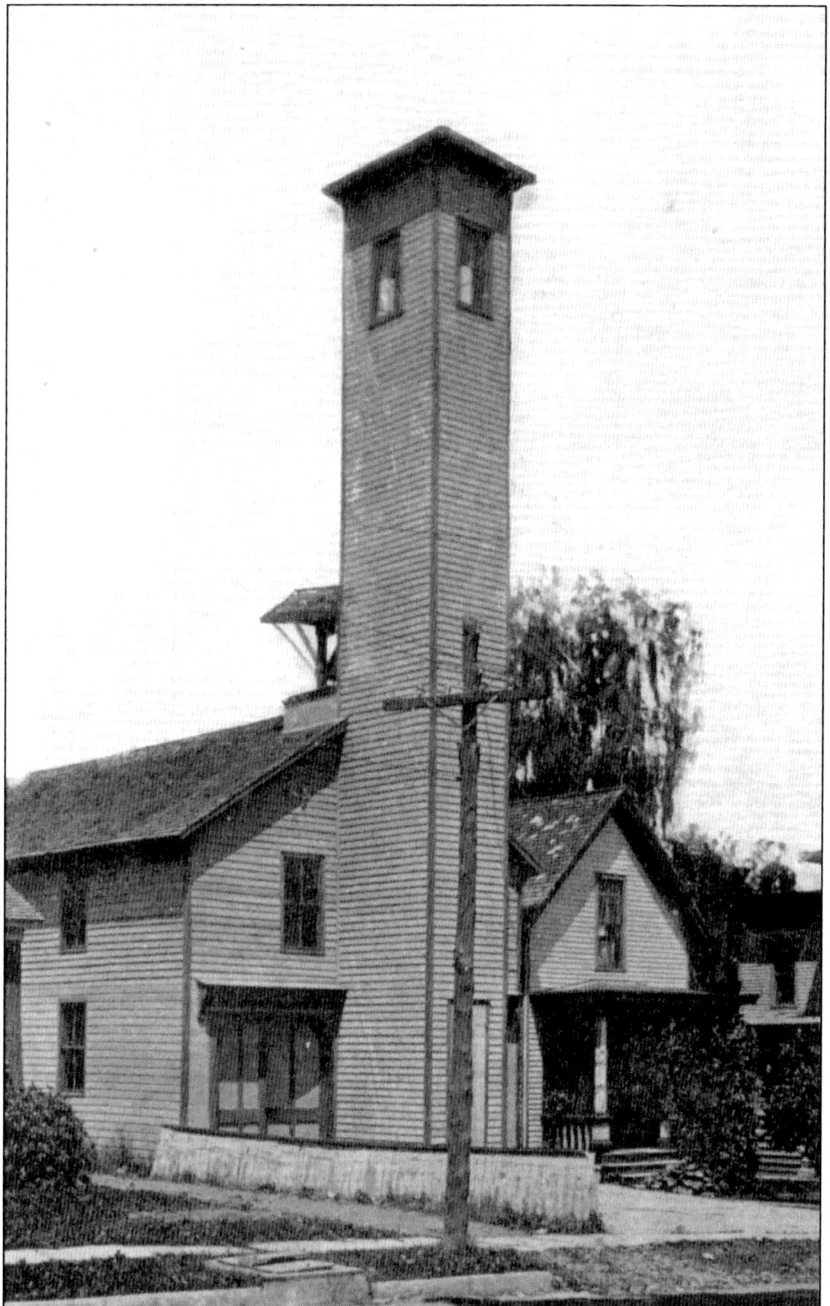

This tall hose tower was added to the fire station early in the 20th century. A picture of a band, taken in 1906, shows the station without the tower, but this photograph is labeled 1917. The tower was used often when the fire truck had been out to a fire. The hose was pulled to the top of the tower, and any water left in the hose drained out, drying the hose. This fire engine hall was burned in 1938, and when it was rebuilt, the tower was deemed unnecessary. The little house on the right was used at different times as a home and a public library and was the American Legion rooms before it was destroyed in the 1938 fire.

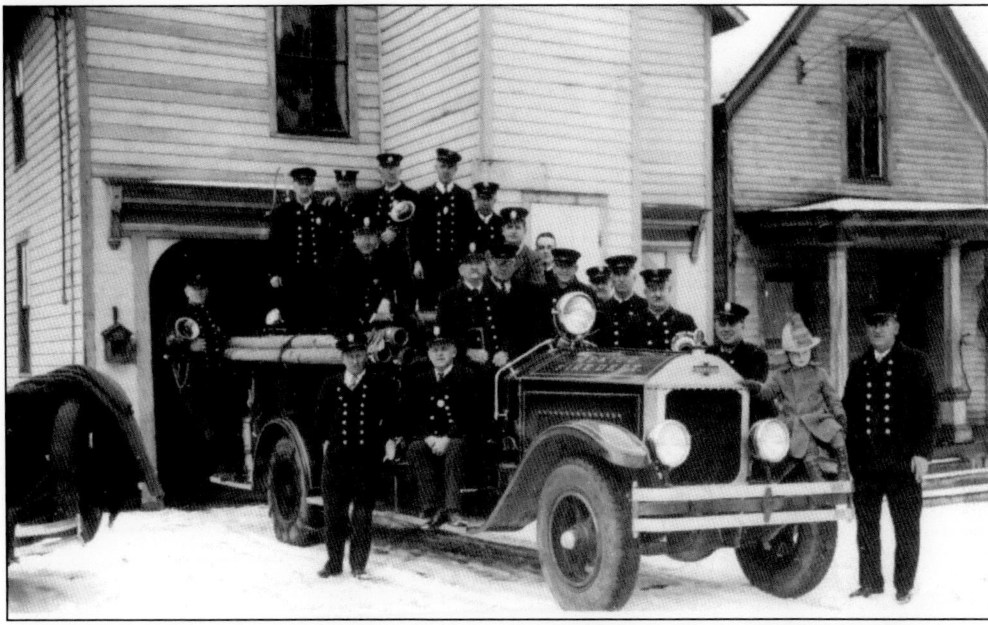

The Mexico Volunteer Fire Department is shown here in dress uniforms in 1935. The officers were Luke S. Clearwater, chief; Ray E. Dailey, assistant chief; Harry C. Varce, treasurer; Lawrence M. Bateman, secretary and truck driver; John Humbert, hose foreman; Fred Kellogg Jr., assistant hose foreman; and truck drivers Glen A. Buck and John Lum. The boy sitting on the mudguard of the engine is Donald Halstead. (Author's collection.)

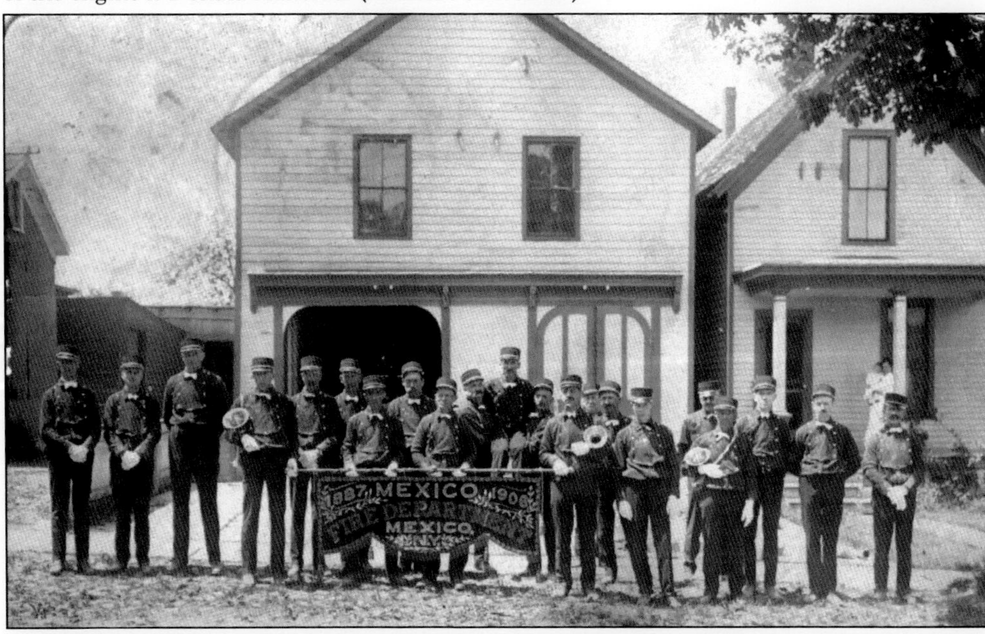

The Mexico Volunteer Fire Department prepares for a parade in 1906. The volunteers always marched in the Memorial Day parade and the Fourth of July parade. The firemen planned an all-day celebration for the "glorious Fourth" for many years. Activities included a parade, a ball game, field sports, and such attractions as rope walking over the Little Salmon River, climbing a greased pole, or riding an animal of one's choice. (Courtesy of the Barry Haynes collection.)

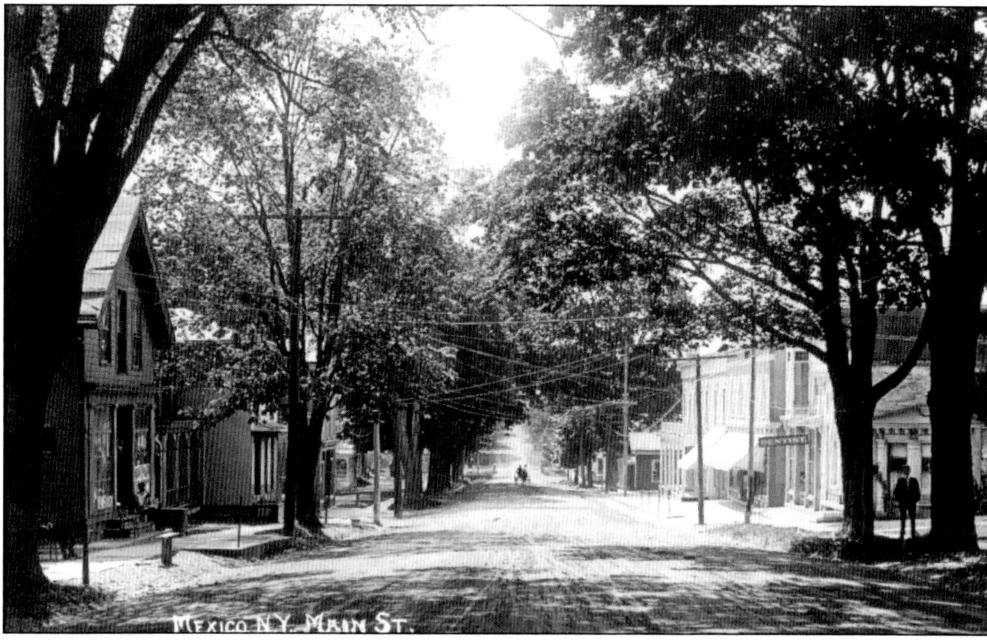

Maple and elm trees gracefully frame Main Street, shading the people and their homes. Some of the trees were very old, but some were planted along the road as the village grew with new homes. Age, disease, and highways destroyed most of these beautiful trees, and only a few have been replaced. (Courtesy of the John Castle collection.)

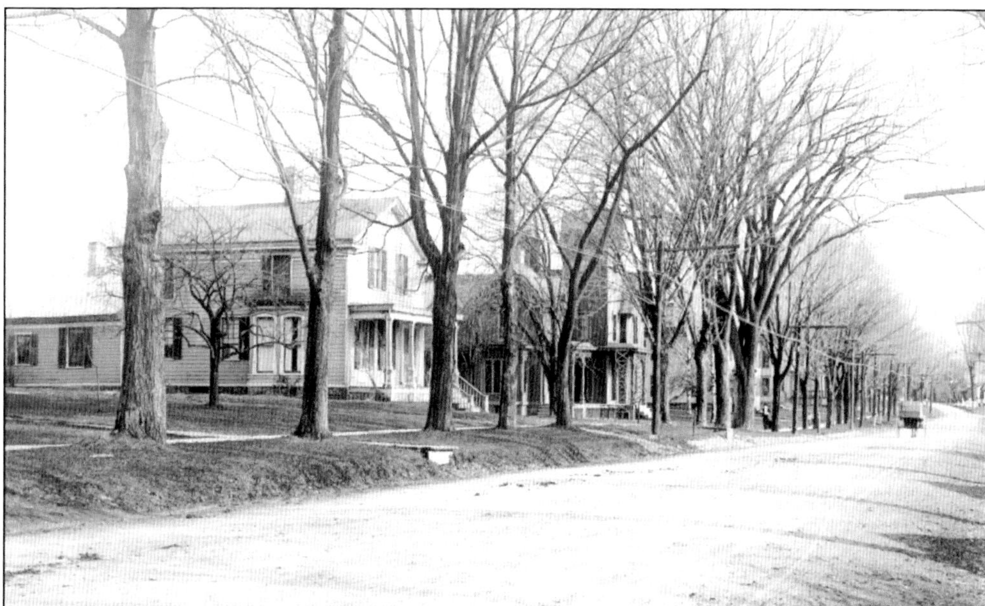

Looking south on Church Street in 1910, the first house on the left was the home of Henry Humphries, editor of the *Mexico Independent* from the newspaper's beginning to his retirement in 1917. The house is no longer standing. A display of monuments made by Anthony Salladin can be seen at the bend in the road at the far right. Many Salladin stones are found in the Mexico Cemetery.

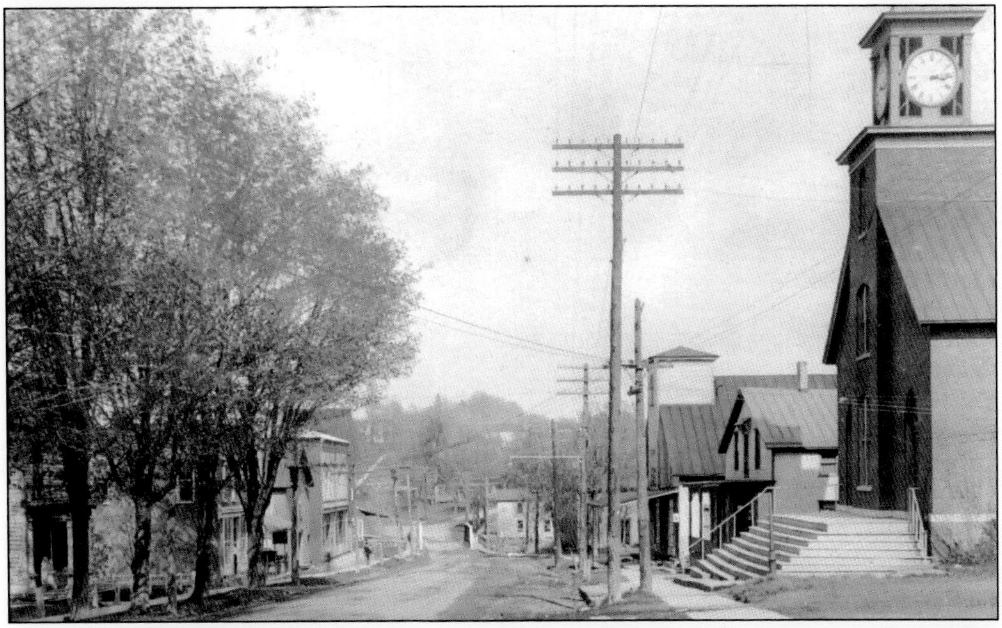

The town hall, right, was built in 1879 with a door on each side of the entrance and a window in the middle. It was named Washington Hall. The clock tower was added in 1882, leaving screen-covered openings on all four sides so the bell could be heard clearly all around the village. The hall became the town's political headquarters and the scene of theatricals, dances, lectures, and Mexico Academy commencements. (Courtesy of the Barry Haynes collection.)

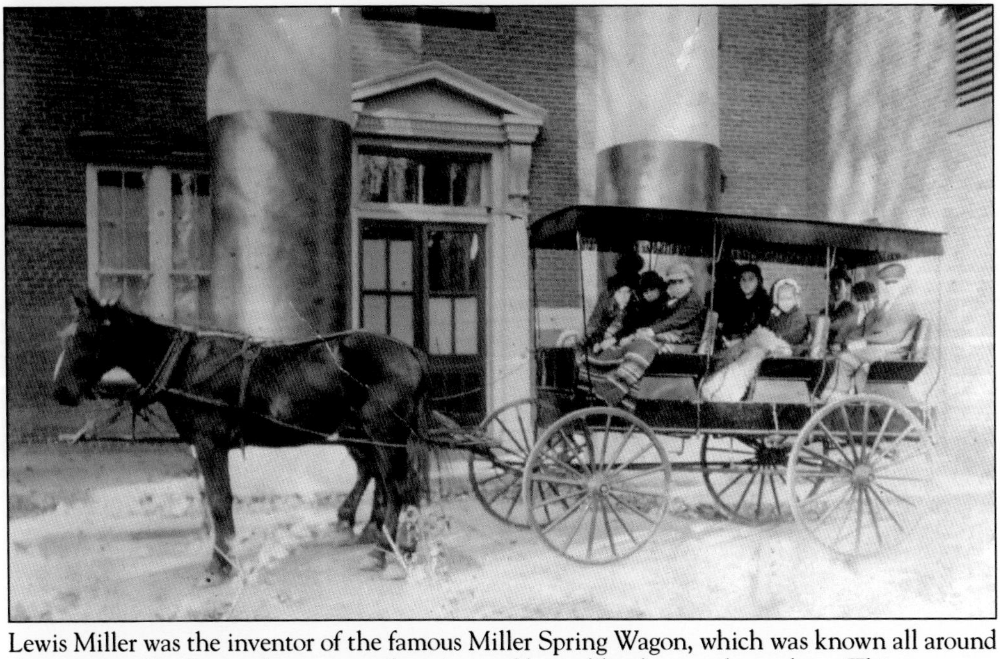

Lewis Miller was the inventor of the famous Miller Spring Wagon, which was known all around the country. He also made carriages, buggies, and buses like the one shown here. This was not a school bus like the ones known today but a privately owned bus that picked up both young and old. If the bus was coming from the railroad station, it would not be unusual for the driver to stop for children walking along the road and take them to school.

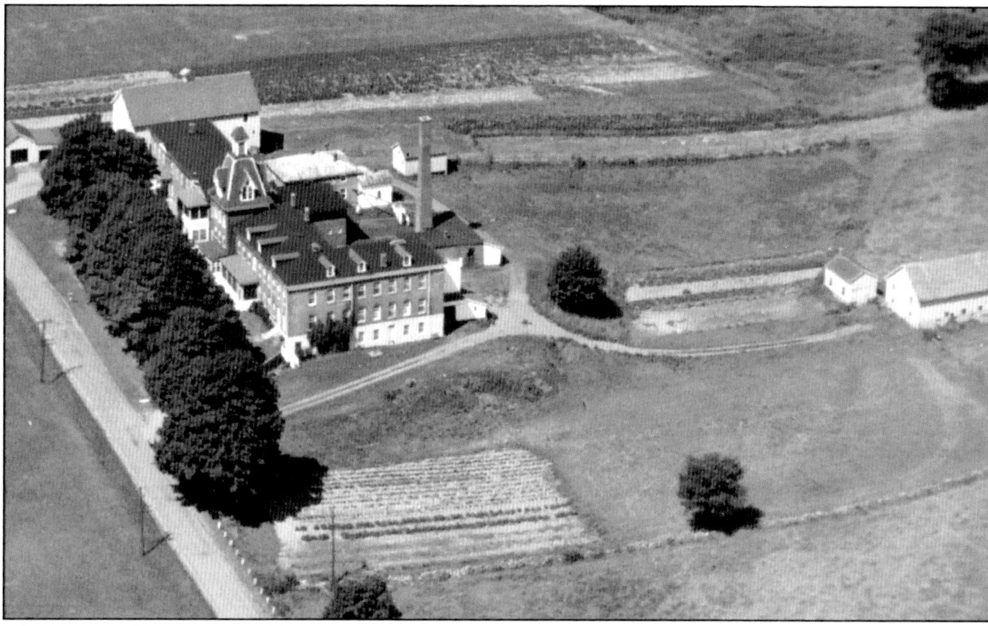

The Town of Mexico established a home for the needy in 1828 in a small farmhouse on County Route 64. A large brick building was soon constructed, with additions put on through the years. The men at the county home helped with the work on the farm to help provide much of the needed food. This site is now the Board of Cooperative Educational Services (BOCES) heavy equipment training area. (Courtesy of the John Castle collection.)

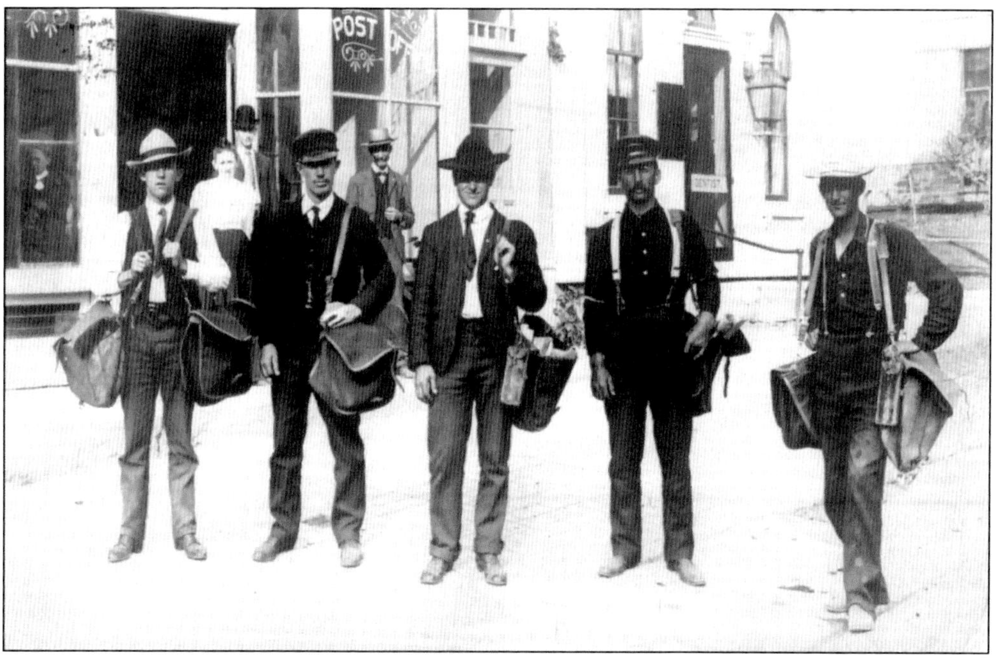

From left to right, Captain Boyd, Ray Wilcox, M. C. Fellows, Ralph Walton, and Perley H. Doil stand in front of the Mexico Post Office ready to leave on rural free delivery service in 1905. This postcard was mailed at 10:00 a.m. on October 20, went to Fulton, and is marked "rec'd on the 21st at 7am" in Oneida. The five men retired from the postal service together in 1935.

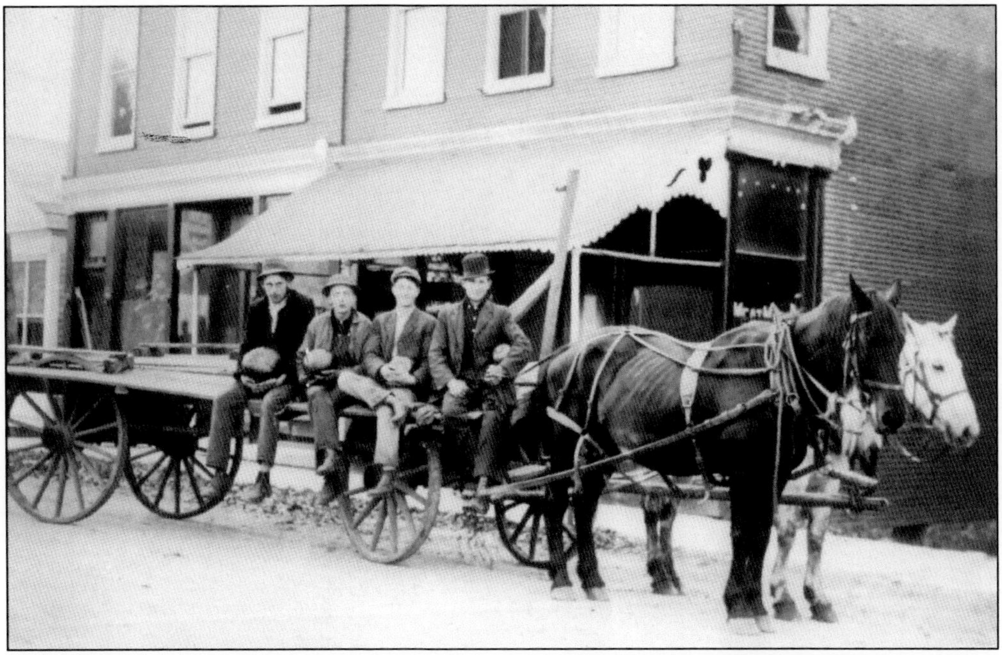

South Jefferson Street was home to a number of businesses at the dawn of the 20th century. In this 1910 photograph, from left to right, Will Clark, Jay Wheaton, Lin Jeffers, and Austin Gosier pause in front of two buildings then located on the present location of the Key Bank driveway behind today's Hart and Stone Store.

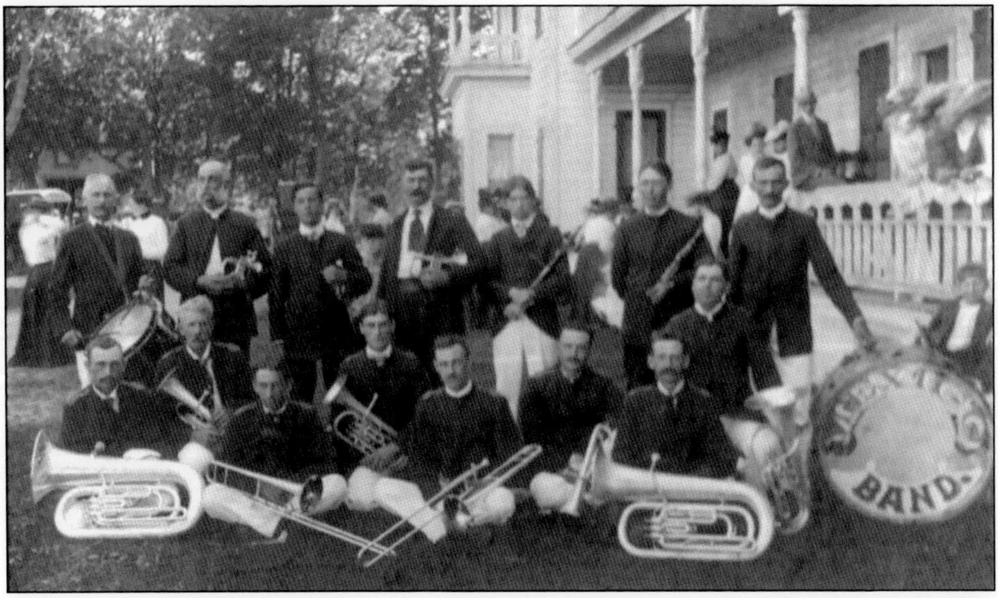

The Mexico Helicon band, organized in 1868, was reorganized as the Silver Cornet band in 1880. In the summer of 1901, the band played at the Twice Told Hotel under the direction of Frank Hoose. Members include, from left to right, (first row) Warner Buck, Oliver Mowry, Ward Walton, Bert Buck, Lee Houghton, Warren Gardner, George Burdick, and Jesse Lawton; (second row) John Cobb, Henry Penfield, Charles Steinburg, Will Buck, Glen A. Buck, Frank Hoose, and Julious Furney.

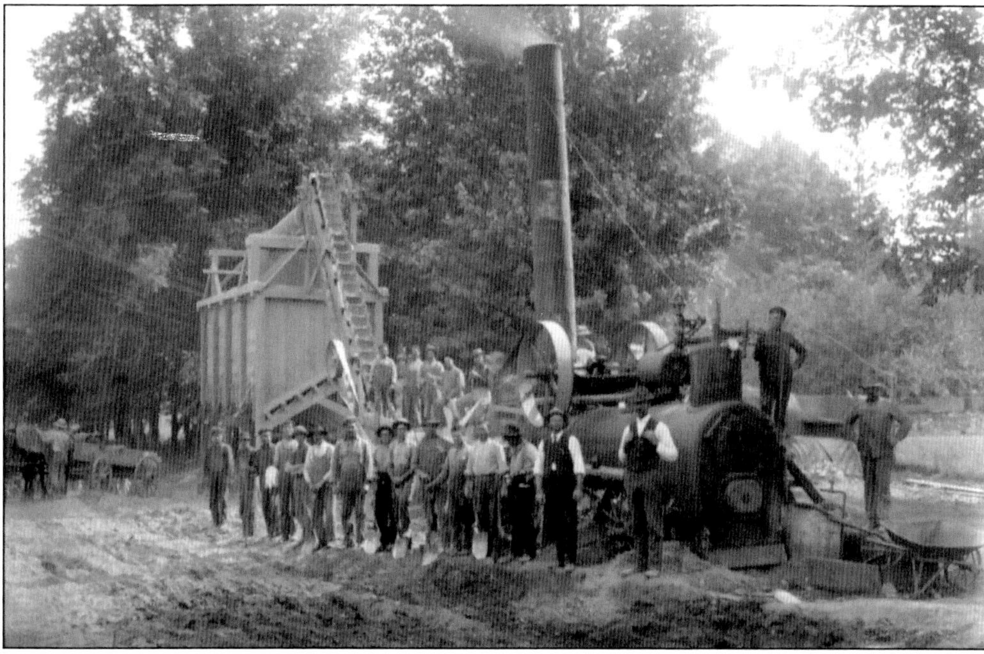

This stone crusher was once a common sight in Mexico. Robert Roach remembered seeing it on State Route 3 north near the apple grove stand in 1935. It was also used on Cole Road and at Dewey's Corners. The old farm stone walls were crushed up and used to make roads. The farmers hauled the stones in their wagons, and for this they were given credit on their taxes.

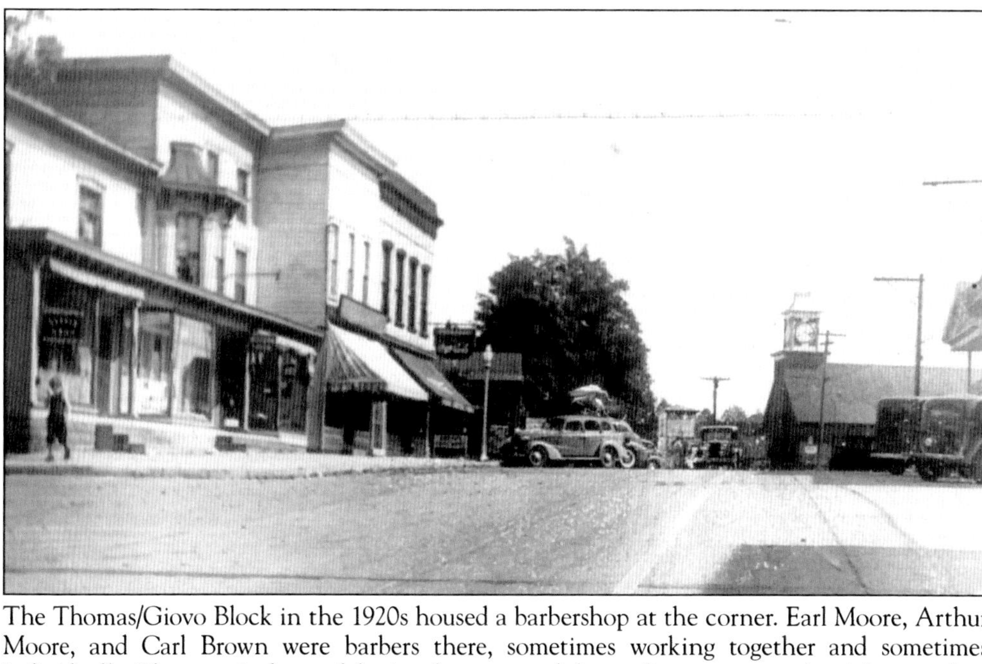

The Thomas/Giovo Block in the 1920s housed a barbershop at the corner. Earl Moore, Arthur Moore, and Carl Brown were barbers there, sometimes working together and sometimes individually. The steps in front of the jewelry store and the appliance store to the right were dear to the village boys. Most nights after supper, the boys gathered on the steps to talk, laugh, argue, and enjoy the companionship of the "boys only" club.

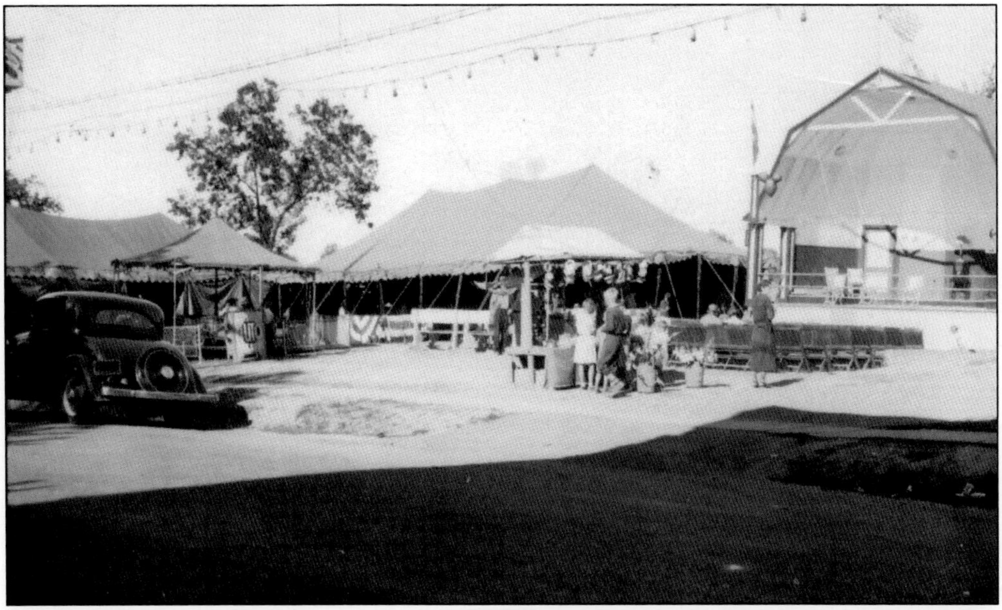

The band shell on North Jefferson Street was finished in time for the old home week celebration in 1936. The adjoining lot was given to the village by R. Austin Backus to be used as a park. The area was used for a band concert in 1936 and for closing ceremonies that Sunday. The firemen used the park for a bazaar in 1950, as did other groups through the years. (Courtesy of the Barry Haynes collection.)

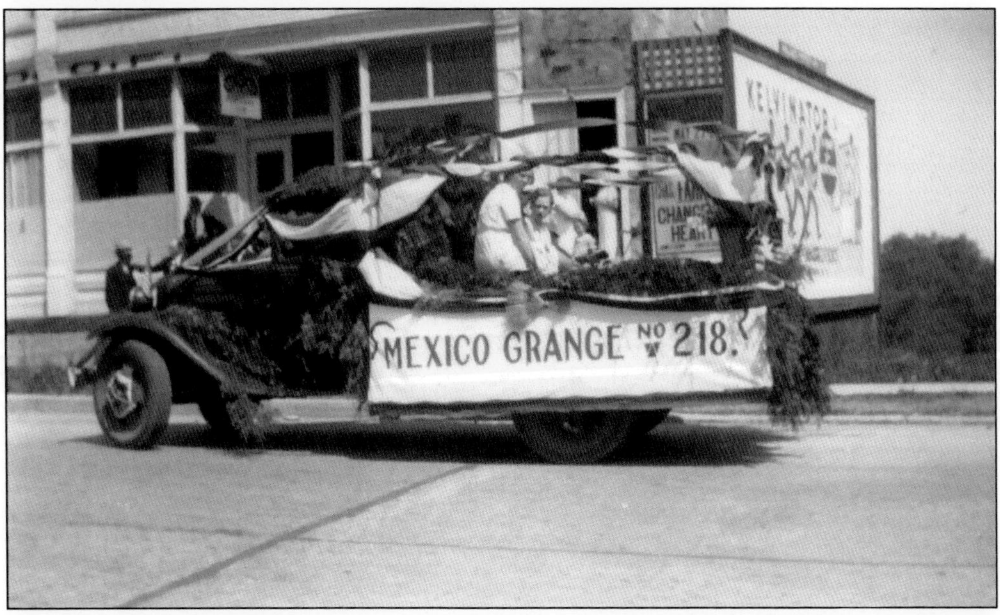

For many years in the 20th century, the Memorial Day parade involved most of the organizations in Mexico. In this picture from about 1934, the Grange float passes Fraternity Hall on East Main Street. The Odd Fellows and Rebekahs, the Masons, the Order of the Eastern Star, the Boy Scouts, and the 4-H group made floats for the parade. Usually the American Legion and VFW led the parade and the school band supplied the music. Horses and decorated bicycles added interest and fun. (Courtesy of the Barry Haynes collection.)

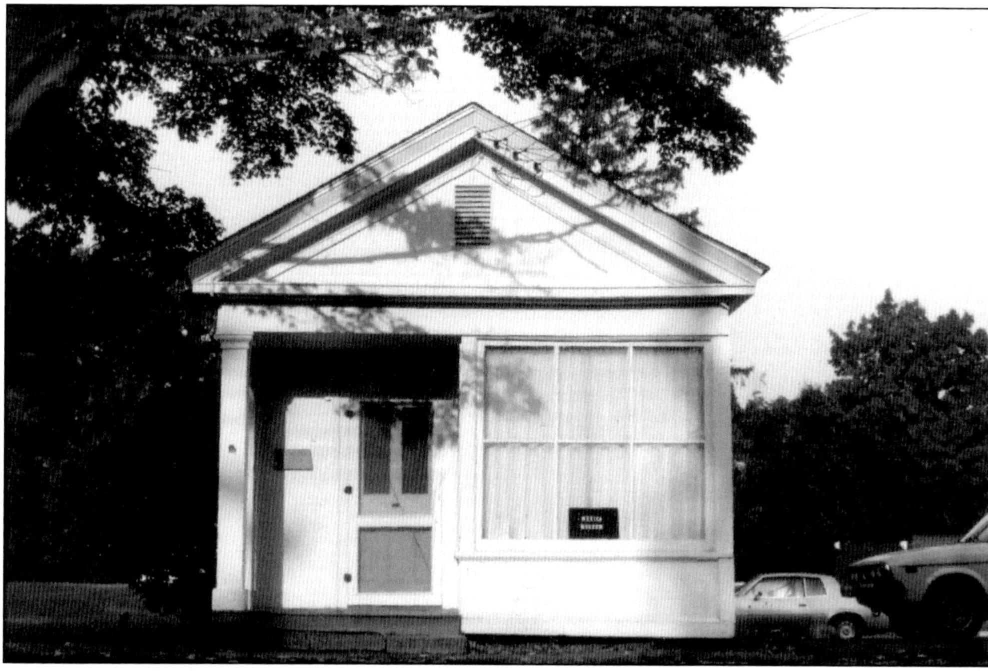

Levi Downing built this Greek Revival building for his law office in the mid-1800s. It had many uses through the years. Finally the owners, Worth and Frances Dygert, rented it as an apartment. In 1980, the Dygerts sold the building to the Town of Mexico for use as a museum and to be maintained by the historical society. (Author's collection.)

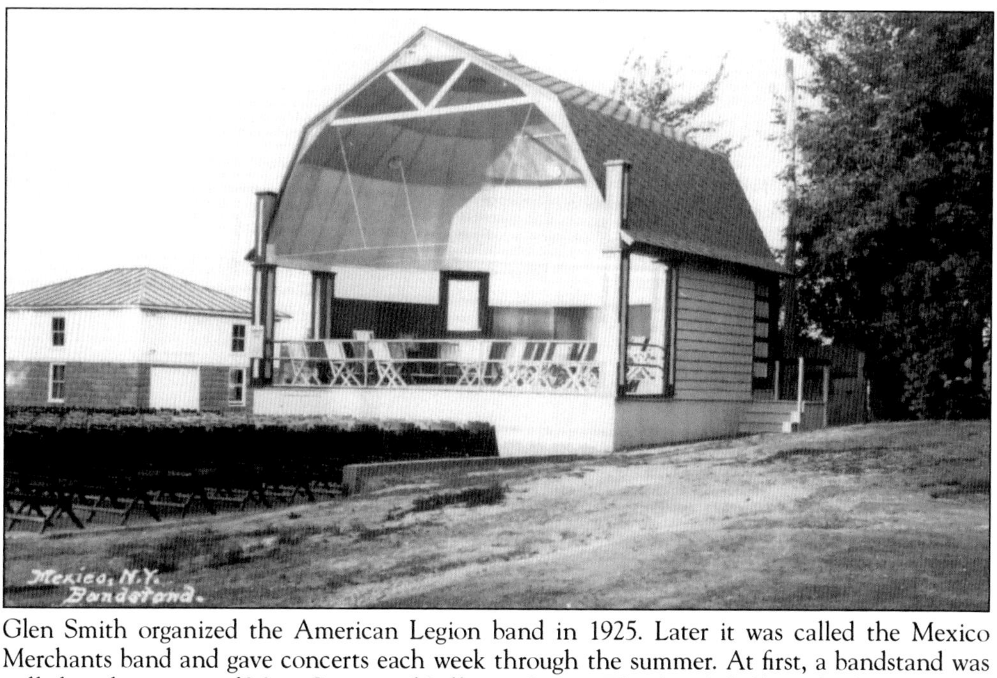

Glen Smith organized the American Legion band in 1925. Later it was called the Mexico Merchants band and gave concerts each week through the summer. At first, a bandstand was pulled to the corner of Main Street and Jefferson Street. This band shell was built in 1936 on North Jefferson Street. One evening each week, the village enjoyed this casual entertainment much like the block parties of the modern days. (Author's collection.)

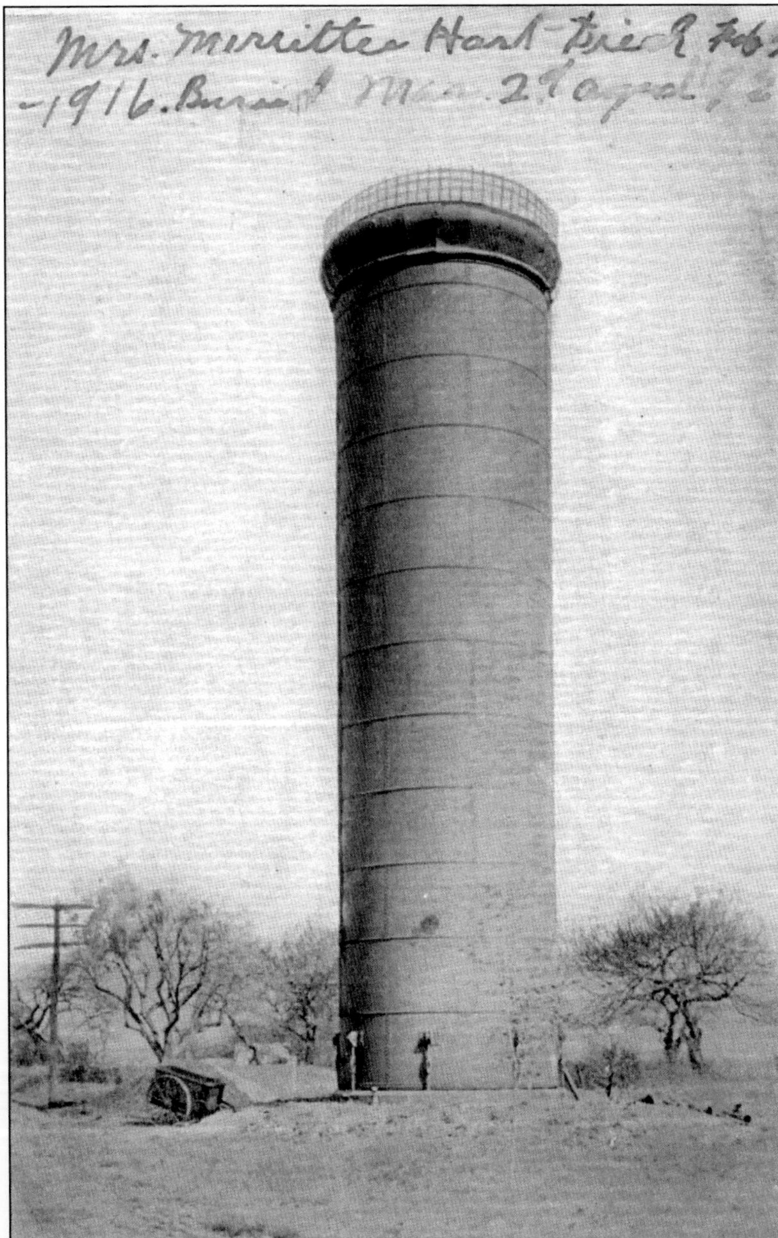

The Mexico water system was completed in 1913. Mains were laid in trenches dug by hand, which piped water to this standpipe on East Hill from springs on Pump House Road. The total cost of the system was $56,000. Over the years, many additions and extensions have been made. In 1931, led by Mayor Earle A. Mowry, three more acres were bought with two new big springs. The new system started operation in 1934. A new standpipe was erected in 1950, and a booster was added to the system in 1954. New wells and pumps were added in 1956 and 1958. In 2008, work was begun to supply water to residents in the town beyond the village. A new water tank has been built on State Route 3, south of the village. Mexico water remains among the most pure in New York, but the state has recently demanded that chlorine be added to the water supply. (Courtesy of the John Castle collection.)

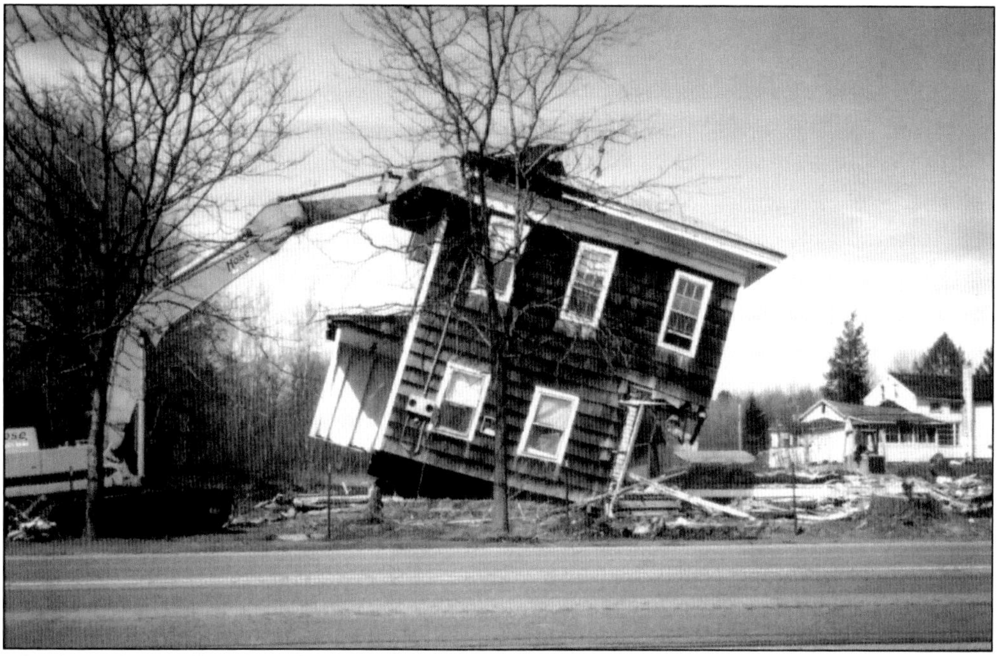

The face of the village has changed greatly since 1990. Bob Cone's home and barbershop were demolished to make room for Fastrac's convenience store and gasoline pumps. At the same time, the corner lot was leveled for McDonald's. Although such corporations want their businesses on the Main Street of the village, most side streets still maintain their small-town ambiance.

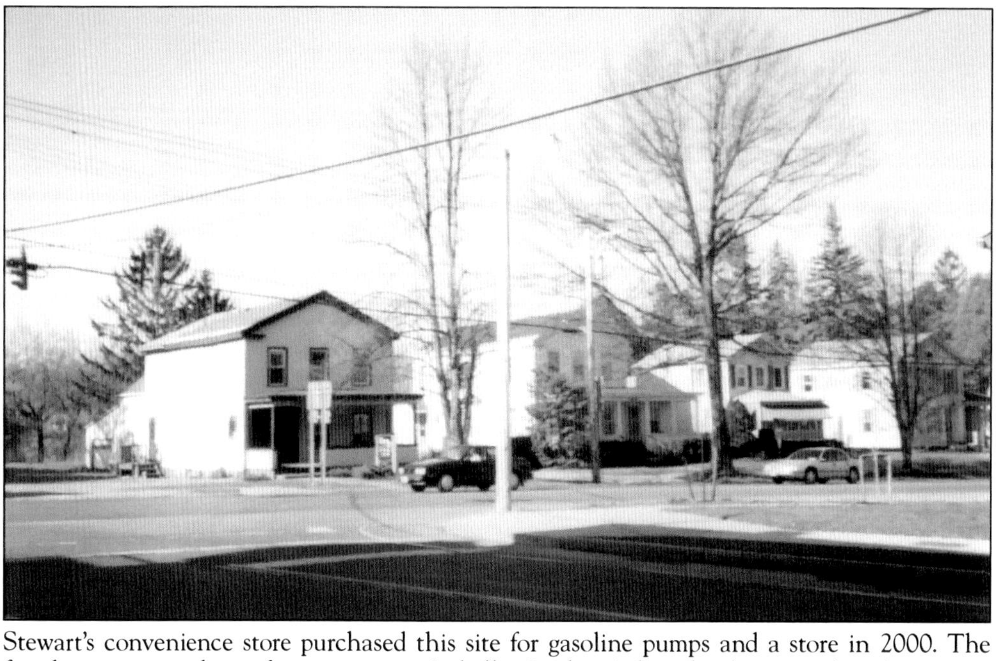

Stewart's convenience store purchased this site for gasoline pumps and a store in 2000. The first home removed was for many years Isabelle Gardiner's boardinghouse and in later years a Century 21 office. The second house will be remembered by many as the Gibbs funeral home. It was an apartment house during the last few years before removal. (Courtesy of Nancy Ramsey Murray.)

Two

WORSHIPPING TOGETHER

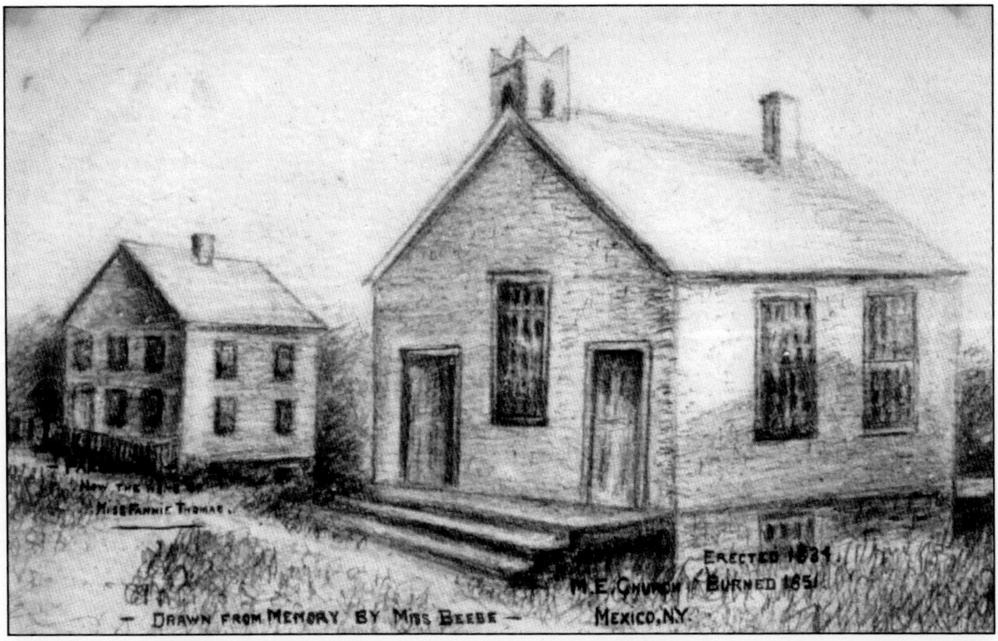

This first Methodist church building was constructed in 1833, and it was drawn from memory by Emma N. Beebe in 1908. It was on the south side of Main Street just east of Black Creek. It was made of brick, had a pulpit of the old-fashioned kind with three or four steps, and had a basement with two rooms. It burned in 1851.

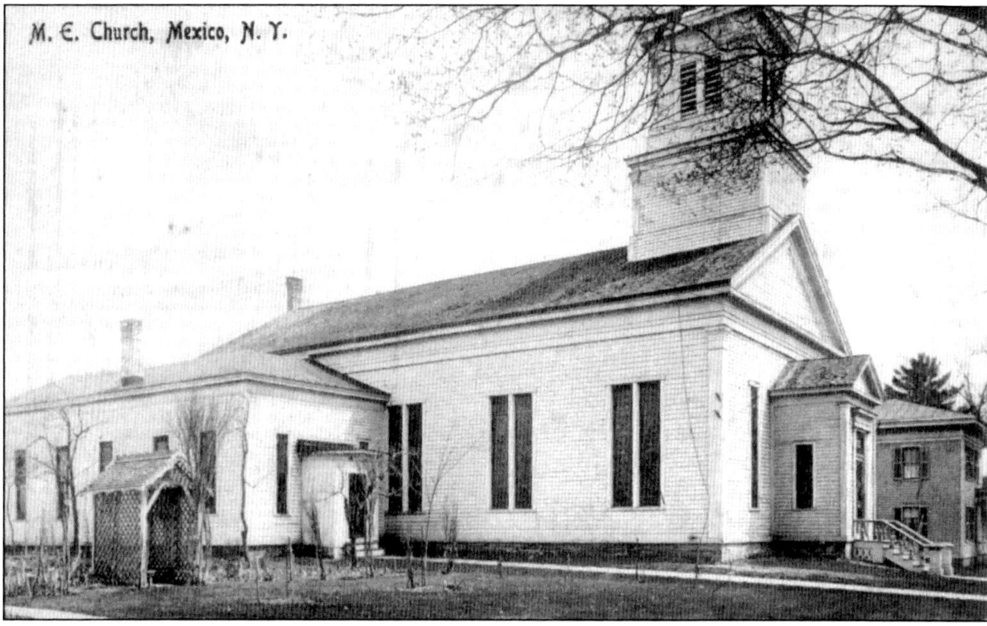

In 2008, the First United Methodist Church celebrated its 200th anniversary. Services were first held in the home of Minerva and Leonard Ames. As the congregation grew, services were held in a schoolhouse or Orson Ames' Tannery until the little church of 1833 was built. When that church burned, the present building was erected on Church Street. In 1926, the wing on the north side was replaced by a large annex. (Author's collection.)

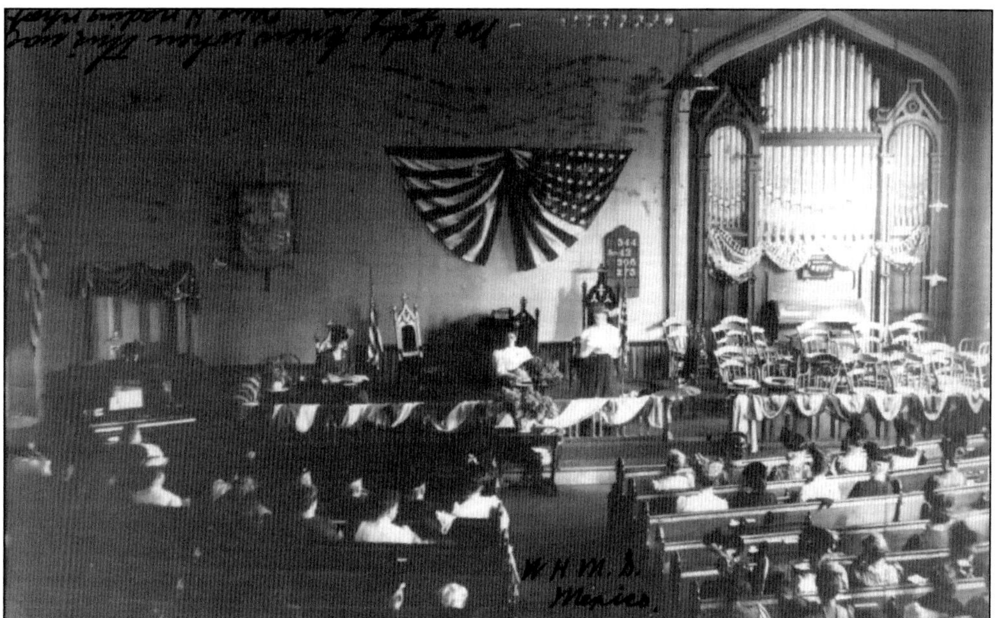

The Woman's Home Missionary Auxiliary of the Methodist Church was organized in 1891. The auxiliary members were found wherever the Stars and Stripes was displayed, working with other auxiliaries in industrial southern states, immigrant homes in New York City, frontier ministries, and those in need in the Mexico area. (Courtesy of the Barry Haynes collection.)

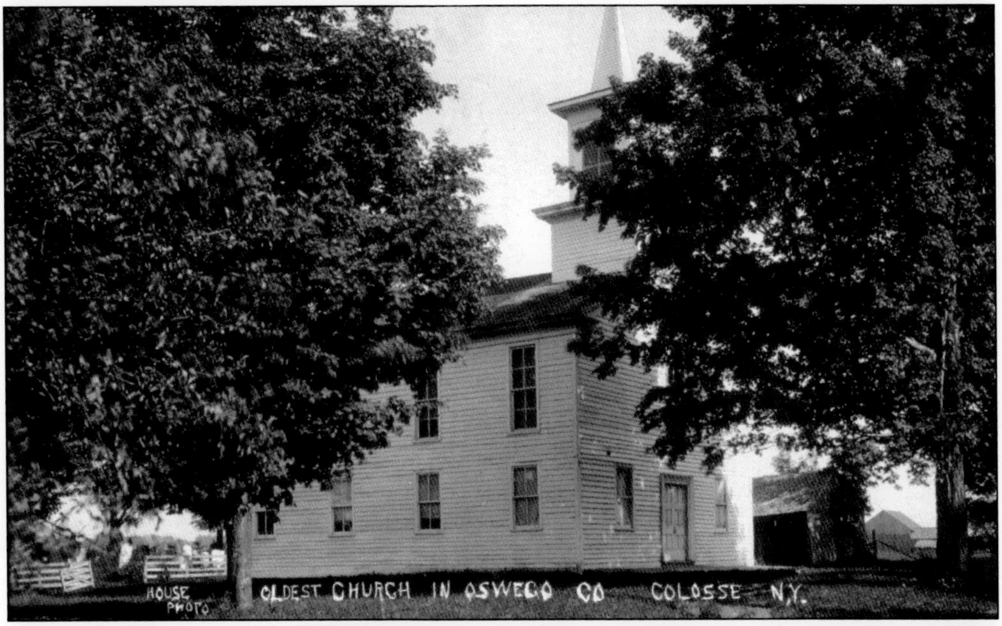

The settlement of Colosse built the first church edifice in Oswego County in 1823 and 1824. The congregation's membership continued to grow and reached 400 but declined as churches were built in neighboring communities. For many years, the Colosse Baptist Church was the oldest active parish in Oswego County until it was torn down and a new building was erected in 1963.

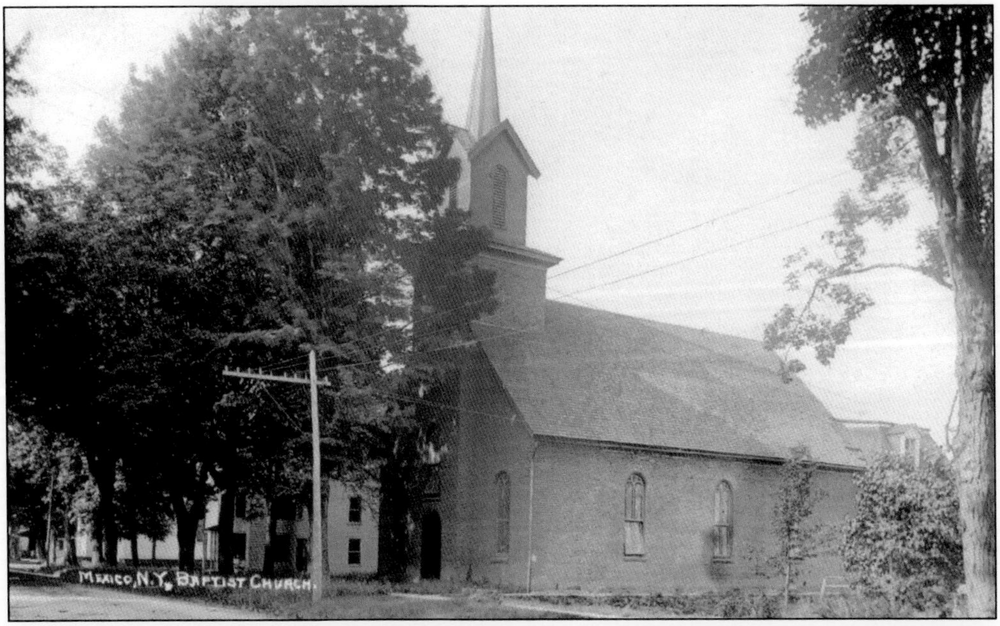

The Baptist congregation of Mexico built its church in 1832. In 1872, the building was extended toward Church Street. A vestibule took the place of the old piazza, the roof was raised, a steeple was built, and stained-glass windows were installed. Through the years, many changes have been made, including Sunday school rooms, a dining room and kitchen, chandeliers, and carpet. The steeple was removed in 1954.

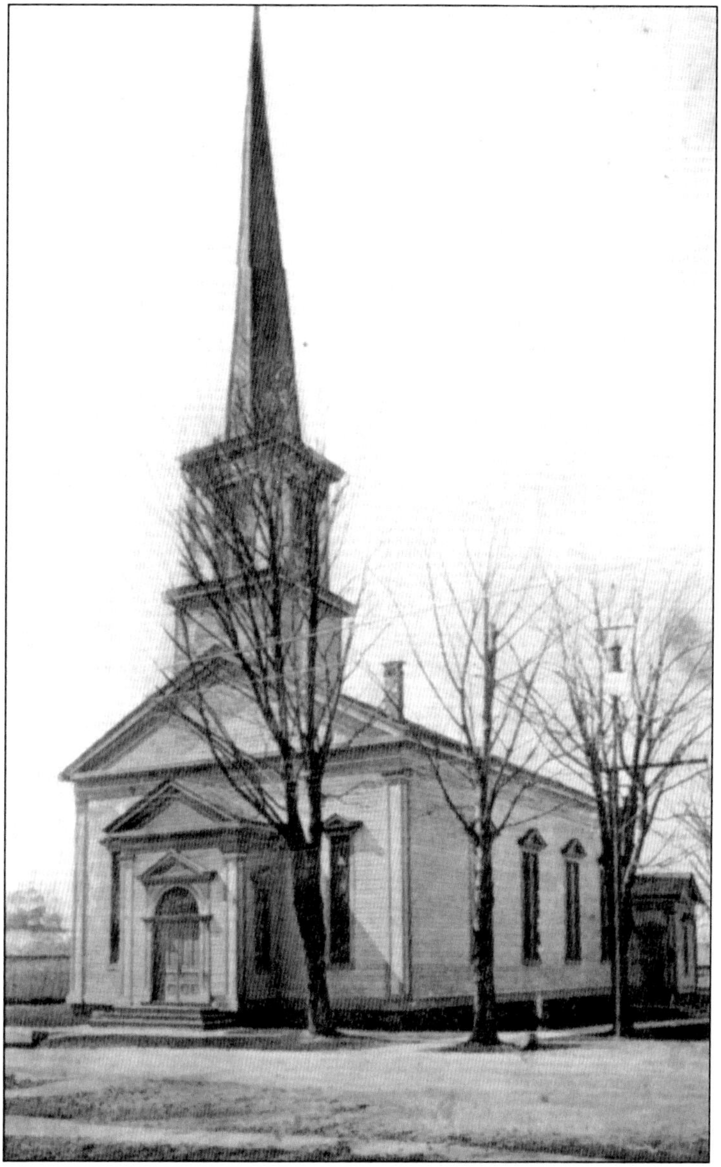

On August 27, 1810, seven women with fresh memories of New England white churches with tall spires met in Shubal Alfred's barn to form a religious society. It was not until 1811 when there were enough men to serve as trustees that the church was legally formed. In 1818, it reorganized and became a Presbyterian church. Prior to this, meetings were held in homes or schoolhouses. Early in 1831, a small meetinghouse was completed on the corner of Church and Spring Streets. In 1840, a bell was raised in the small belfry. The church planned to toll the bell for deaths with 10 strokes, a pause, and 10 more ending with the extra years of a person's age. The first time the bell tolled was for a Mrs. Hamilton, age 99, and its slow, solemn notes seemed to go on forever. The practice was discontinued. In 1858, major changes were made to the edifice, including the addition of a lecture room and the present style. The exterior changes in 1879 and 1880 included an added vestibule that greatly changed the front of the church. Stained-glass windows were added, and the interior of the sanctuary was completely renovated. The church remains the same today.

In the winter of 1950, a member of the Presbyterian church opened its door to find disaster. The engineers said four plaster ceilings had been put over the original ceiling, but they were not solid enough to hold firmly. The theory is that the vibration of a passing snowplow caused a beam to move slightly and loosen those four ceilings, causing them to break loose and crash down. (Author's collection.)

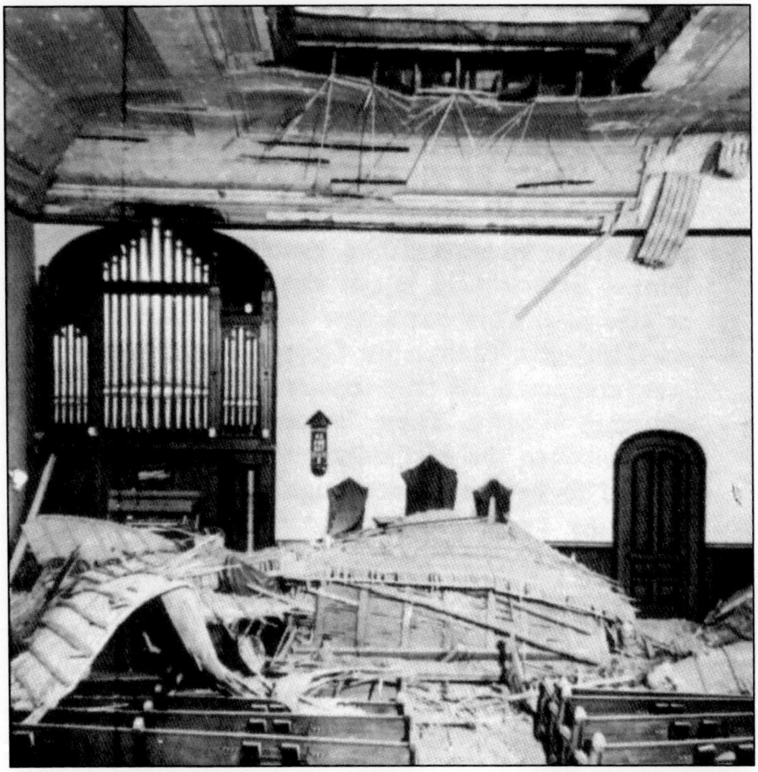

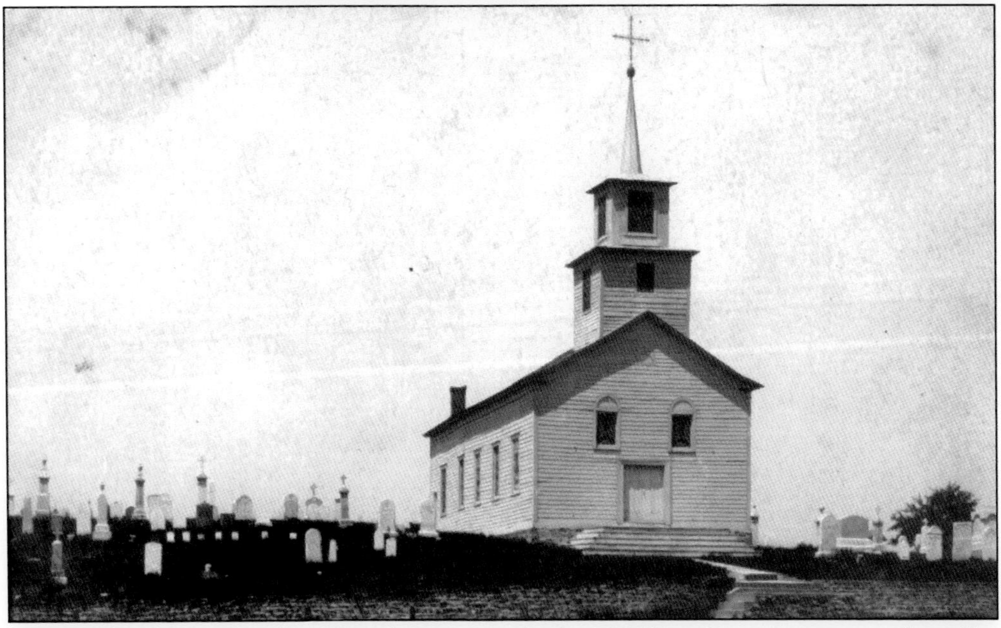

St. Ann's Catholic Church on French Street was built in 1840, and services were conducted by a Franciscan father from Syracuse. Later the parish became an out mission of other churches. In 1914, Mexico erected St. Mary's Star of the Sea Roman Catholic Church, and St. Ann's became an out mission of that church. Many of the gravestones in the adjoining cemetery are the work of the Salladin family and are noted for their excellent workmanship.

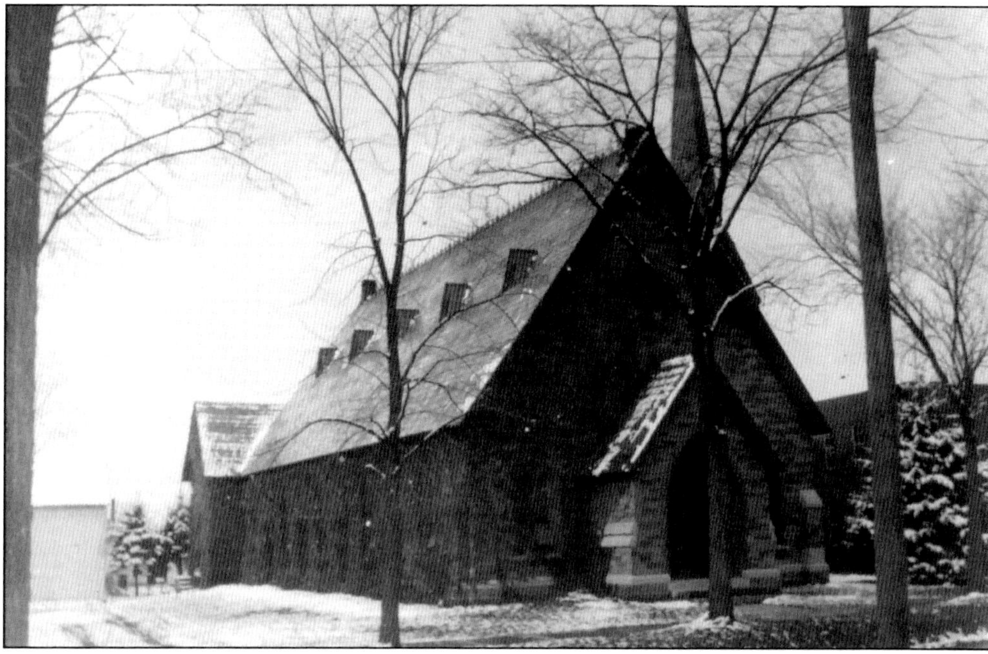

The Grace Episcopal Church was built in 1848 with the blue-gray stone from the Arthur quarry. The church bell, hung in the belfry in 1871, is in the key of A, while the Presbyterian bell is in the key of C and the Methodist bell is in the key of F, together making a minor cord. (Author's collection.)

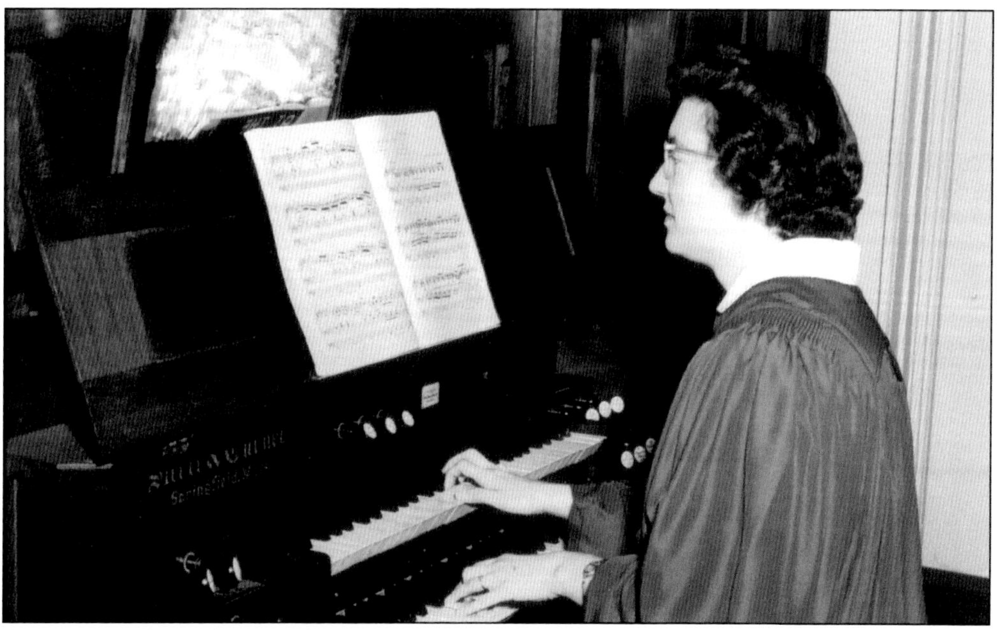

Organist Cecile Buck sits at the Steer and Turner organ in the Grace Episcopal Church where she was organist for 50 years. First used in 1874, it is the oldest Steer and Turner pipe organ in New York State that remains intact and unaltered at the original setting. The National Organ Historical Society has presented a plaque to the church to recognize this unique and beautiful instrument. (Author's collection.)

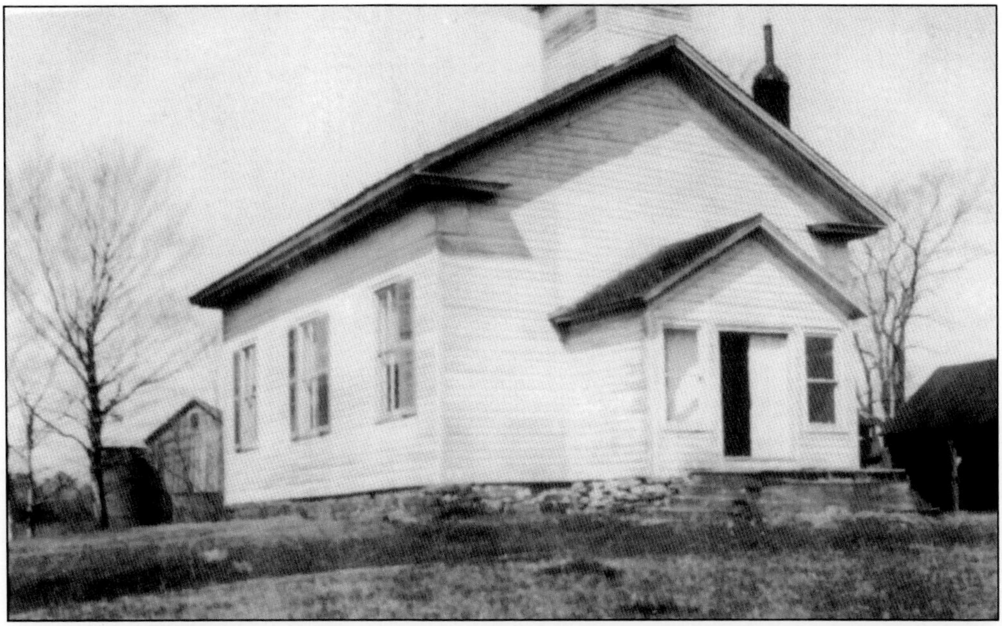

The Baptists and the Methodists living in the Texas–Fort Leazier area constructed North Church in 1845, using the building on alternate Sundays. In 1875, the Methodists bought the interests of the Baptists. In 1901, the congregation began having suppers as fund-raisers. Since there was no kitchen in the church, the meals were served in the homes of members who lived nearby. (Courtesy of the Barry Haynes collection.)

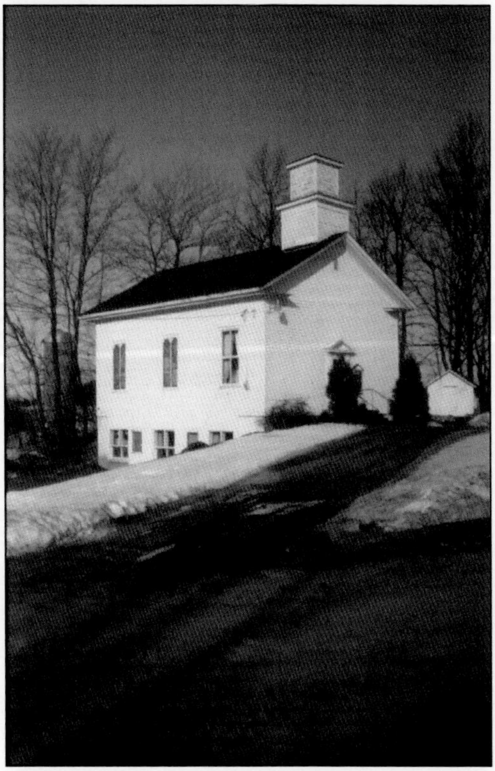

The front of North Church burned in 1939. Repairs and other remodeling were done, including enlarging the sanctuary and adding a small kitchen and a dining room. The famous dinners could now be held at the church, and the chicken barbecue became a regular event. Renovation in 1975 made the lower level into a larger kitchen, a dining room, and Sunday school rooms.

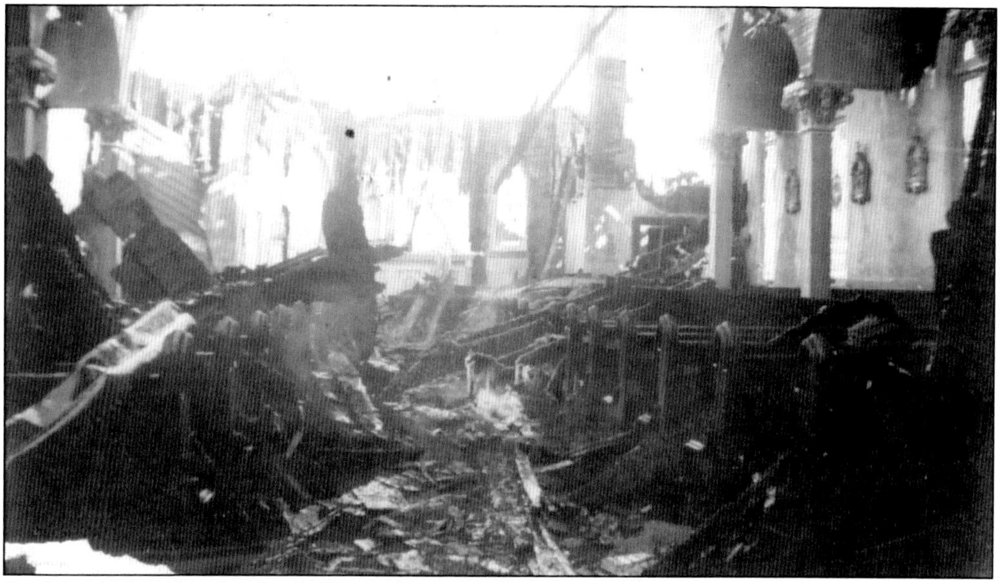

On March 6, 1938, the fire hall was destroyed by a blaze. So when St. Mary's Star of the Sea Roman Catholic Church burned three days later, the fire alarm was out of commission. Margaret Buck Ruth was the local telephone operator on duty. She called the pastors of the churches to have the bells rung as an alarm. Then she called as many firemen as possible. The church was gutted but restored by Christmas. (Author's collection.)

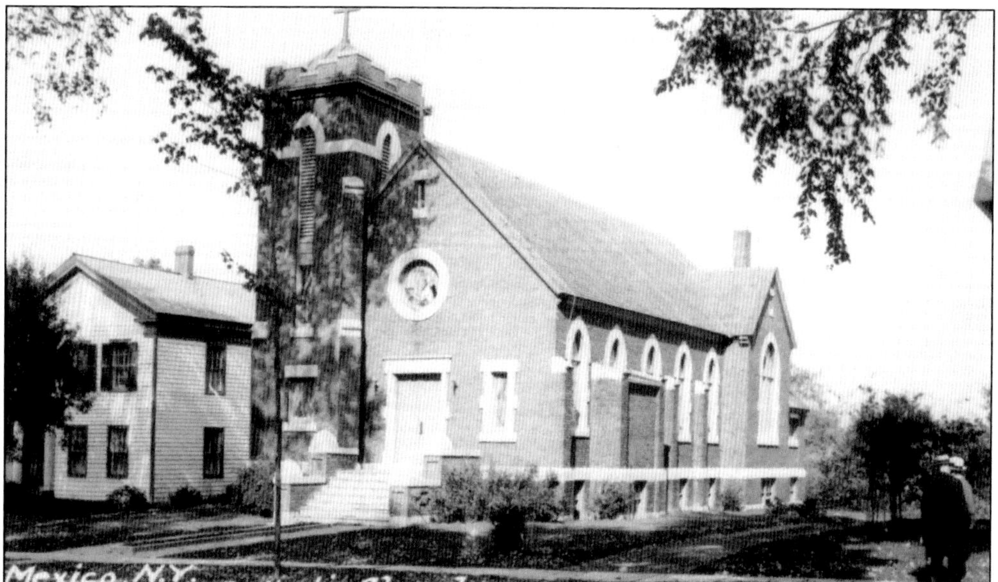

The cornerstone of St. Mary's Star of the Sea Roman Catholic Church was laid in 1916. After the disastrous fire in 1938, the church had to be rebuilt. An entrance for the handicapped, a signboard, new steps, and doors were some of the improvements made during the years. St. Anne's Catholic Church of Parish has united with St. Mary's Star of the Sea Roman Catholic Church in Mexico to form St. Anne Mother of Mary.

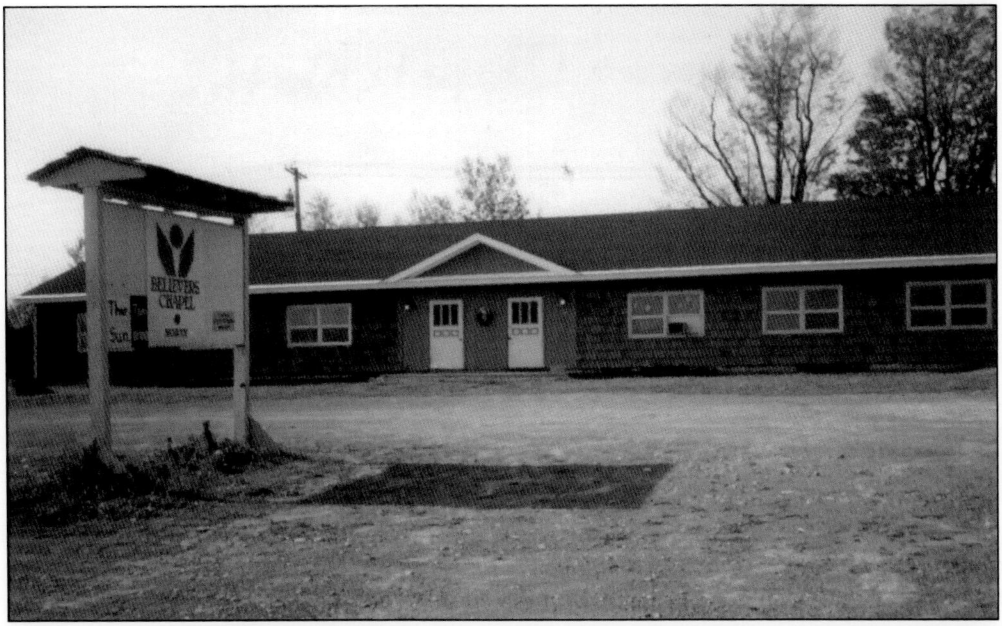

Believer's Chapel North is a nondenominational church that began meeting in 1992 in a vacant building south of the village of Mexico on State Route 3. Manny Josbena was the first pastor of the young congregation. The building was purchased two years later, and many improvements were made as the membership increased. Paul Anderson, a lifelong resident of Mexico, is the present minister.

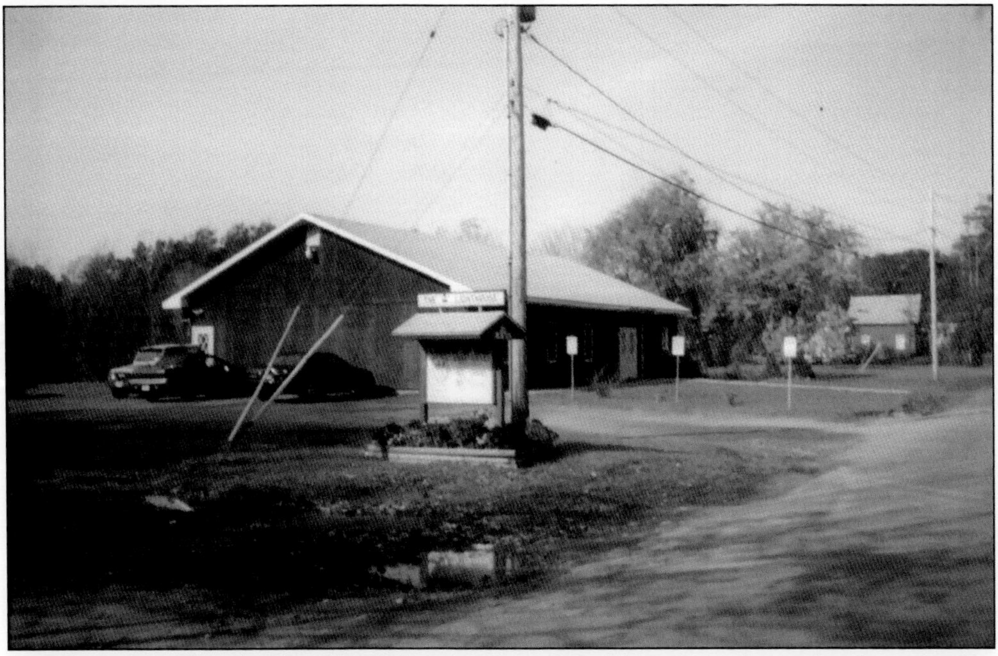

Members of the Church of God built their parish in 1978. The pastors changed and membership varied until Pastor Ronald Russell came in 1994. Membership grew and large additions have been made to the church. The name was changed to the Lighthouse Church of God, and outreach programs were added to the mission, as other churches have done in the community.

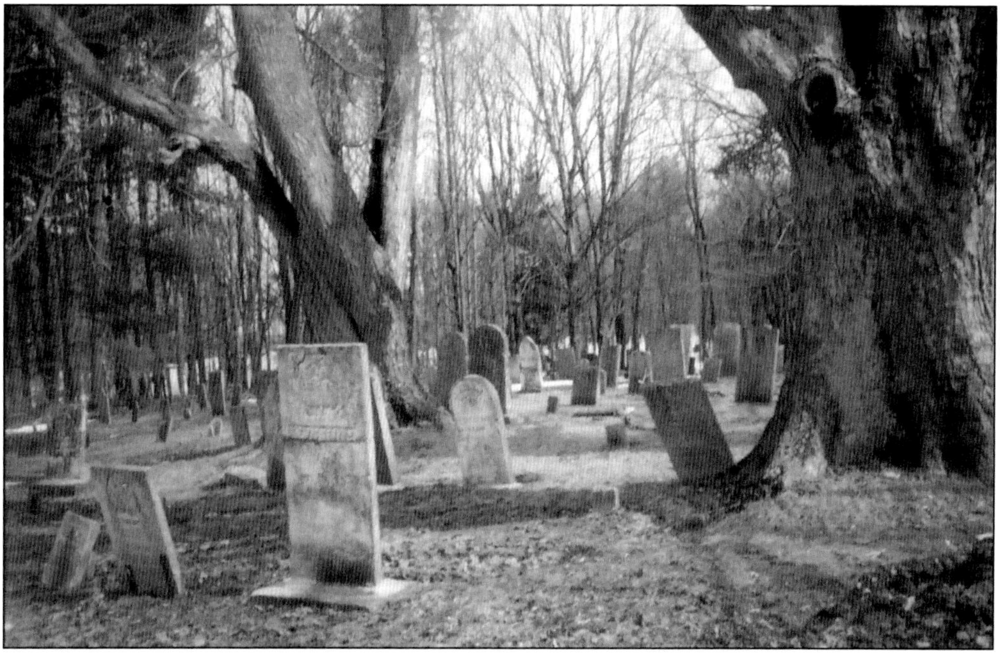

The Colosse Cemetery is on State Route 11 next to the Baptist church. The first two burials were a mother and her baby in 1810. The last burial was in 1912. The site of the Colosse Baptist Church was chosen close to the burying ground. It was the first church edifice in the town, built in 1823 and 1824. The church has always taken care of the cemetery. (Author's collection.)

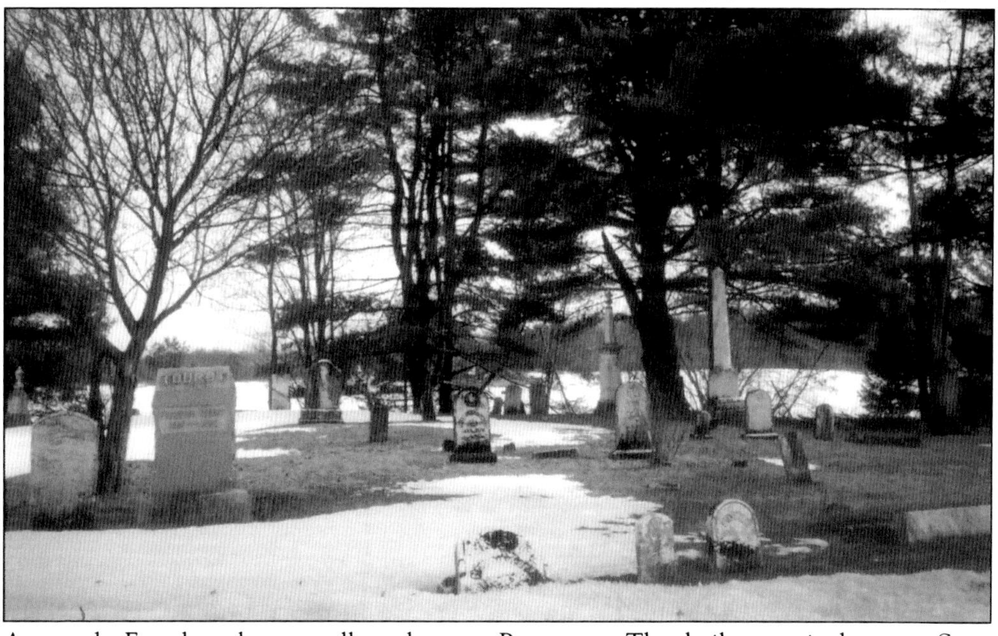

Among the French settlers, a small number were Protestants. They built a meetinghouse on State Route 11 about the same time St. Ann's Catholic Church was built on French Street in 1840. The building was sold in 1904 and razed for the lumber. Many of the bodies and gravestones were moved to the Parish and Central Square Cemeteries. Of the remaining stones, the earliest is 1844 and the latest is 1954. (Author's collection.)

Three

TEACHER SAID SO

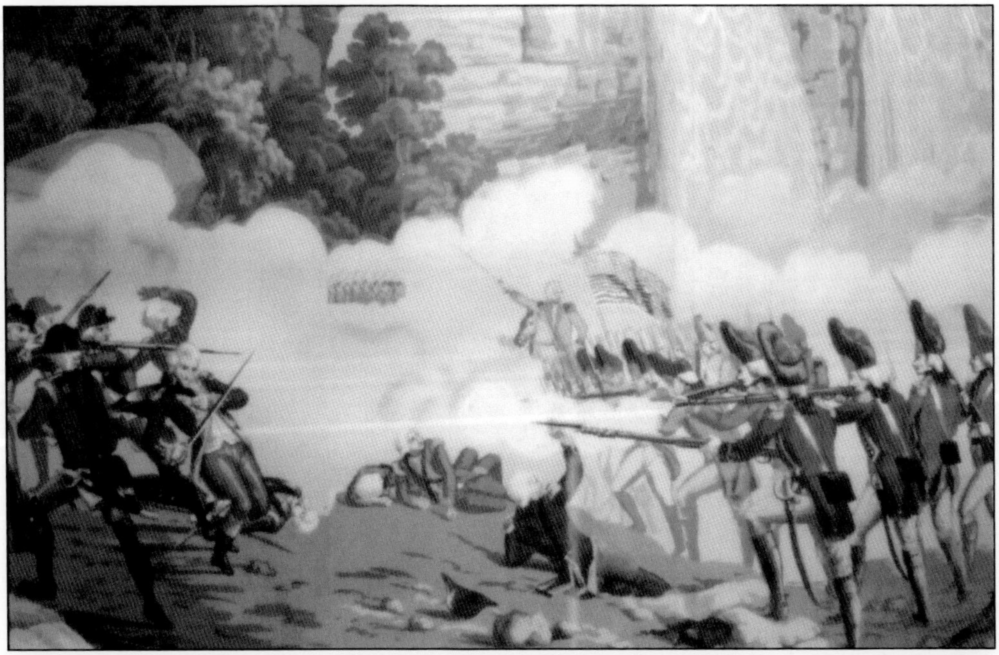

LaGuerre d'Independence is a colored, 32-strip, hand-carved wood block scenic mural located in the lobby of Mexico High School. The mural was printed in France in 1852 and in 1930. The Mexico mural is from the second printing. It is designed in five distinct scenes of historical significance depicting the war of independence. A significant number of the wood blocks were lost or destroyed in World War II. Mexico High School is the only site in the world where the mural is shown in its entirety.

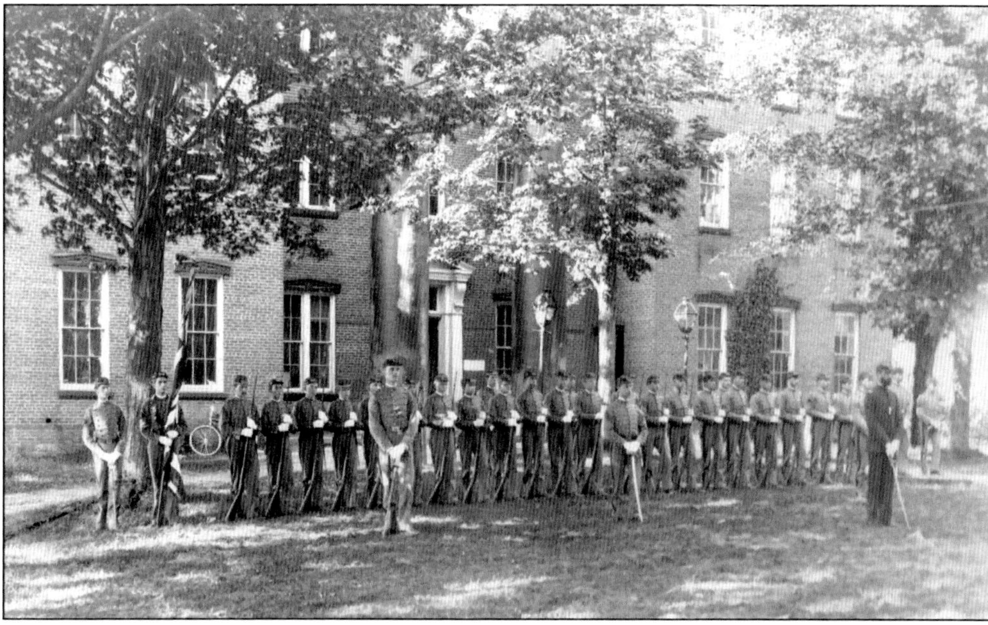

All schools were private in the 1800s and often leased to the principal. In 1893, Col. Melzar C. Richards (retired) of the U.S. Army leased the academy and organized Mexico Military Academy with a large faculty, military staff, and a cadet battalion fully officered. The military academy was short-lived because, in 1895, the state no longer recognized private academies. All children then attended free public schools.

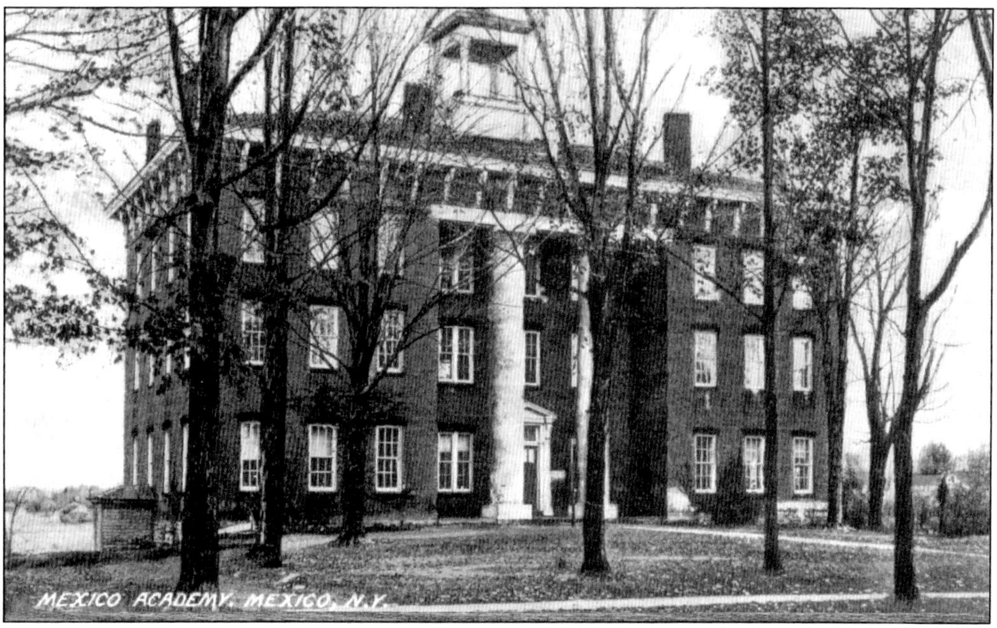

In 1854, with attendance increasing, the necessity of replacing Mexico Academy was inescapable. A sum of $7,500 was needed, and the people went to work, raising money by voluntary subscription and loan from the state (which was paid back). This dignified redbrick edifice was dedicated debt free in December 1855. The old academy was sold, but the bell was removed and hung in the belfry of the new school. (Author's collection.)

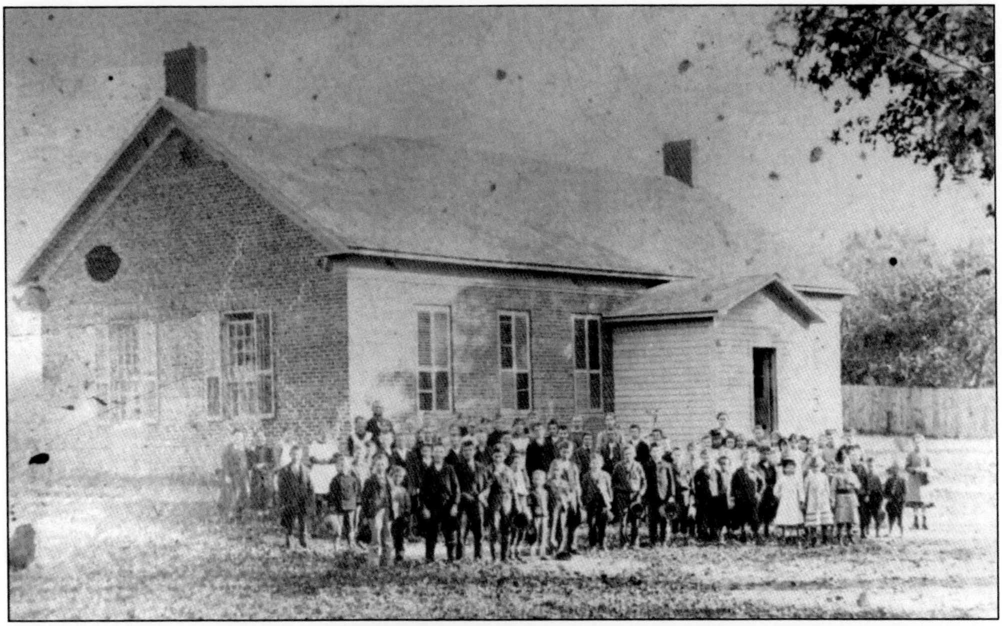

School District No. 8 was a two-room school built on the corner of Church Street and Madison Avenue in 1851. In 1854, John Ladd was paid $64 for teaching the four-month school in the upper room, and Julia Ladd was paid $20 for the four-month school in the primary room. Attendance was so great that a third room was added in 1886. It consolidated with the academy in 1895. (Courtesy of the Barry Haynes collection.)

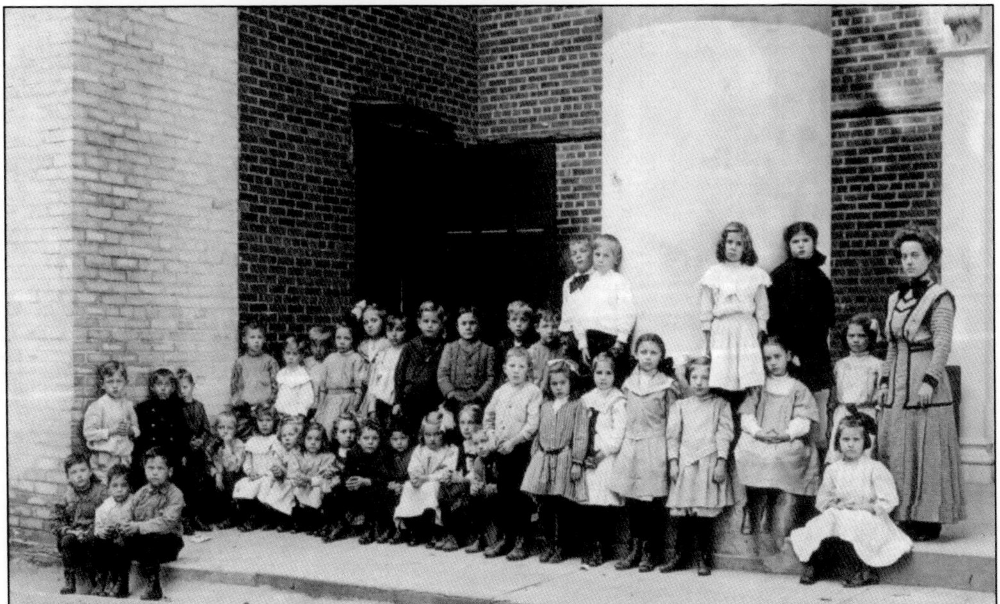

The three village schools consolidated with the academy in 1895 after changes in state laws. School No. 7 was on the west end of Main Street, school No. 9 was on North Street, and school No. 8 was on the corner of Church Street and Madison Avenue. Miss Norton's first-grade class of 1909 is an example of the size of the classes after the village schools consolidated. (Courtesy of the John Castle collection.)

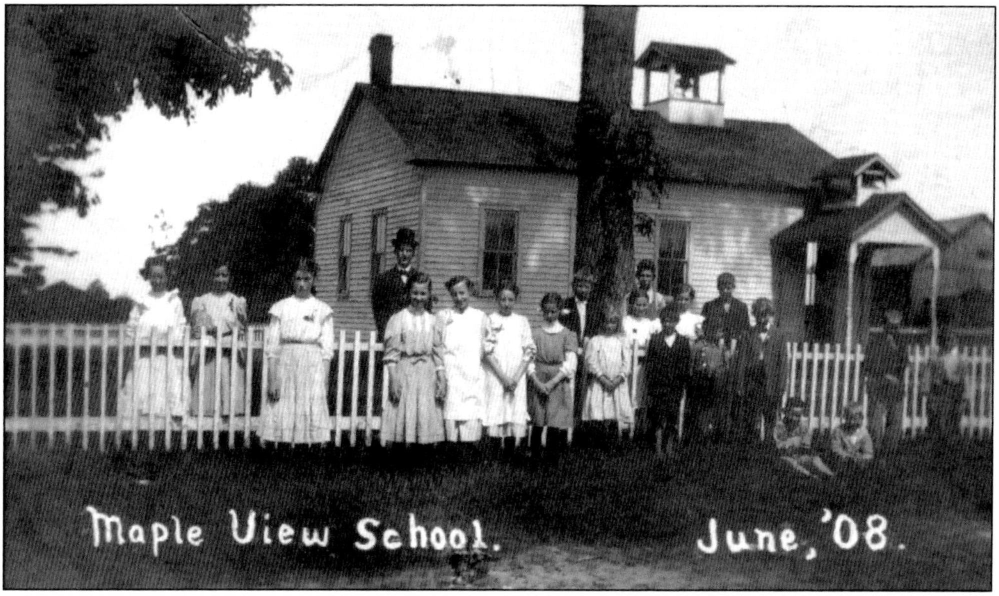

There were 18 common school districts in the town of Mexico in 1908. Most of the districts had one-room schools like the Maple View School shown here. Centralization of all schools in the town of Mexico, with the exception of Colosse, took place in 1936. Other districts in adjoining towns were added, making a total of 31 districts attending Mexico Academy and Central School in the village.

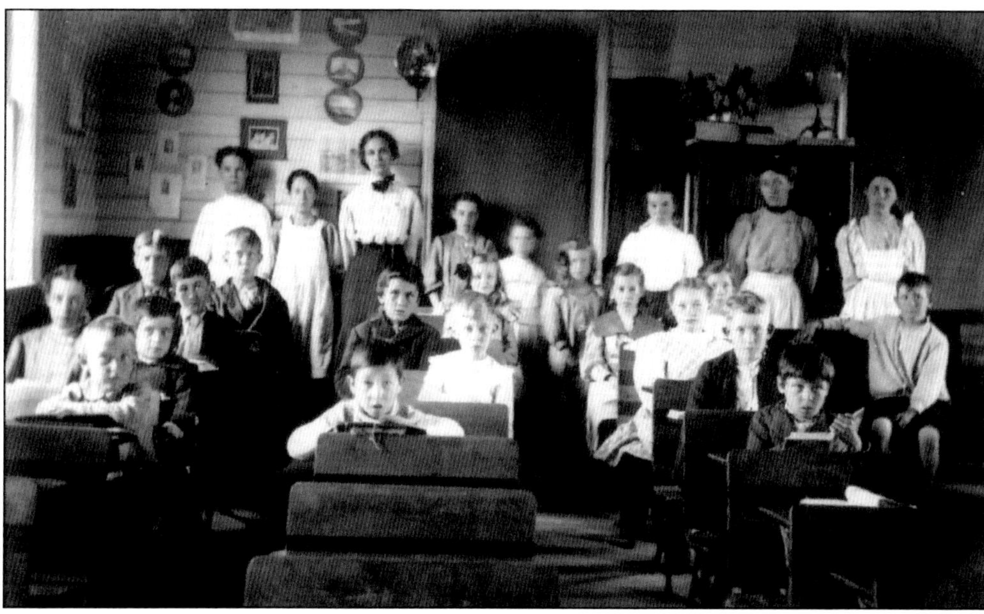

Judge Avery Skinner gave land in Union Square (Maple View) for a school in 1848. Here is the inside of the school with Ruth Patterson Geer as the teacher in the early 1900s. The district became famous in 1902 and won a second prize of $50 for having the best-kept school grounds in the state. In 1937, it was voted to be included in the Mexico school centralization plan.

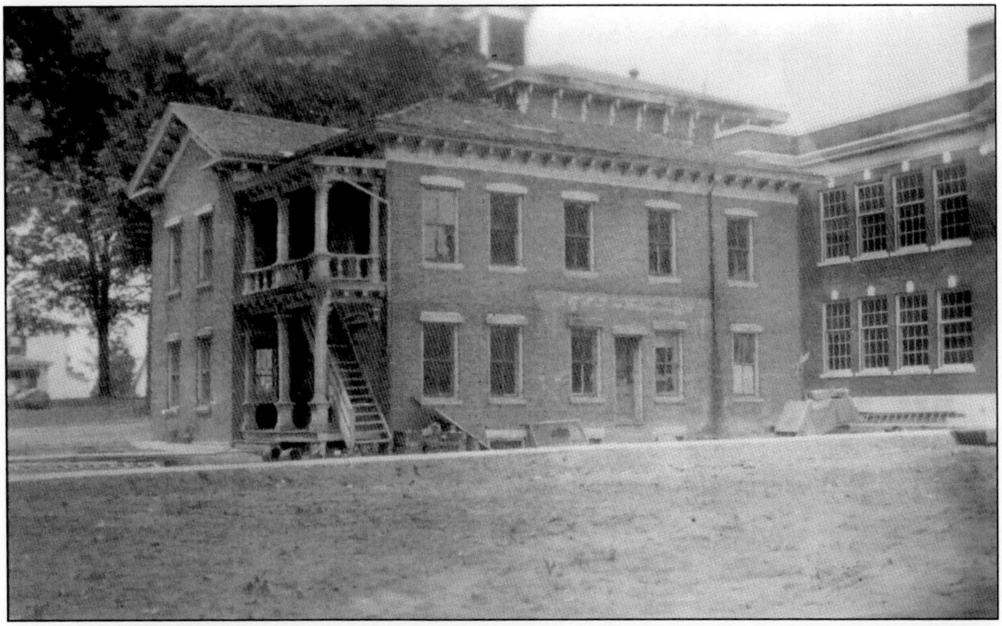

When the state ruled that all schools must be free public schools, Mexico reorganized the district. The three village elementary schools closed, and all the children went to the academy. The roof of that building can be seen over the Lewis Miller house in the foreground. The Miller house was bought in 1919 for grades one through three and the agriculture department. The 1929 school is seen on the right. (Courtesy of the John Castle collection.)

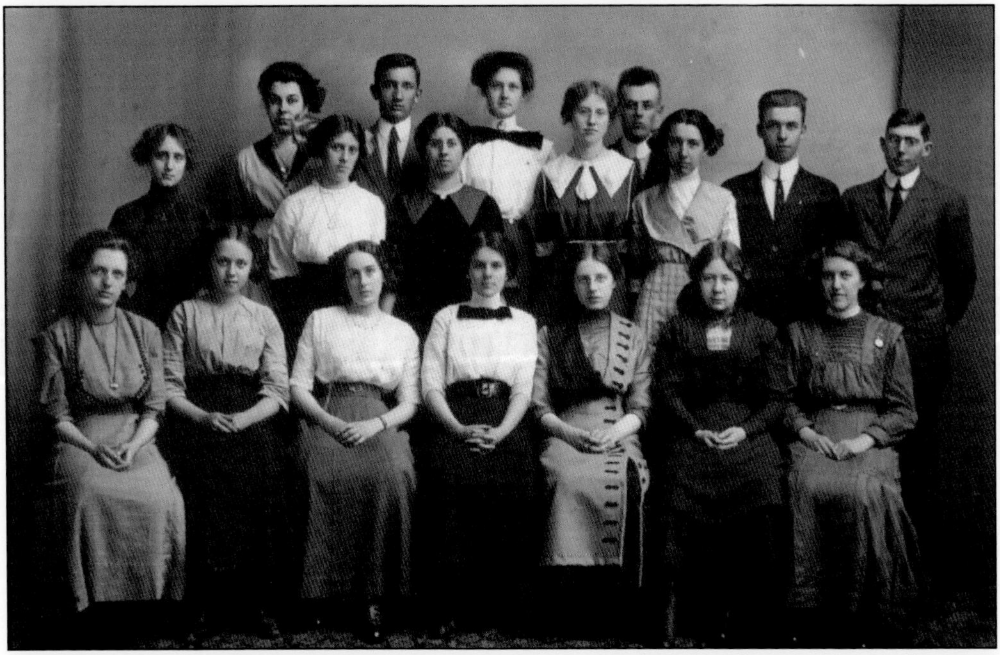

The senior class of 1912 had 18 members; the freshmen class had 40. This was the usual pattern of the high school in the early 20th century. The young people dropped out to go to work and learned a business by experience or a trade by becoming an apprentice. Ina B. Stone, teacher at Mexico Academy from 1923 to 1958, is the first girl on the left. (Author's collection.)

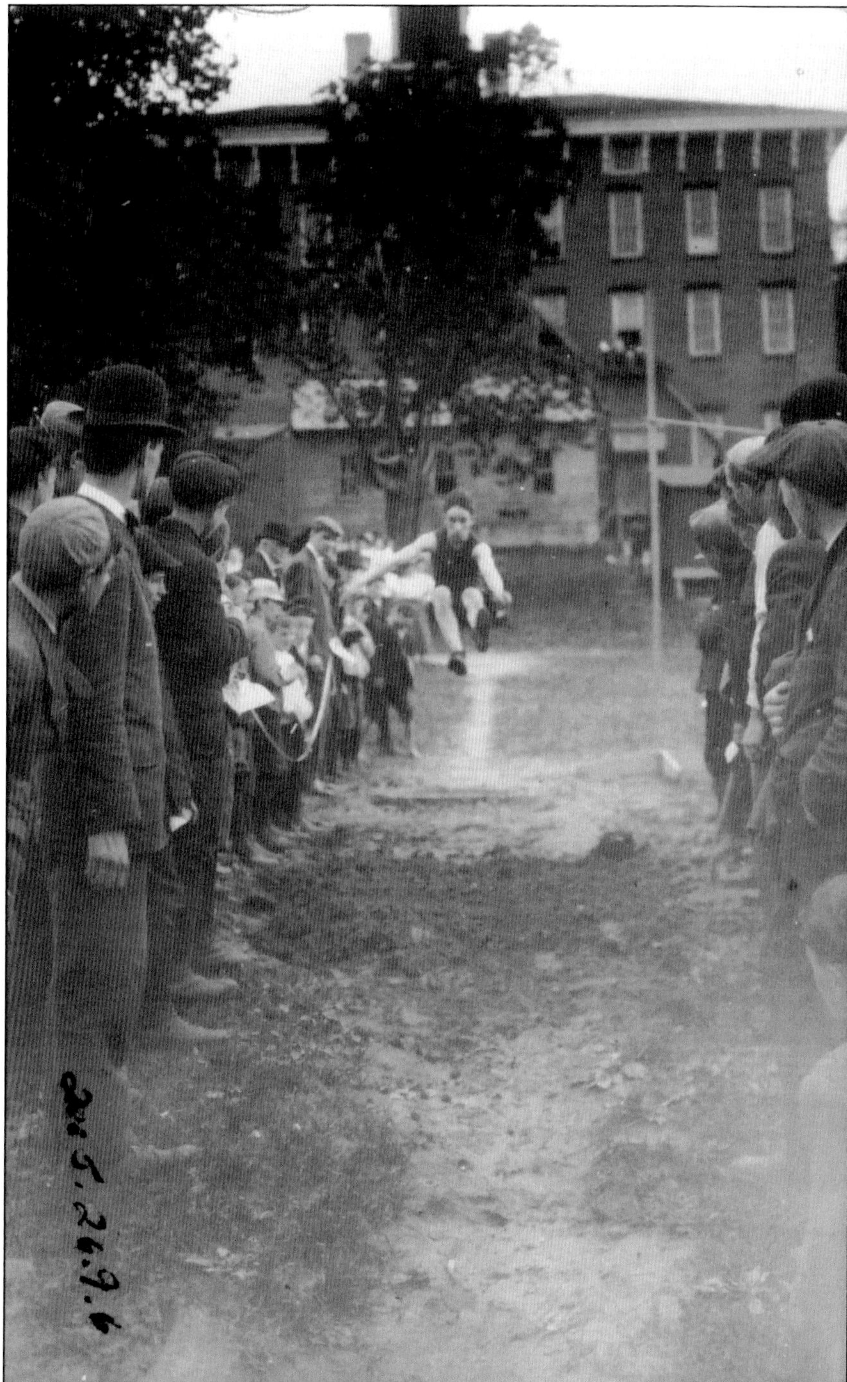

Without a doubt, the event of the school year and the spark of school spirit was the interclass track meet. The townspeople and students lined up as the boys did the broad jump. In 1908, Fred Pond came in first in this event, going a distance of 17 feet, 10.5 inches. In 1907, Professor Woodward presented the high school with a silver cup. Members of the winning team of the interclass track meet had their names engraved on the cup for the next few years.

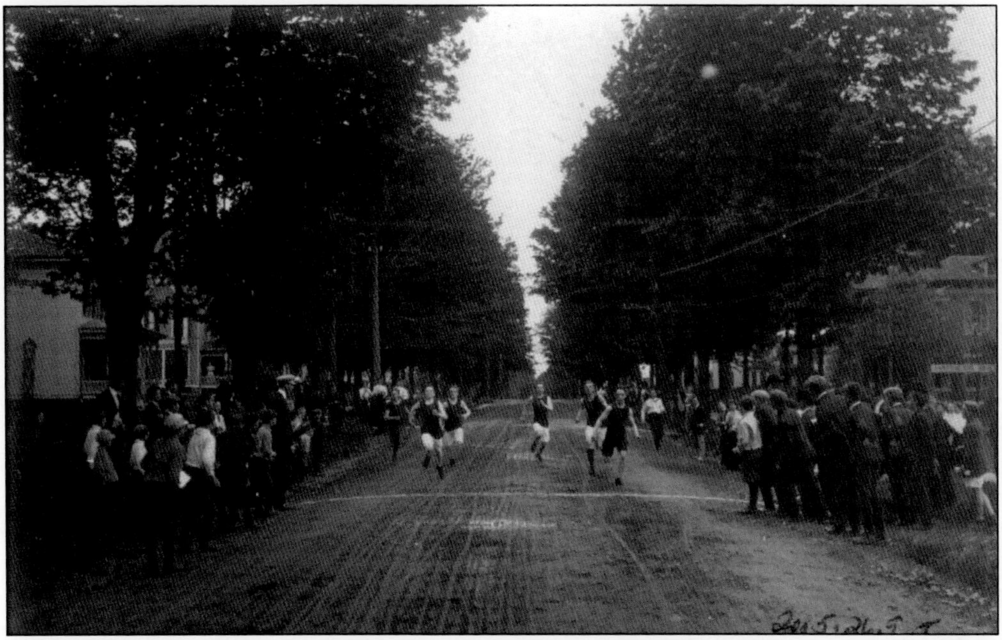

About 100 townspeople lined the street to watch the 100-yard dash in 1908. A fee was charged, and nearly $10 was raised. The money was to be used for supplies for the athletic program the following year. Intramurals continued to be popular until school buses became available to transport teams to neighboring schools.

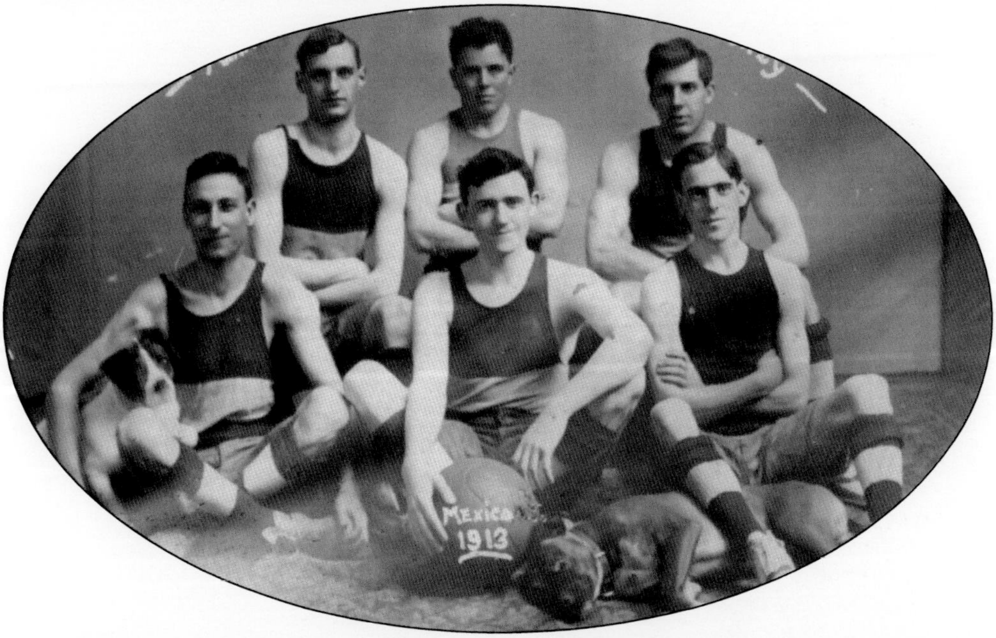

The 1913 Mexico High School basketball team of Davis, Day, Dolph, Maybie, Stevens, and Taylor played the first game with the Sandy Creek High School team at Sandy Creek. The team played well, although the floor was about 30 feet by 20 feet, and the fast forwards could not get around the room without blowing out the lights. They also played an Oswego Church team and town teams from Phoenix and Manlius. (Courtesy of the John Castle collection.)

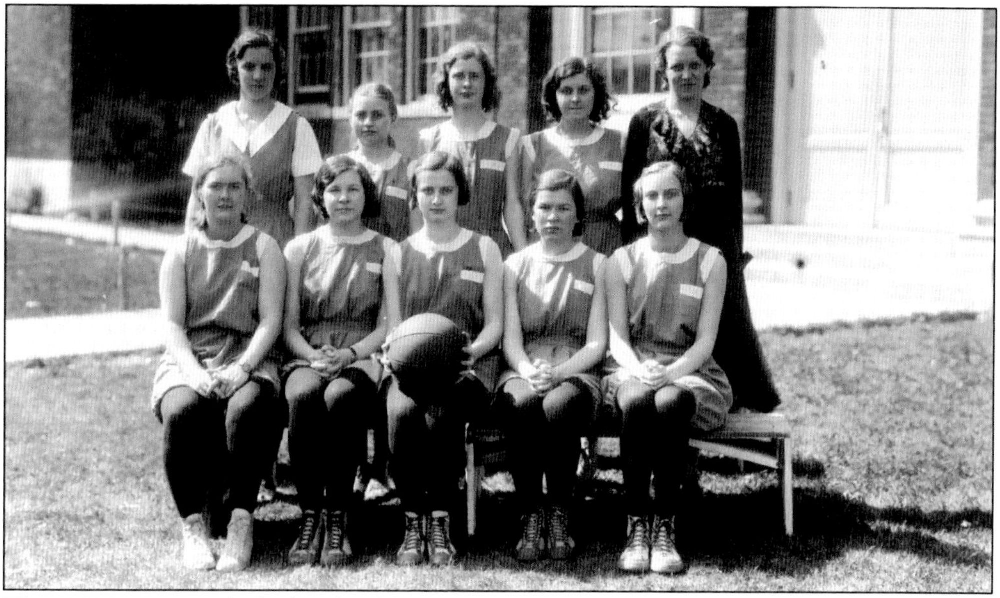

The 1932 Mexico girls' high school basketball team tied with Camden for first place in the league. The team lost the play-off game by one point at the final whistle. Pictured are, from left to right, (first row) Lois Switts, Frances Jones, Charlotte Smith, Elma Jones, and Hilda Barton; (second row) Seraphine Rose, Margaret Armstrong, Merle Graves, Zirita Bloodgood, and Jean Robinson. (Author's collection.)

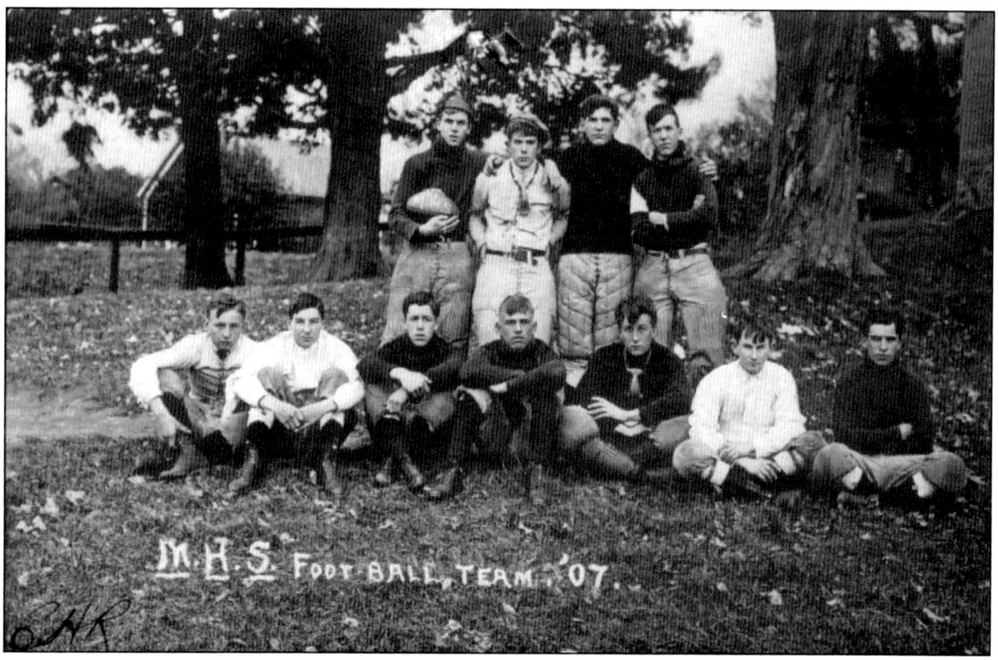

The first real football team from Mexico High School was organized in 1903. That year, the team was undefeated and won the first championship in the history of the academy. The banner was won again in 1904. In 1909, Mexico won the Oswego County championship. The players wore new suits that were purchased from monies raised by subscription. The 1907 football team had a great year. (Author's collection.)

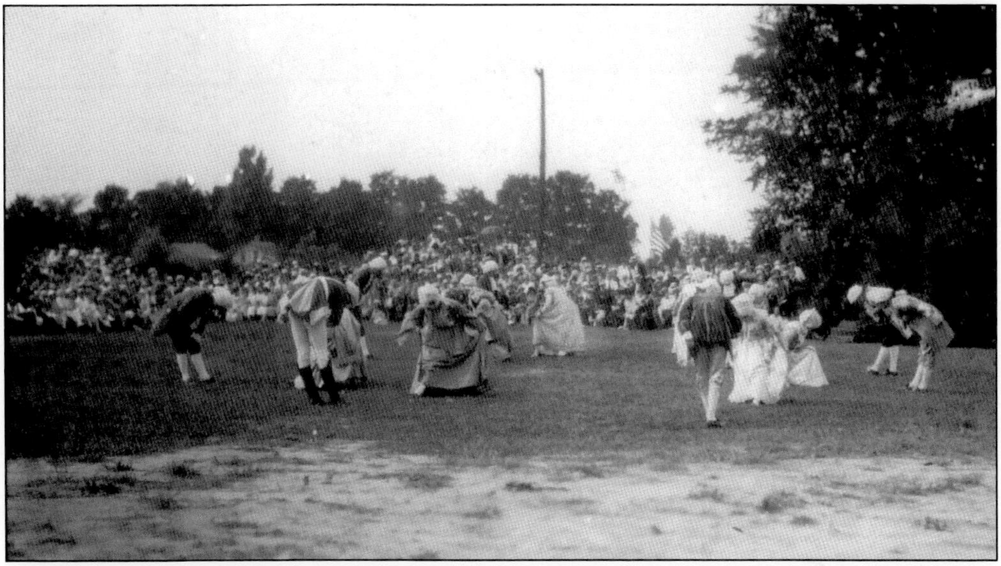

One of the most outstanding community events of the 20th century was the centennial celebration of Mexico Academy in 1926. The entire community was involved in committee planning or in pageant participation. A group of 11 committees coordinated all planning and logistics for the grand occasion. Because the celebration was scheduled over four days, considerations for lodging, meals, and transportation were essential. Each of the four days centered on a specific theme: Sunday for church services, Monday for registration and a reception banquet at Oswego's Hotel Pontiac, Tuesday for the historical pageant, and Wednesday for a festive picnic at the lake. Since the pageant attracted an estimated 1,000 spectators and involved hundreds more in performance and support activities, community resources were tightly stretched. The six-episode performance featuring music, dance and scenery, and requiring 14 field marshals, was a triumphant success as shown in these two photographs. Above, Colonial ladies and gentlemen dance the minuet while below, the "Sprit Triumphant" shows the Spirit of the Flanders Field in her golden chariot. (Above, courtesy of the Barry Haynes collection.)

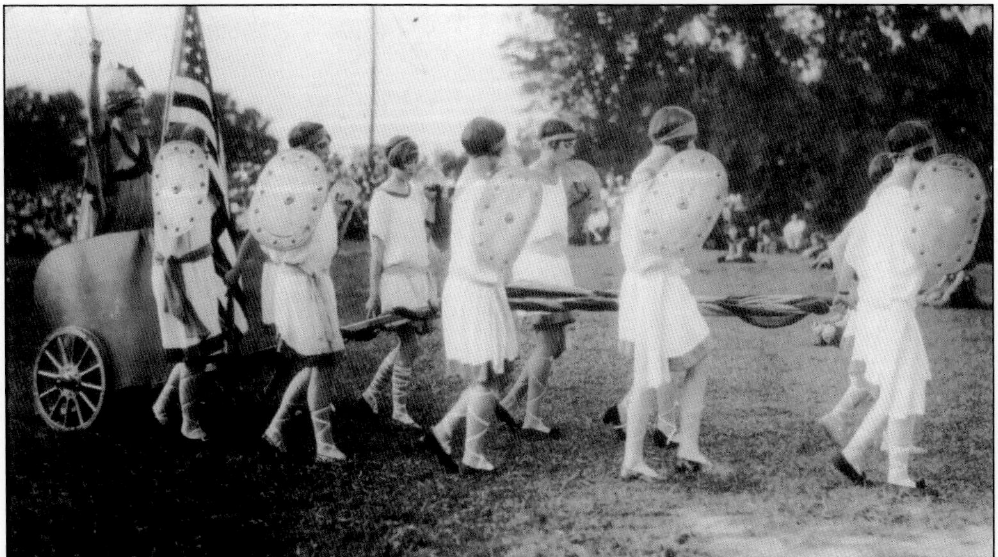

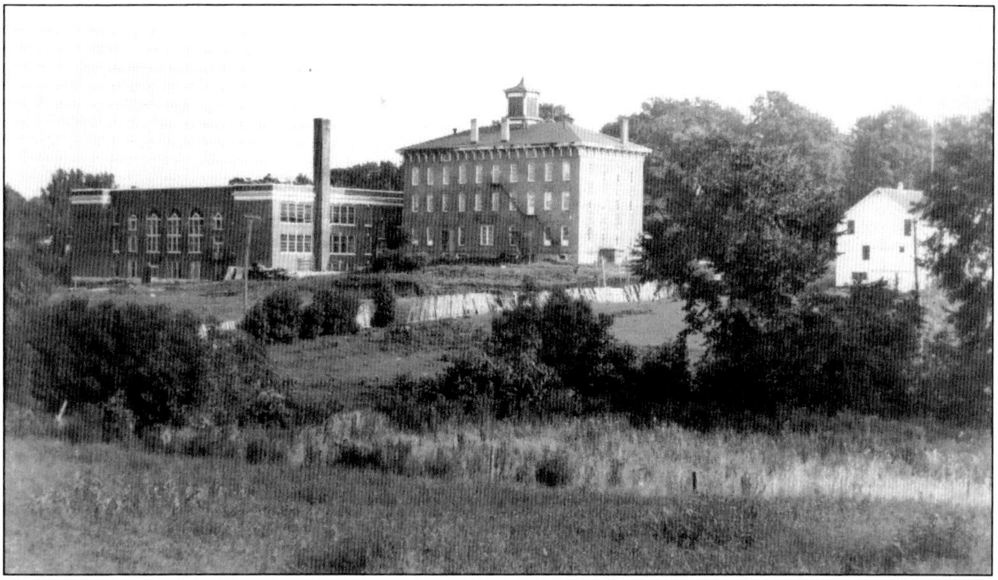

The back of the 1928 academy and the previous academy stood side by side until 1930 when the 1855 building was razed. The bell from that school was saved in one of the classrooms in the new school. Most of the land in the foreground was privately owned until 1937 when the academy was completed and the campus was enlarged. (Courtesy of the Barry Haynes collection.)

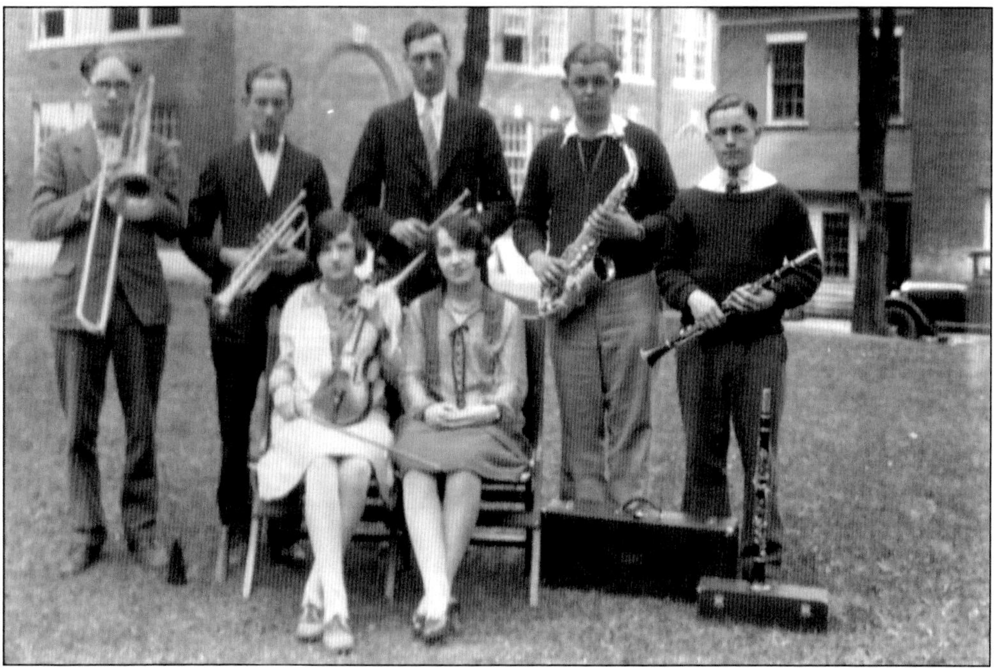

The orchestra was first organized by these high school students in 1928. The group was led by Glen Smith. Members are, from left to right, (first row) Grace Buck and Mary Hurlbut; (second row) Walter Weeden, Charles Whitney, Laverne Leavitte, Ross Stevens, and Warner Buck. Every Friday, the orchestra played during morning exercise and also at several dances that were held throughout the year. A music teacher initiated a wood and instrumental music program in 1929.

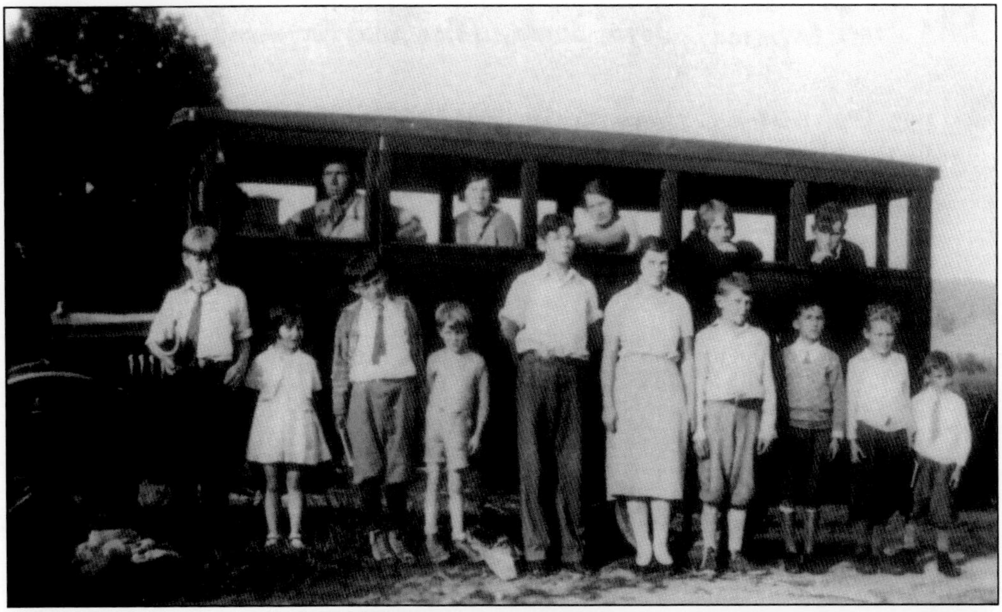

Some of the country schools closed before centralization. The Butterfly School was one of them. A bus was purchased to bring those children to the village school. Sitting in the bus with driver Ollie Thompson are, from left to right, Frances Jones (Eggleston), Rita Jones (Raymond), Joyce Jones, and Allie Raymond. Standing by the bus are, from left to right, Richard Guile, Dawn Emlaw, Jack Tessier, Calvin Jordal, Floyd Jones, Elma Jones, David Jones, Timothy Sachel, Ralph Schmidt, and George Sachel. (Courtesy of Allen Humbert.)

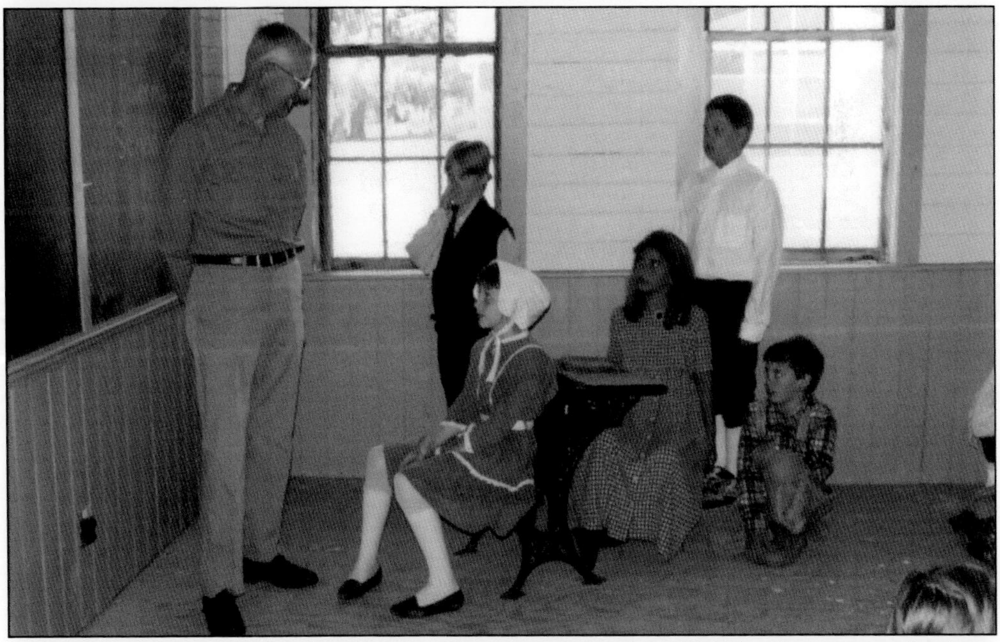

Palermo joined the Mexico school system when it centralized in 1936. An elementary school was built next to the one-room school. The old building was used for a bus garage until it was recently restored. It is now used as a teaching tool for classes to come for the day, and they often dress as children who attended the school years ago. Dr. Ken Richards leads the class on this day.

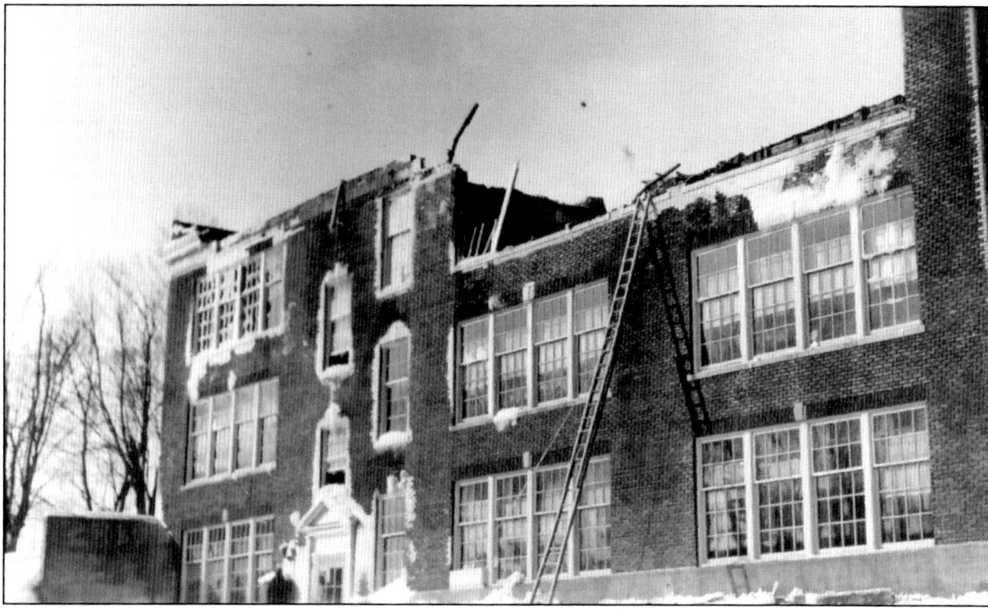

The newly built 1928 Mexico High School was short-lived when it was ruined by fire in February 1936. Oswego and Pulaski answered a call for help and brought extra hose and pumpers. The new electric village water pump stood up under the heavy strain, and water from Black Creek helped quench the fire. By dawn, the entire roof was gone and the upper floor in ruins. Crews of men and boys cleared the debris from the second floor and swept water out of the lower floors to prevent damage from freezing. Electricity and heat were restored to the lower floors to prevent damage to the walls. Books were taken to the town hall for safekeeping. For the next two years, grades one through eight and all the high school classes had makeshift housing.

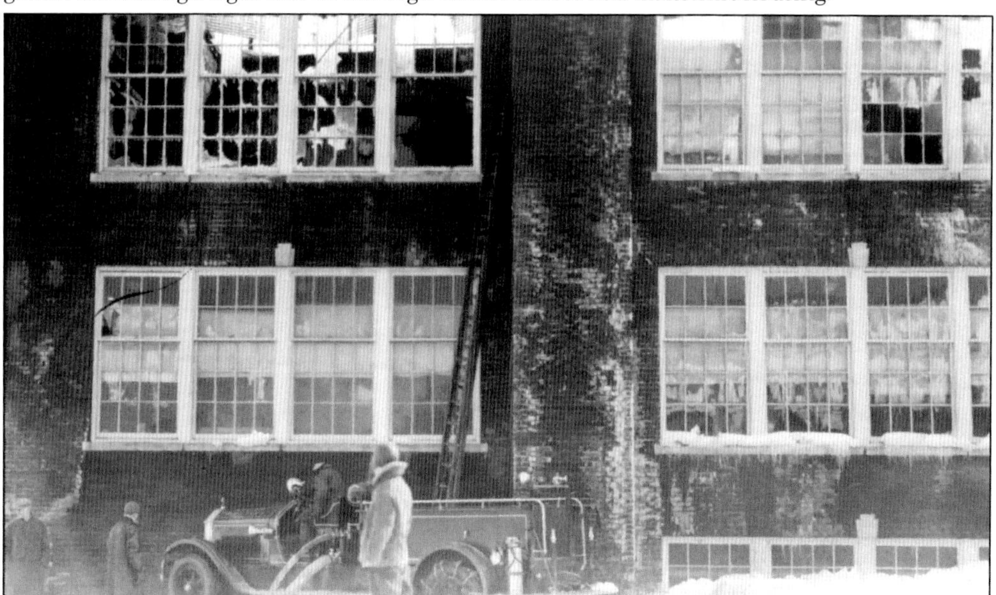

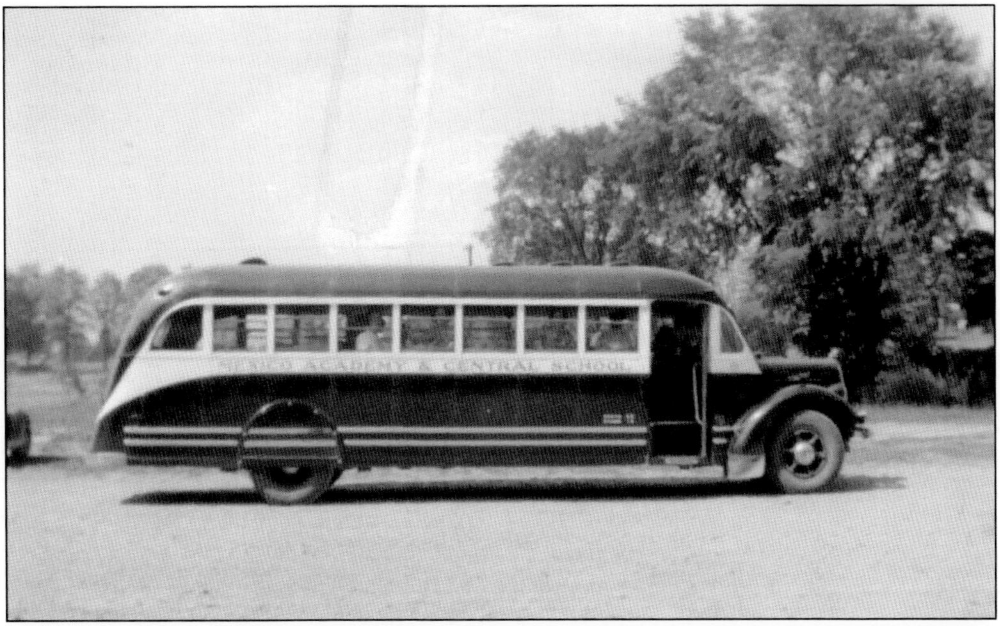

When the Mexico Academy centralized in 1937, more buses were needed to bring in the children from the neighborhood one-room schools that were closing. This was bus no. 9, the highest number in the fleet of buses. The early buses were painted with the school colors—orange and black. Later the color had been changed to the standard yellow. (Courtesy of Allen Humbert.)

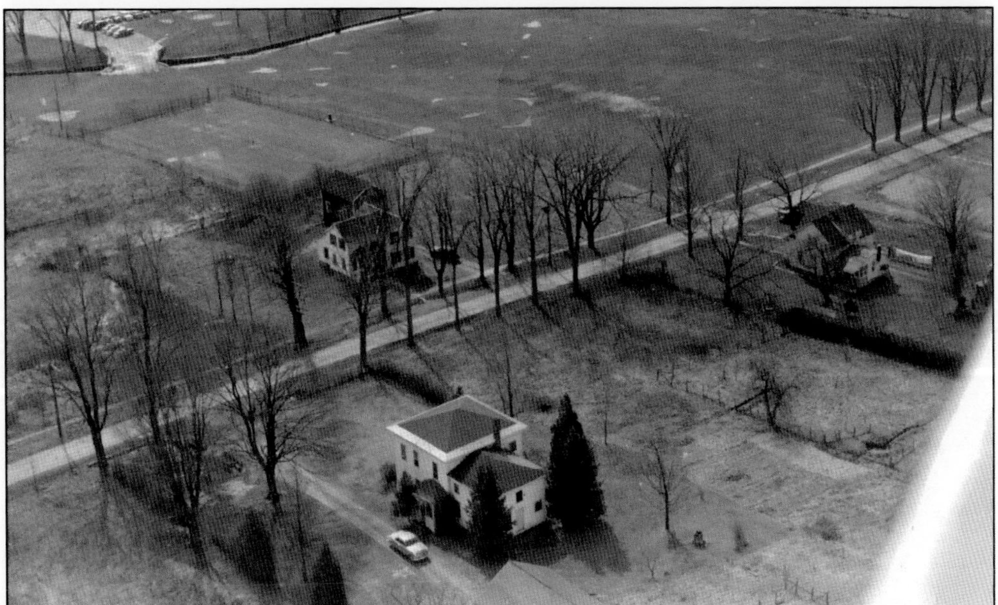

A large athletic field was included with the new school in 1937. The house by the tennis court was the home and studio of Doris and James Murphy. The house in the foreground was the home of Howard and Florence Fultz and is now owned by Richard Beck. The house on the right was the home of Charles and Mildred Graves and is now owned by their son DeMilt Graves. (Author's collection.)

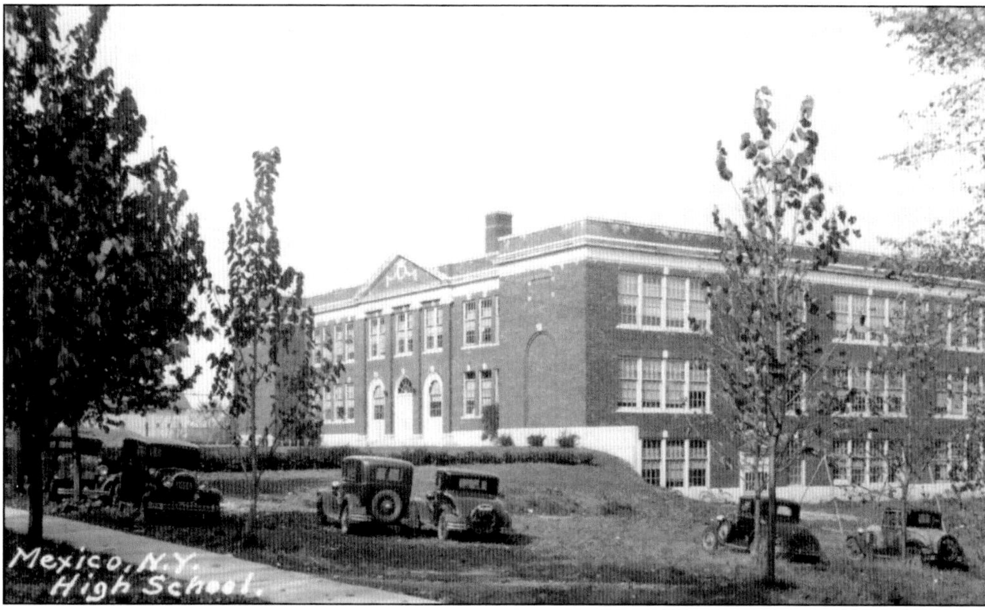

In 1926, the state department of education declared the academy inadequate and demanded a new school be built. In 1928, this building, the fourth academy, was dedicated. It had no belfry, so the bell was placed in one of the classrooms, and the white marble tablet from the 1855 school was preserved in one of the halls. This building burned in 1936. (Author's collection.)

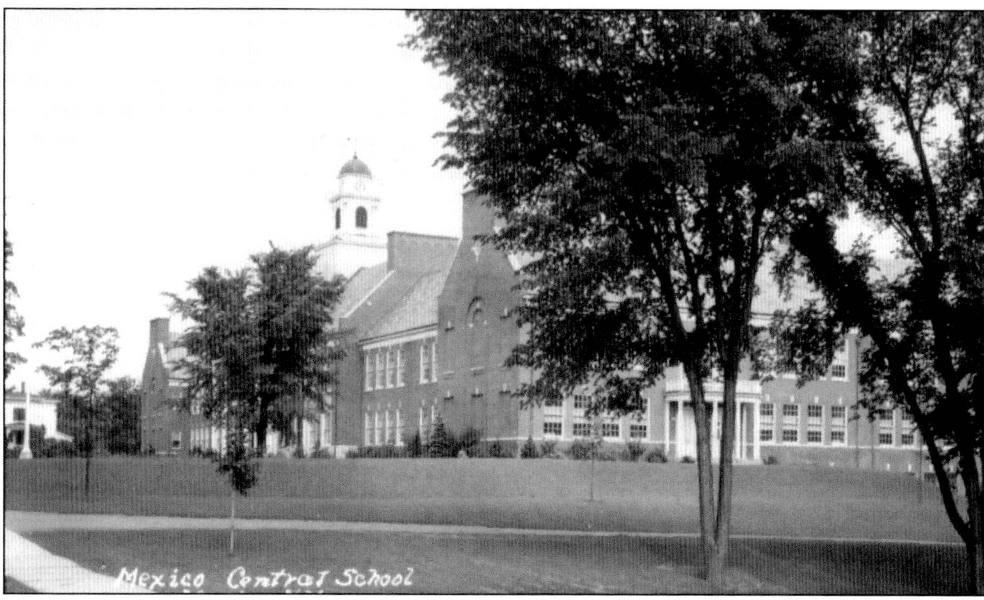

The construction work of the fifth academy was done in 1937 by the Public Works Administration, a division of the Works Progress Administration (WPA). The group consisted of skilled workers, including masons and carpenters. New construction from the front entrance west was necessary. The 1836 bell was hung in the belfry and still rings with the starting of school each September. A kindergarten was included in the school for the first time. (Author's collection.)

Four

Where the *Inn* People Play

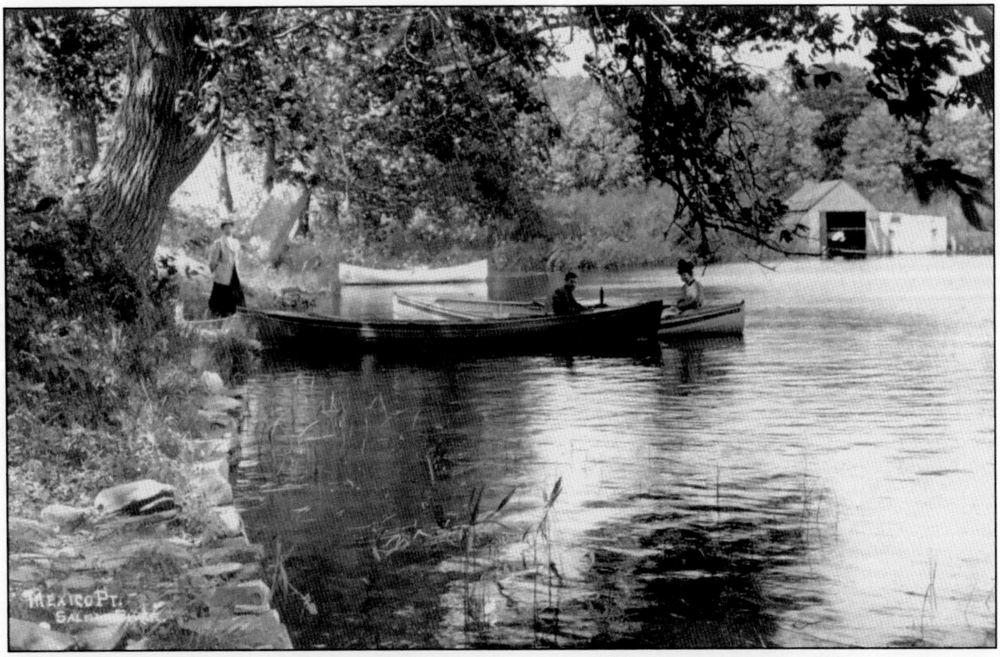

Each of the grand hotels at Mexico Point had boats available for their guests. They could row a short way up the Little Salmon River, drift in the bay, or go out on the lake for the afternoon. Some of the guests enjoyed a few hours catching fish, which the hotel cooks would fix for supper. (Author's collection.)

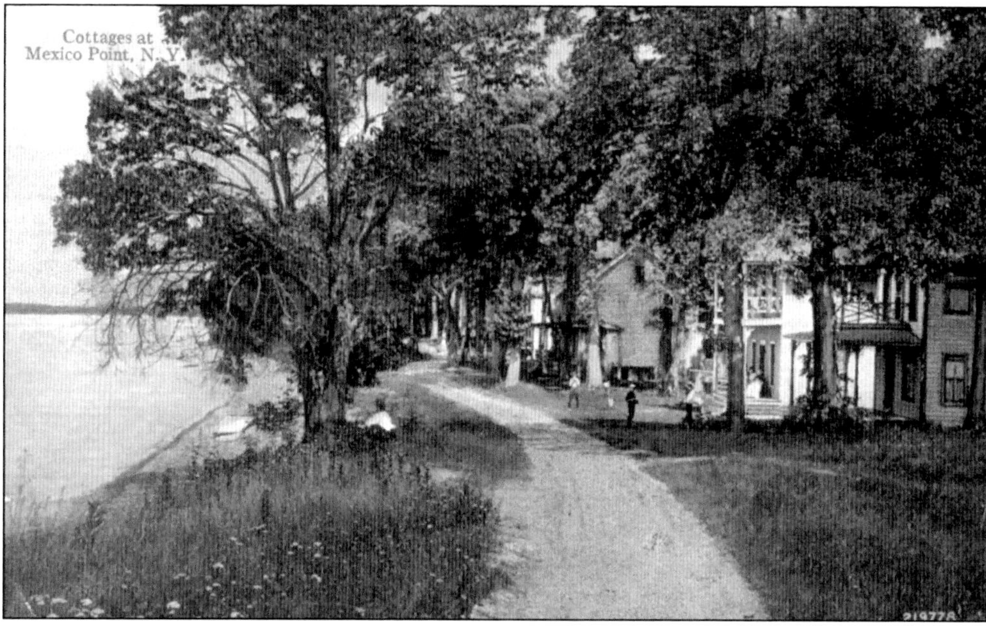

The road from Texas to the lake on the east side of the Little Salmon River was not close to the river, so when the road reached the lake, it was necessary to go west along the water to get to Mexico Point and Twice Told Hotel. Large cottages were built along the road, and families moved to Lake Ontario for extended vacations, staying for weeks at a time. (Author's collection.)

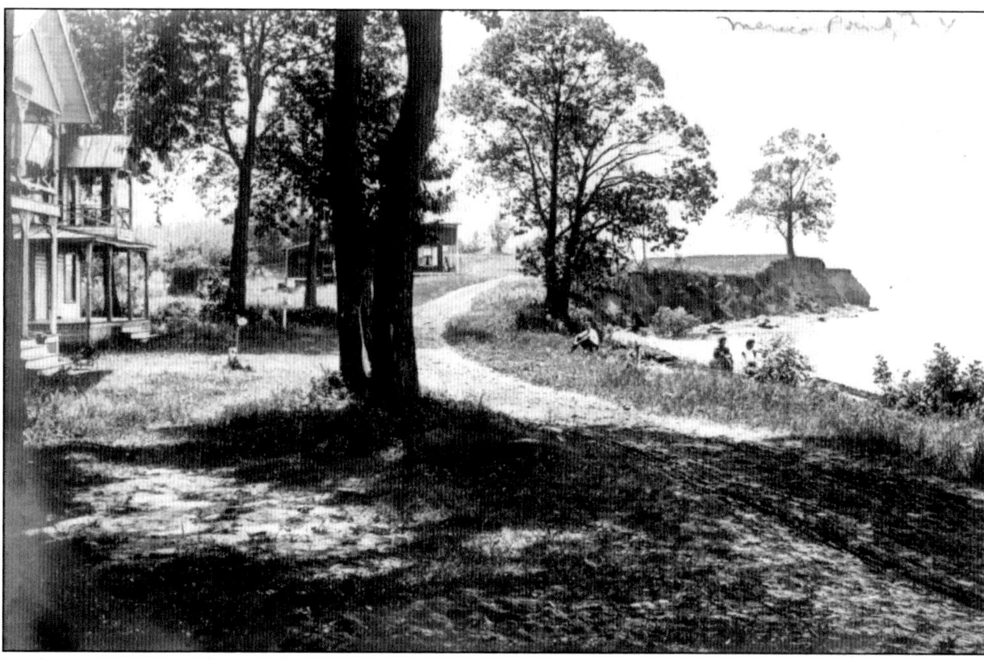

In the early 1900s, the road on the east side of Lake Ontario went west along the water in front of a row of cottages. The waves, ice, and wind undermined the banks every year. The people on the right of the picture look at a tree that had recently fallen into the lake. The tree on the point is ready to fall with the next north wind. (Author's collection.)

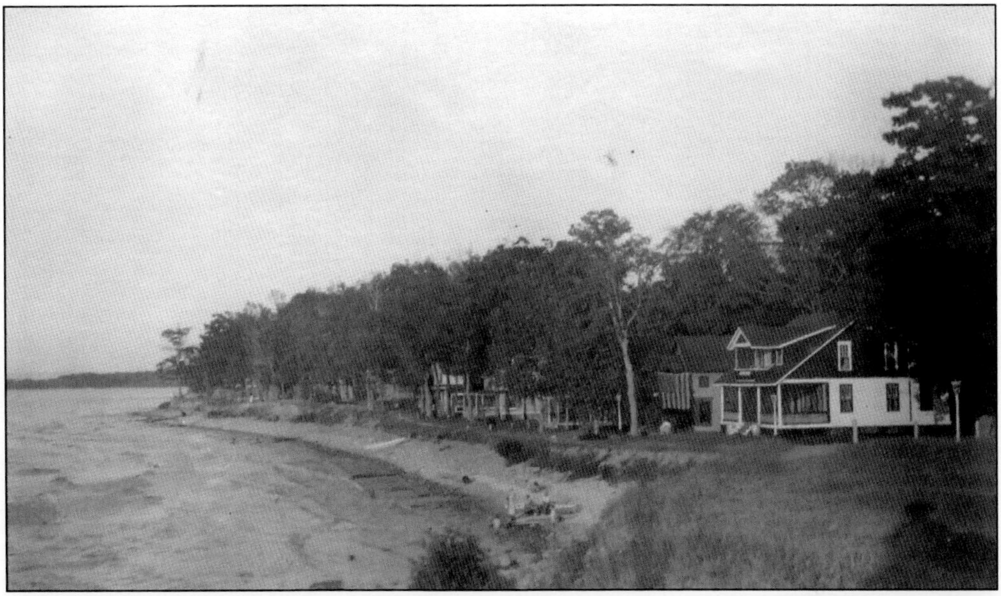

By the 1930s, erosion had taken away the road that was in front of the cottages. The buildings were remodeled, moved back from the lake, or taken down, and new small camps were built farther from the water. The road was constructed behind the camps. The vacationers enjoyed the lake from their porches, and small docks that were put in the water in the spring and taken up in the fall.

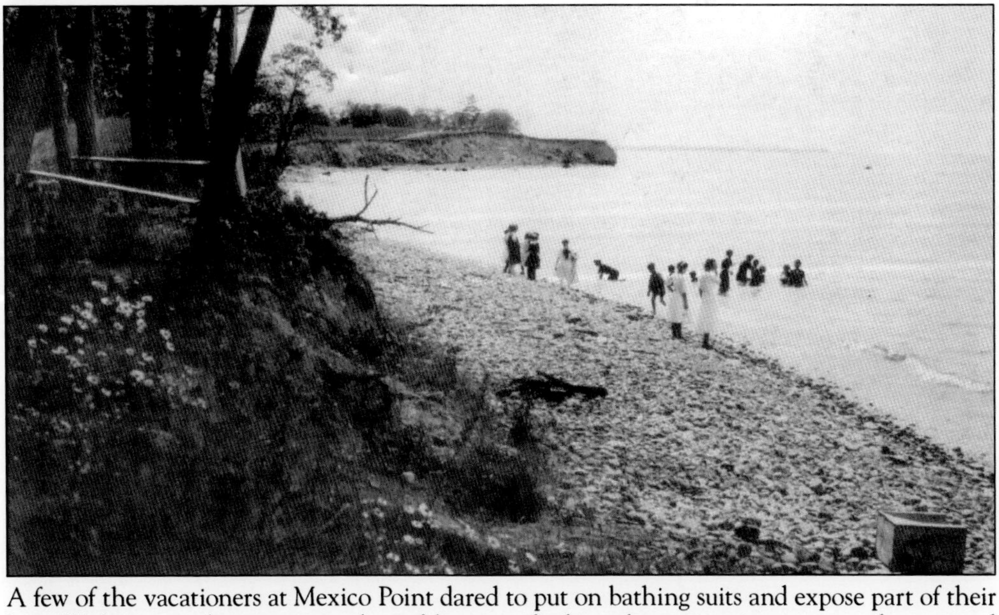

A few of the vacationers at Mexico Point dared to put on bathing suits and expose part of their legs. Wading into the water must have felt very refreshing, but swimming in a wet, heavy wool bathing suit was very difficult. One bather in this photograph has found crawling to be the easiest way to enjoy the water on the rocky shores. (Courtesy of the Barry Haynes collection.)

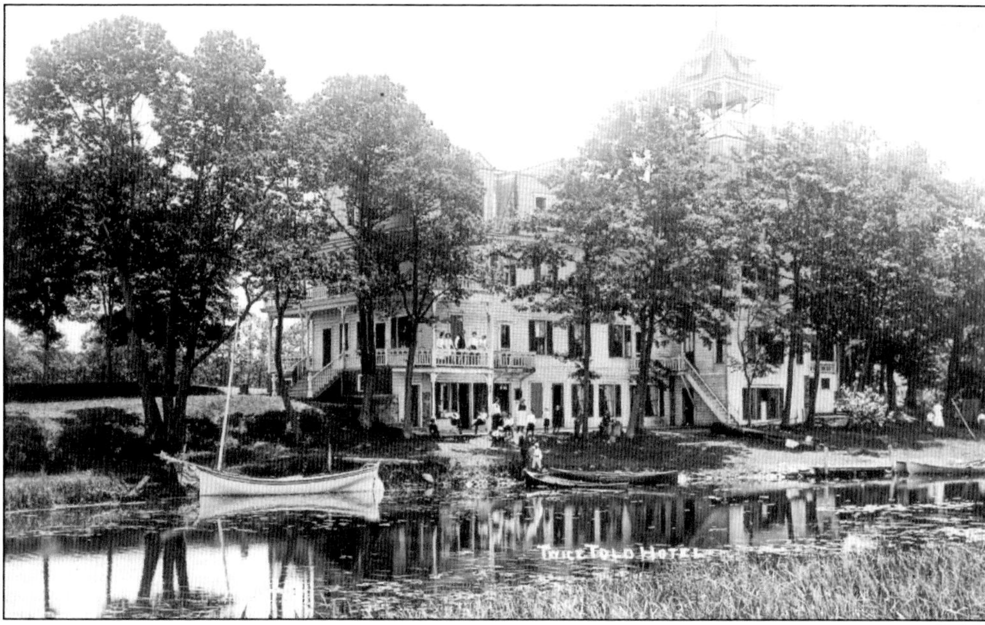

The Twice Told Hotel was the elaborate hotel built in 1891 on the east side of the Little Salmon River at Mexico Point. It accommodated 150 guests and entertained over 400 local people who came for rest and relaxation on the weekends. The hotel burned in 1907 and again in 1914. This view was taken from the west side and shows the front facing the lake. (Courtesy of the John Castle collection.)

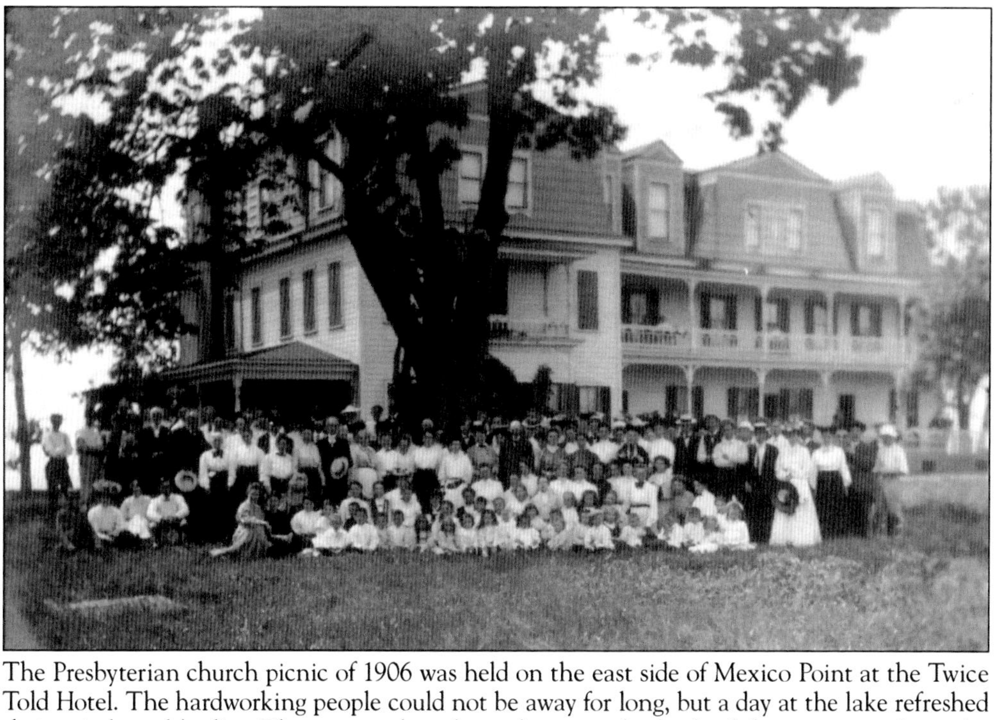

The Presbyterian church picnic of 1906 was held on the east side of Mexico Point at the Twice Told Hotel. The hardworking people could not be away for long, but a day at the lake refreshed their minds and bodies. There was a long horse barn on the back of the property where the animals were hitched, fed, and watered. (Author's collection.)

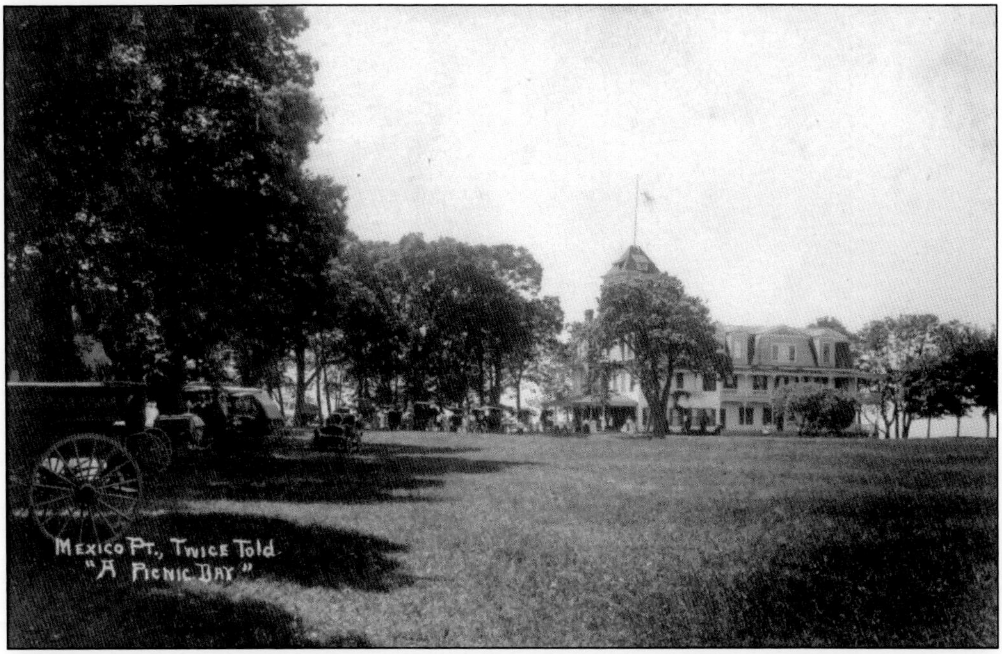

The large field at the Twice Told Hotel added greatly to its popularity with plenty of room for parking near the hotel for automobiles and a horse barn at the back where there was room for horses and carriages. The horses had a shady corral and plenty of water, so they were comfortable for hours as their owners played baseball in the nearby field.

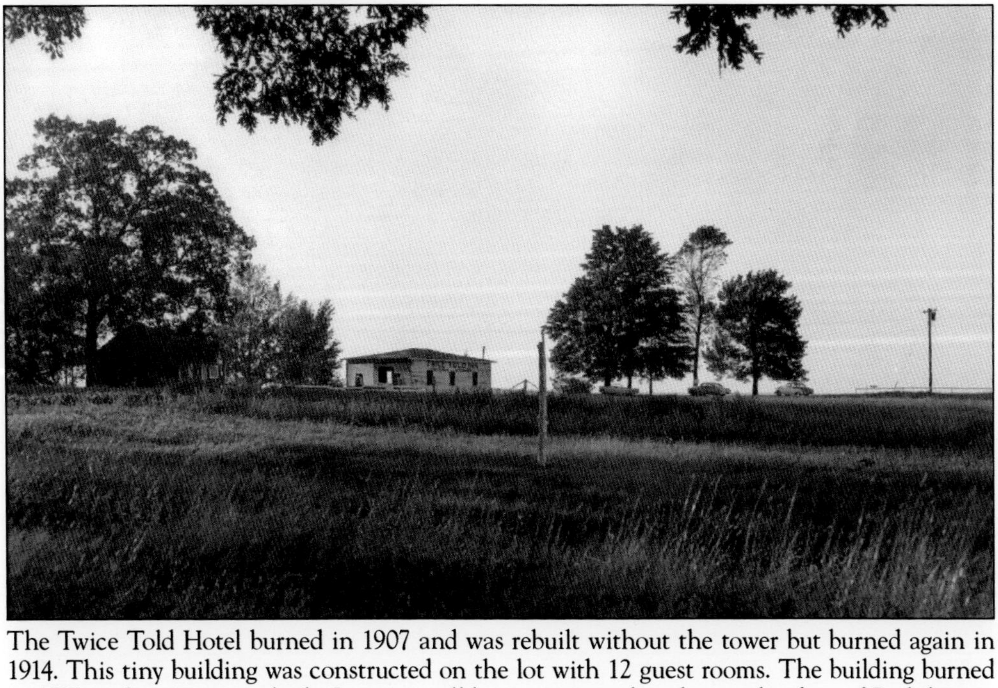

The Twice Told Hotel burned in 1907 and was rebuilt without the tower but burned again in 1914. This tiny building was constructed on the lot with 12 guest rooms. The building burned in 1921 and was never rebuilt. It was a well-known secret that during the days of Prohibition, Mexico Point was a smugglers' harbor to bring in liquor from Canada. (Courtesy of the John Castle collection.)

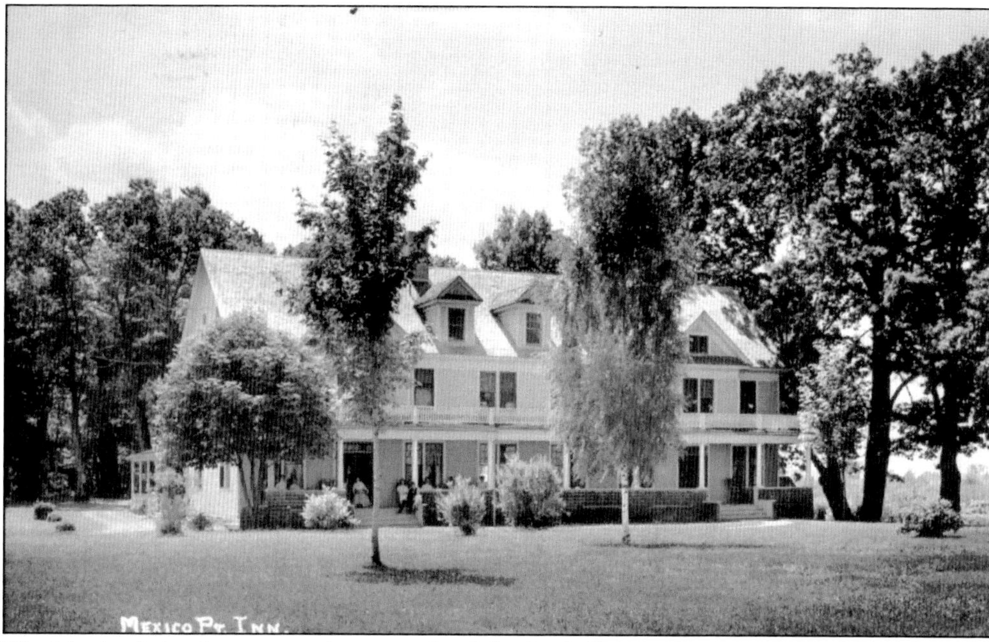

The Mexico Point Inn was on the west side of the Little Salmon River at Mexico Point. Like its sister, the Twice Told Hotel, on the east side of the river, guests came for a week or more to relax and play at Lake Ontario. The inn was badly damaged by fire and rebuilt by the Hungerford estate. (Author's collection.)

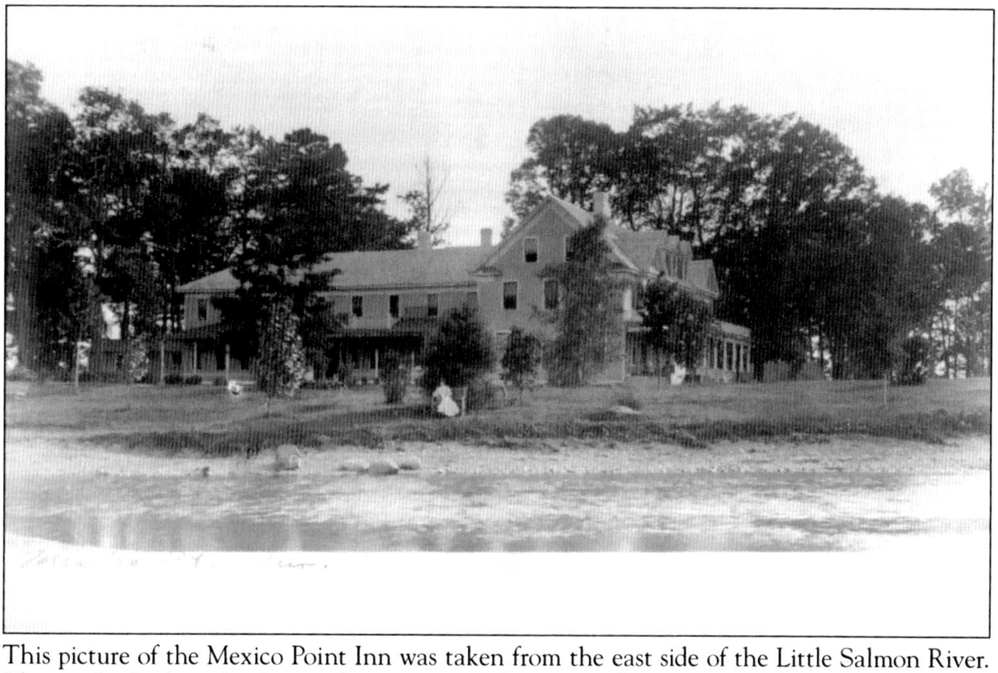

This picture of the Mexico Point Inn was taken from the east side of the Little Salmon River. The inn had a large kitchen, a dining room, a lounge, and many second-floor bedrooms. The public beach was in front of the inn. The land on the west was not sold for cottages until many years later.

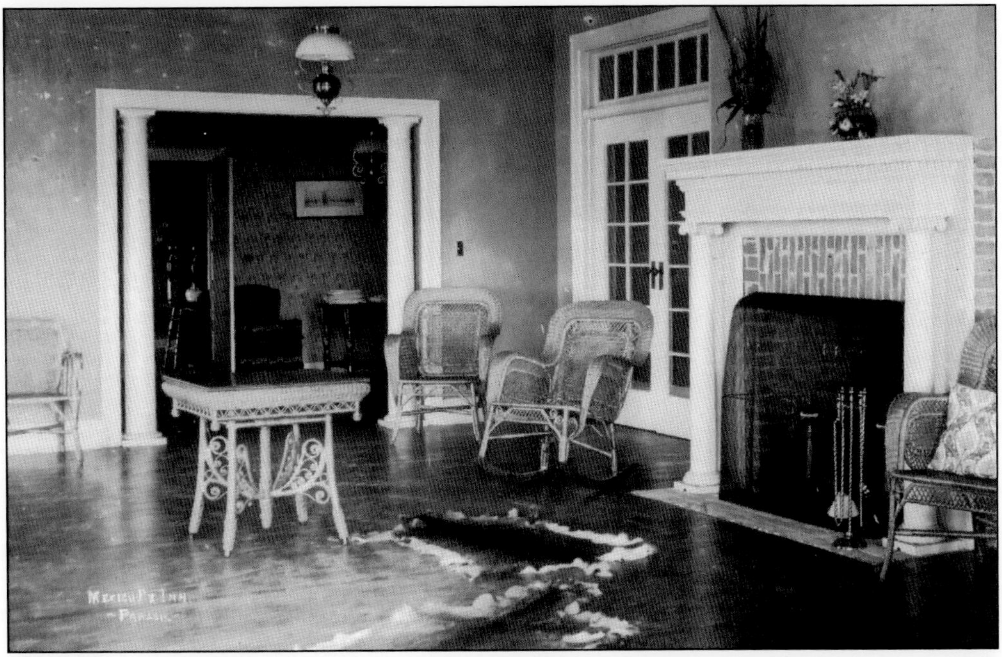

The parlor at the Mexico Point Inn was just inside the veranda and welcomed visitors with comfortable furniture and a "cheerful fire-place." Guests spent time in this room reading, playing cards, and writing. The hotel also boasted of having long-distance telephones, and messages could be sent through Western Union by telephoning the office in the village from the hotel.

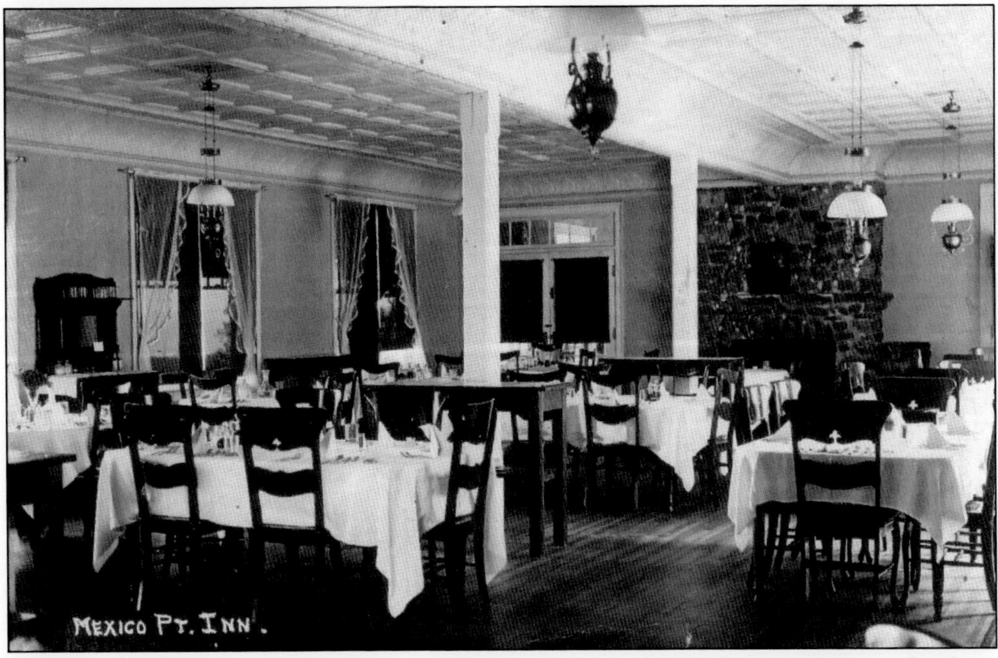

The Mexico Point Inn served meals in a quaint dining room that had a beautiful stone fireplace. The large windows gave diners a view of the lake. Meat, vegetables, and milk were brought in daily by local farmers for the guests. Local groups were welcomed for lunch or dinner, but reservations were necessary to ensure enough food was ready. (Courtesy of the Barry Haynes collection.)

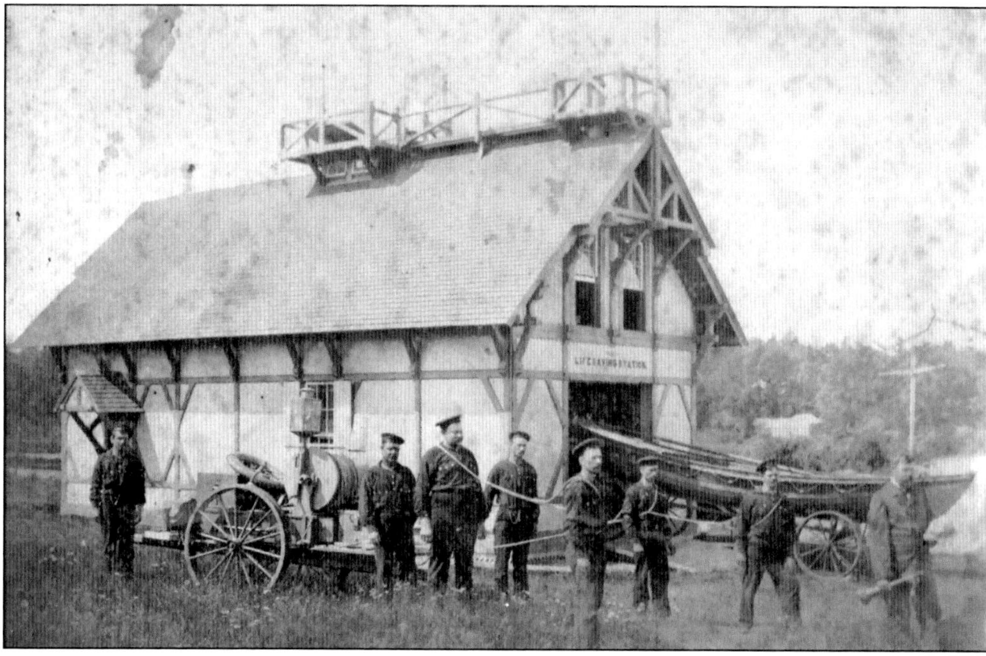

The currents and winds of Mexico Bay were long recognized as treacherous, and many ships went down in these waters. In 1874, Mexico Point was chosen as a site for a lifesaving station. The crews patrolled the shore from April to June and from September to November. They were often called to assist grounded schooners and to rescue their crews. The station burned in 1886 and was never rebuilt.

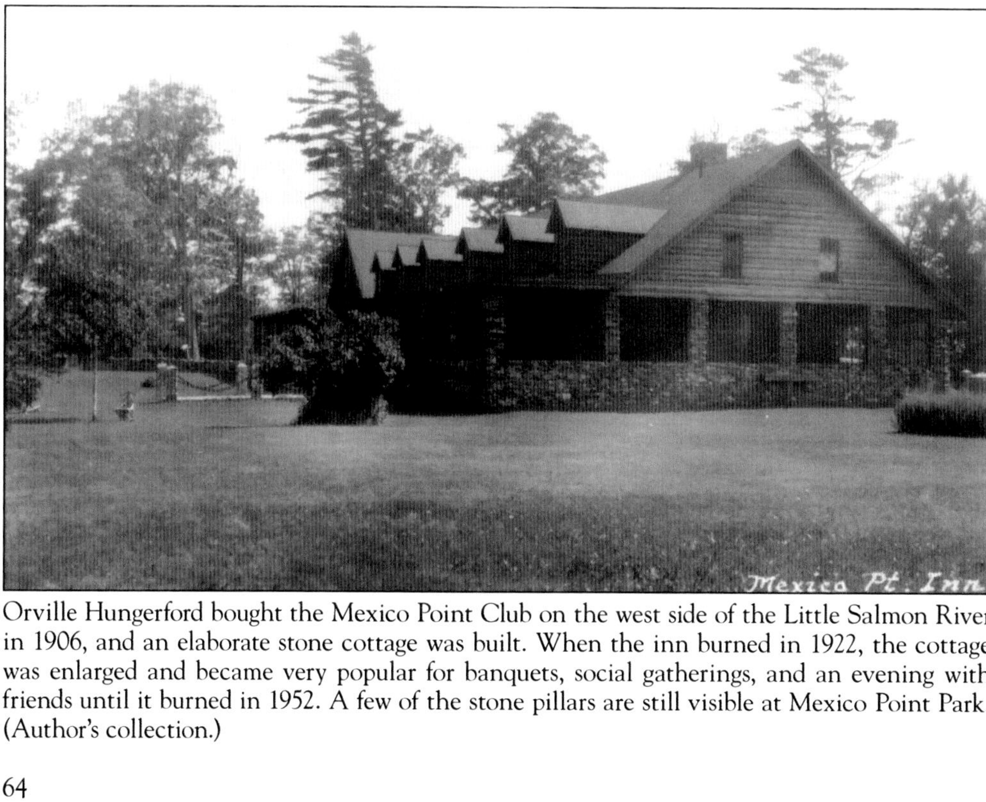

Orville Hungerford bought the Mexico Point Club on the west side of the Little Salmon River in 1906, and an elaborate stone cottage was built. When the inn burned in 1922, the cottage was enlarged and became very popular for banquets, social gatherings, and an evening with friends until it burned in 1952. A few of the stone pillars are still visible at Mexico Point Park. (Author's collection.)

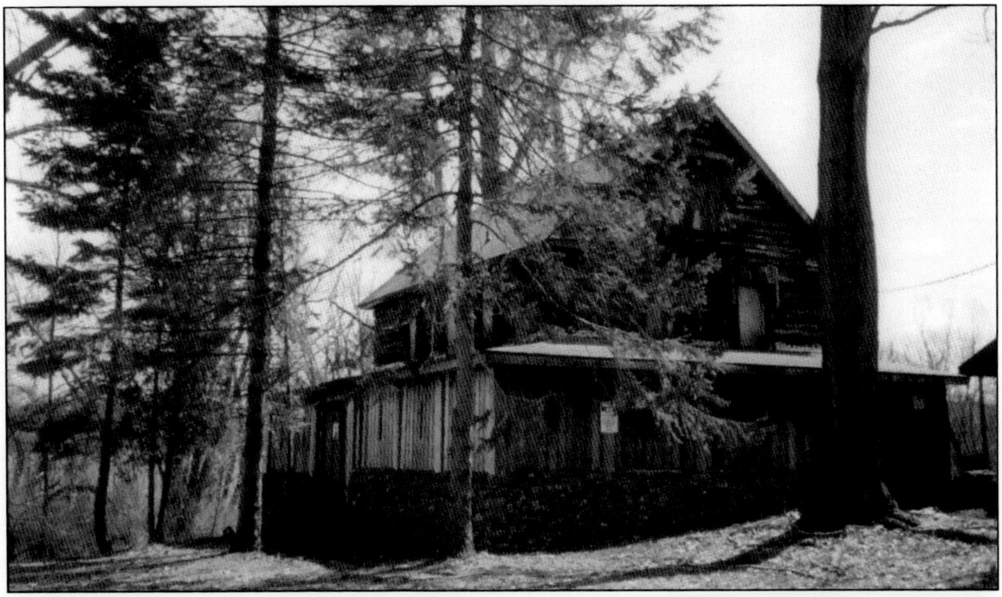

In 1930, William Casey, a professor at Columbia University, and Severin Bischof, a professional artist, turned the carriage house of the Mexico Point Club into an 11th-century manor house. A group of local residents became interested in the preservation of the cottage and formed a group called Friends of Casey's Cottage, later changing the name to Friends of Mexico Point Park. This unique building is now open to the public.

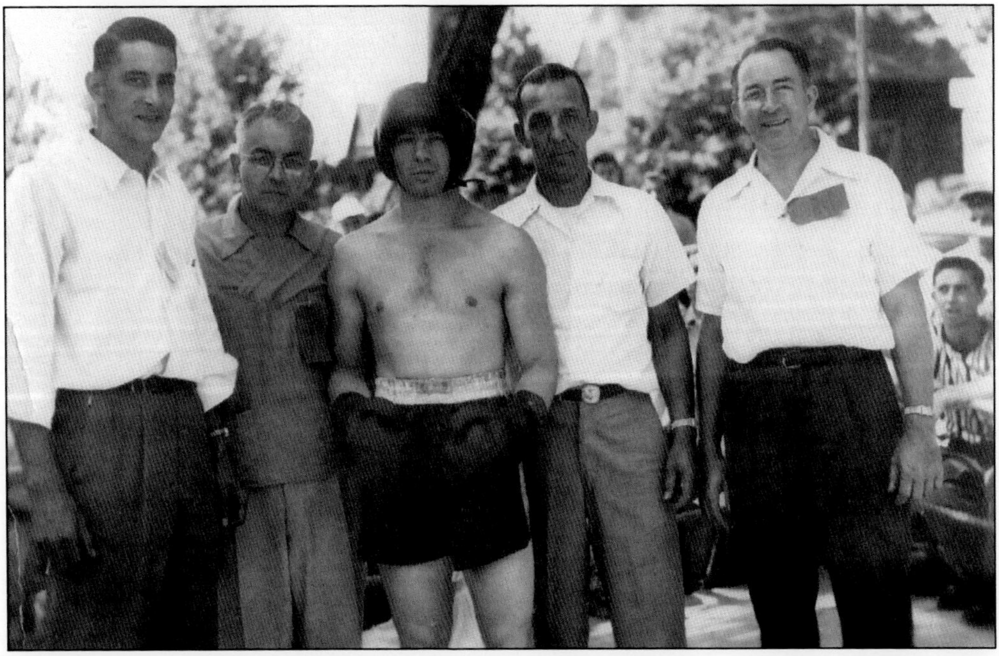

Joey DeJohn, a professional boxer, trained at Mexico Point. Shown in this photograph are, from left to right, unidentified, Barney Cook, DeJohn, Fred Dingman, and Harold Sant of the Mexico Point Club. The other spectators were at the club for the Oswego County Republican Clam Bake in the 1950s. Carmen Basilio, another popular boxer, also trained at the Mexico Point Club. (Courtesy of Friends of Casey's Cottage.)

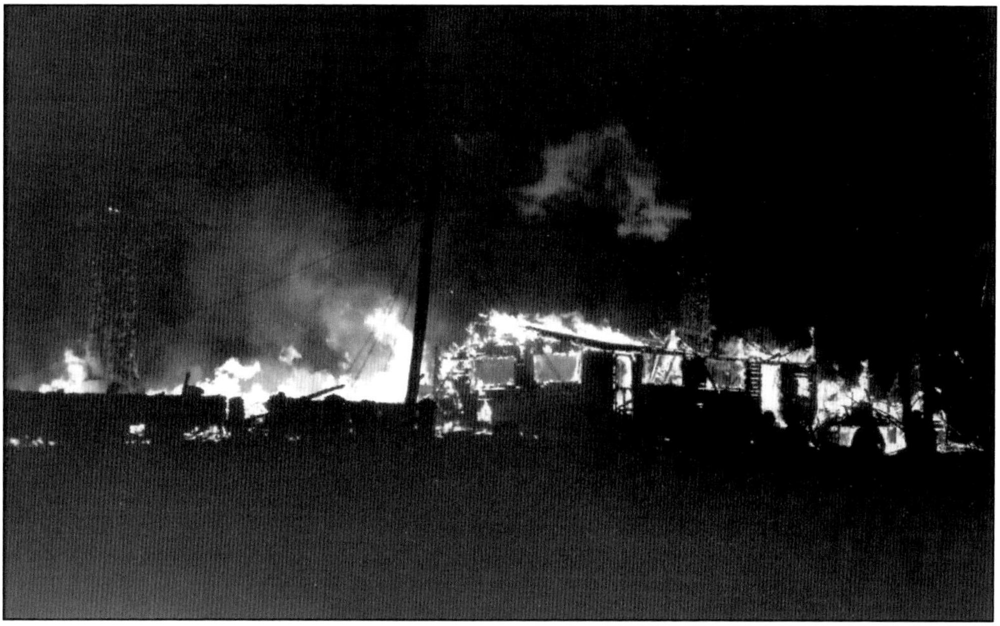

The Mexico Point Club burned at 4:00 a.m. on April 4, 1952. Stone chimneys, foundation walls, and the porch columns were all that remained standing. The Mexico firemen were successful in saving Casey's Cottage and a second building a short distance from the clubhouse. The club was never rebuilt, and the site is now the home of Mexico Point Park. (Courtesy of the John Castle collection.)

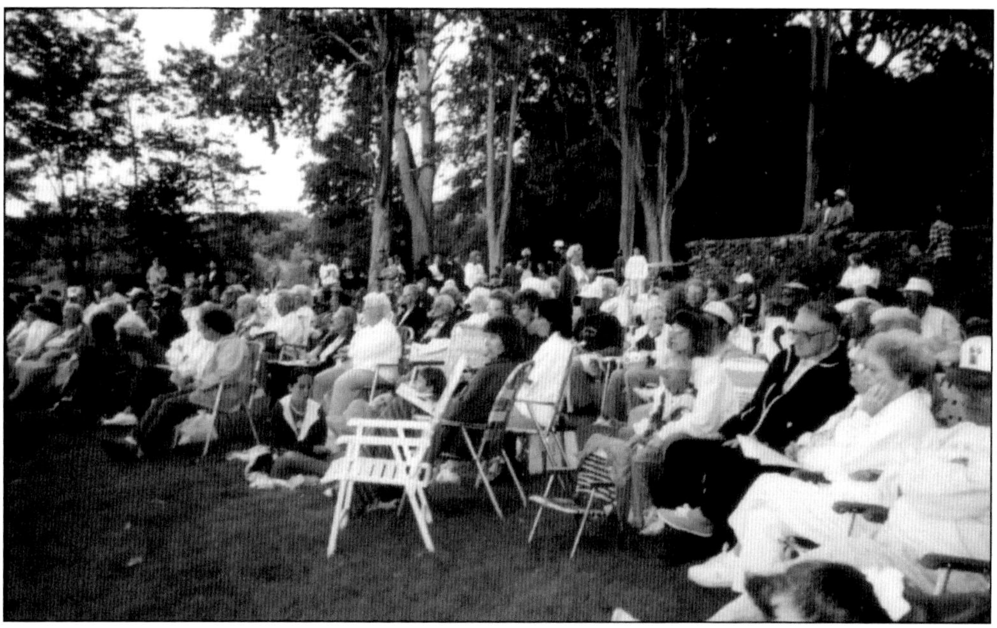

The people of Mexico enjoy Mexico Point today thanks to the effort of Grace Partrick Roop. One of the largest events held yearly is the band concert with fireworks at dark. Another annual event largely attended is the Midsummer's Eve dinner held in August. Weddings, organization picnics, and park-planned events fill the calendar every summer. The park is also open daily for family picnics and swimming. (Courtesy of Friends of Casey's Cottage.)

Five

Living in Snow Country

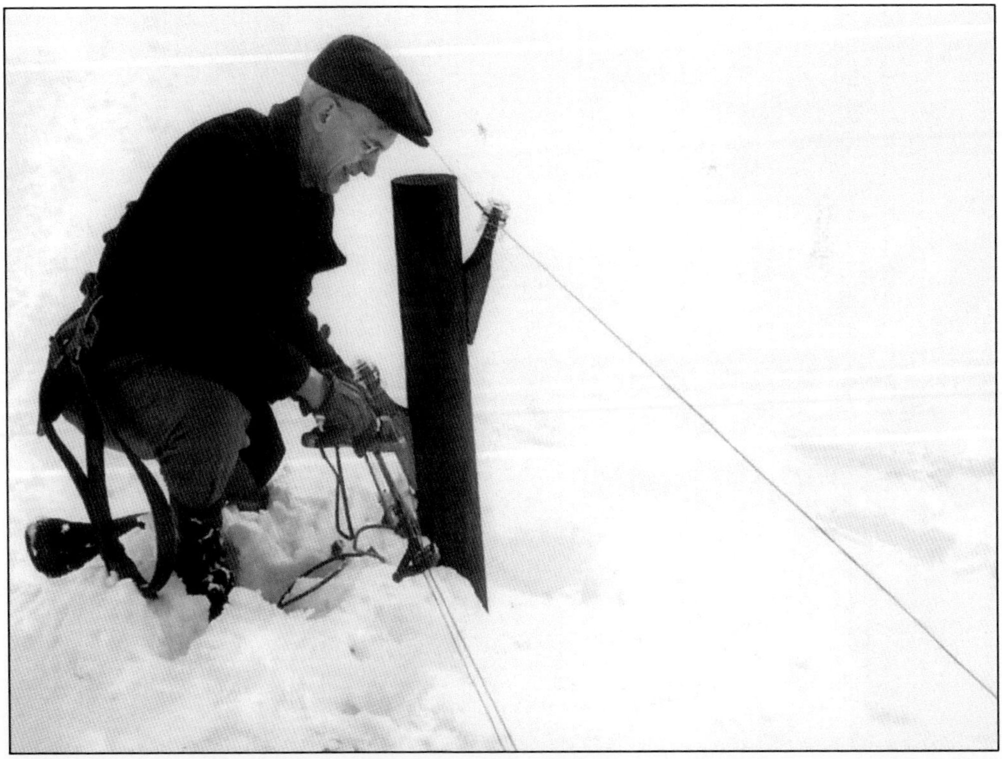

This picture of Charlie Graves kneeling to fix the telephone wires during a storm in March 1947 is a favorite of everyone who has ever spent a winter in Mexico. A blizzard in late February added to the snow on the ground and closed all the roads in Mexico for several days. Clearing the roads was slow work, as the snowbanks grew higher and higher.

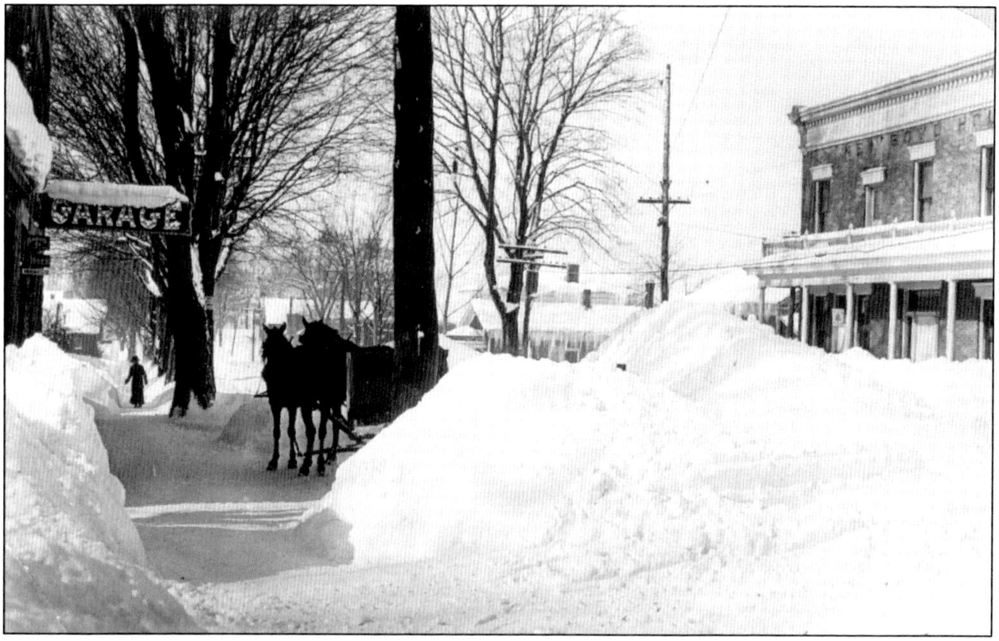

The changing of an era is captured here as the team of horses waits under the sign for the new garage. The Mexico Motor Supply Company and Garage opened in 1911, the first business to come to Mexico with the horseless carriage. A period of years passed before the automobile replaced the faithful horse, especially in the snow. (Author's collection.)

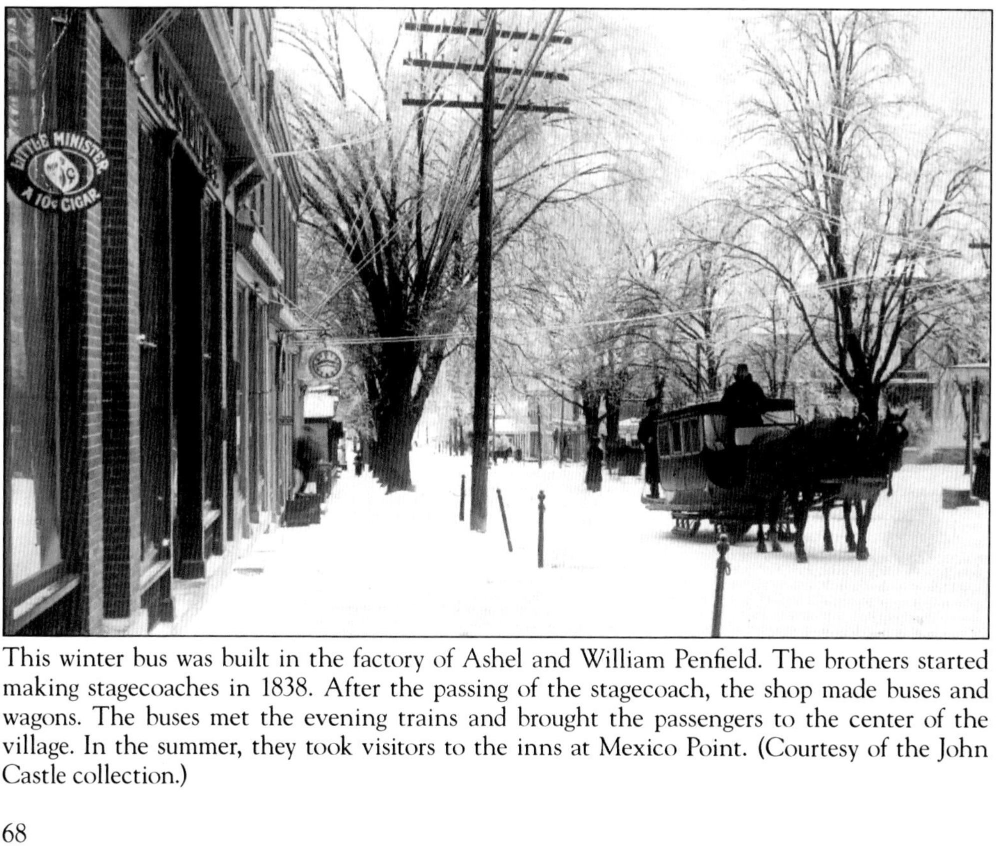

This winter bus was built in the factory of Ashel and William Penfield. The brothers started making stagecoaches in 1838. After the passing of the stagecoach, the shop made buses and wagons. The buses met the evening trains and brought the passengers to the center of the village. In the summer, they took visitors to the inns at Mexico Point. (Courtesy of the John Castle collection.)

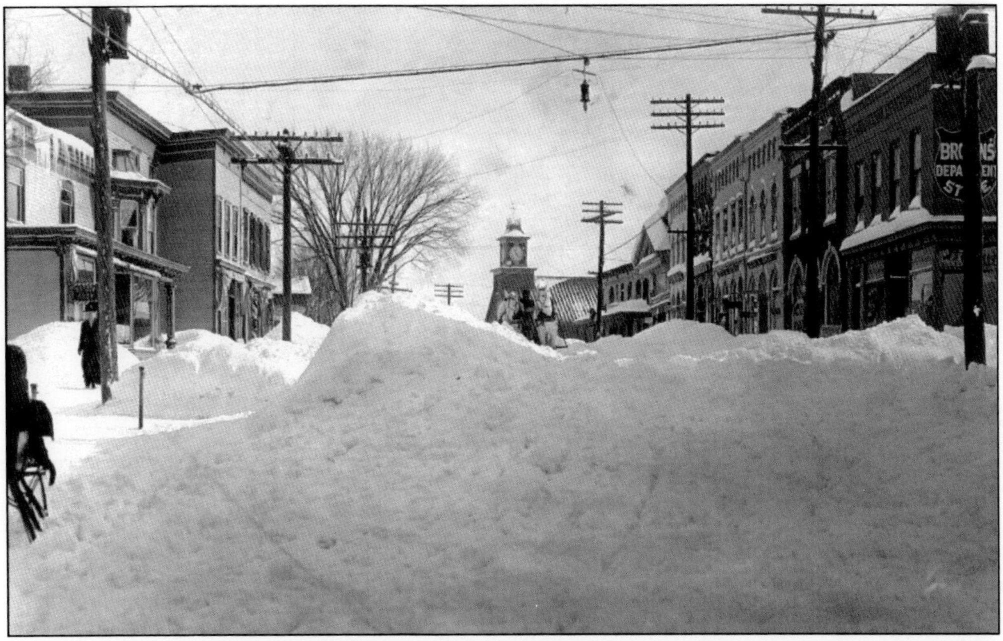

A team of horses worked well pulling a sleigh through deep snow. The team in the center of the picture may also be pulling a large flat board on the back of the sleigh, which was used to pack the snow down. Sometimes a caldron kettle was pulled, and a woman, wishing to pay a visit, rode in the kettle to give it ballast. (Courtesy of the Barry Haynes collection.)

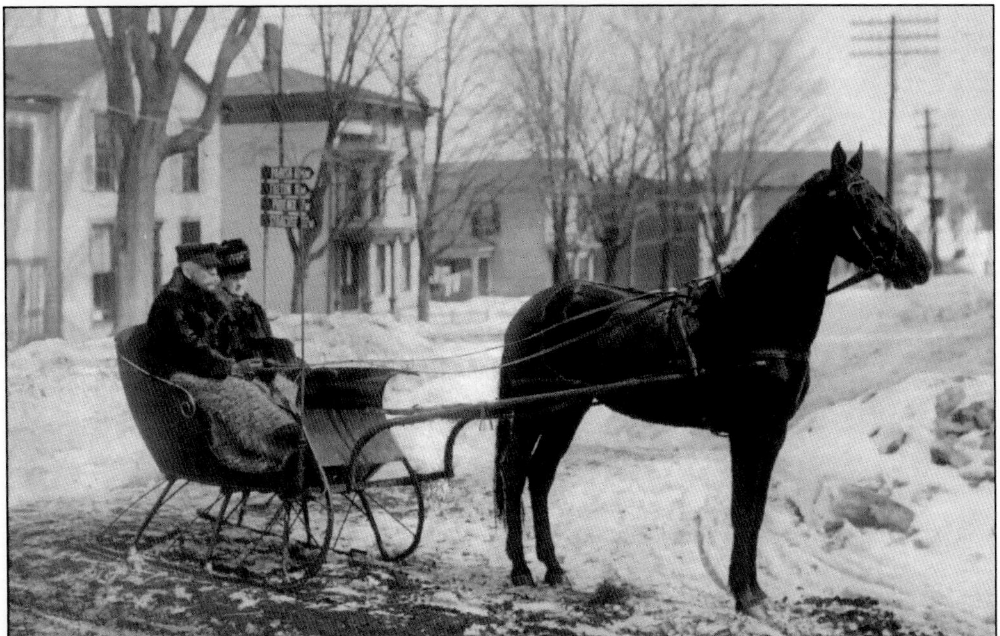

Mr. and Mrs. James Virgil stop at the corner of Main Street and Church Street on a winter day in 1915. They each enjoy a warm fur coat and lap robe, even though the snow seems to have melted on Church Street. The building behind them once housed the business of Starr Clark. Fugitive slaves were hidden by the family in the home next to the store.

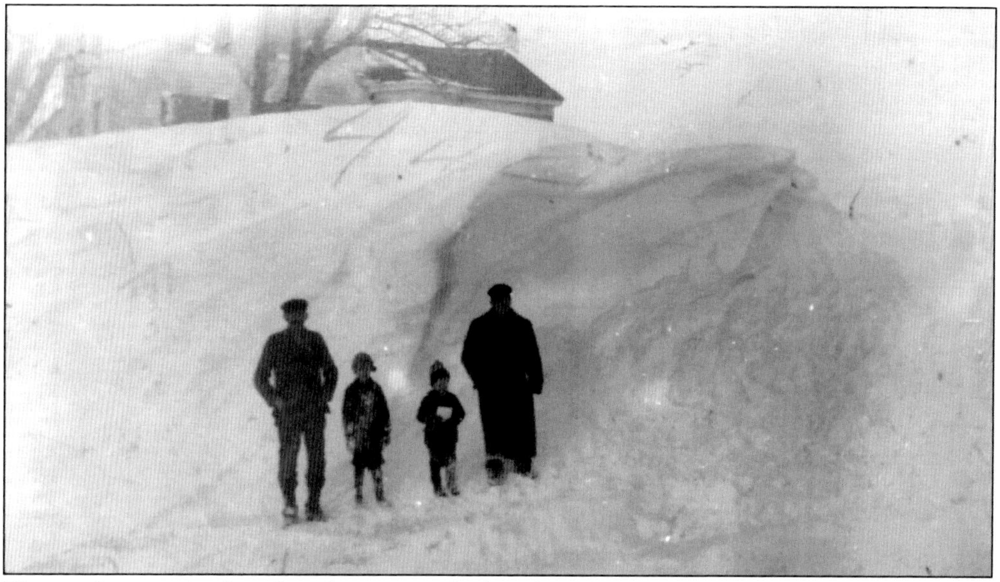

The wind can make the piles of snow even higher than shoveling. In 1915, the snowbanks were so high on State Route 104 west that the telephone wires could be touched by anyone who could climb the banks. Shown in the picture are Richard Backus, his two sons Herbert and Reginald, and milk tester Mr. Waldon. At the time the picture was taken, Backus owned the Taylor-Marsh farm.

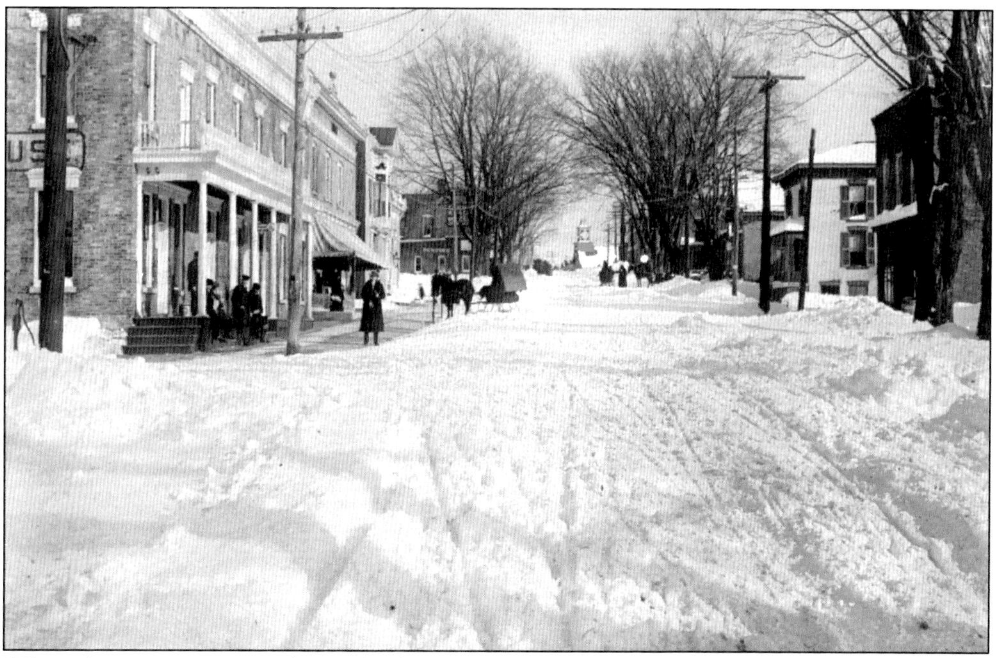

When the snow was not deep, the horses and sleighs could get around town. Sometimes a tentlike shelter was added to the sleigh to protect the riders from the wind and cold. The businessmen kept their sidewalks well shoveled all winter. The Boyd House (Beck's Hotel) was an attractive building on the corner of Railroad Street (Scenic Avenue) and Main Street. (Author's collection.)

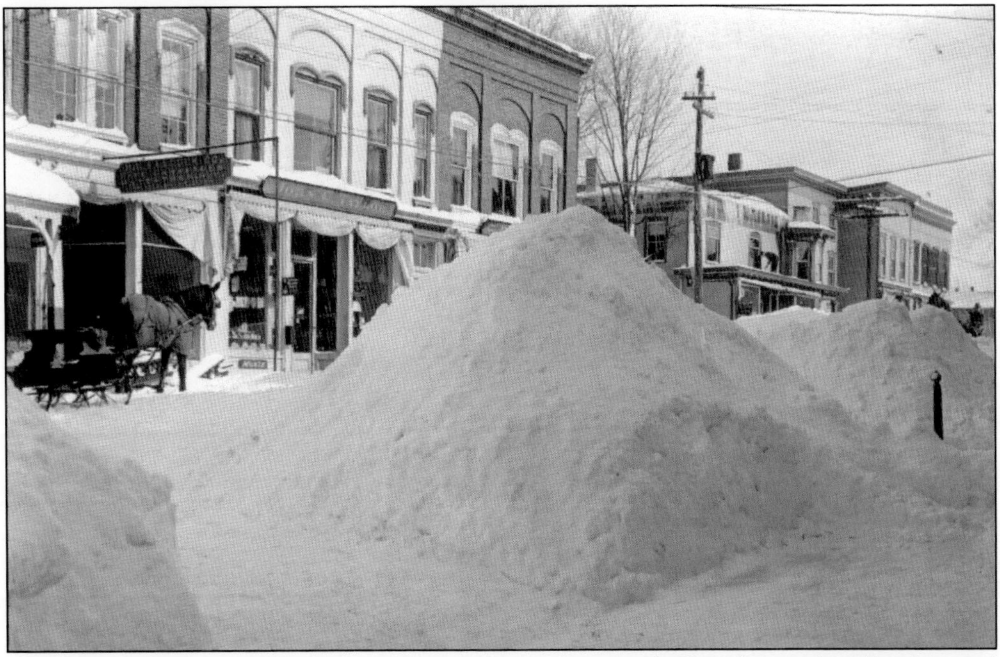

As winter continued, the merchants had to throw the snow high to keep sidewalks clear and to provide passage from the road to their businesses. The air stayed cold with a big snow cover, and by January, the horses needed blankets. Some things never change: on the right is a man shoveling off the roof, a common sight today.

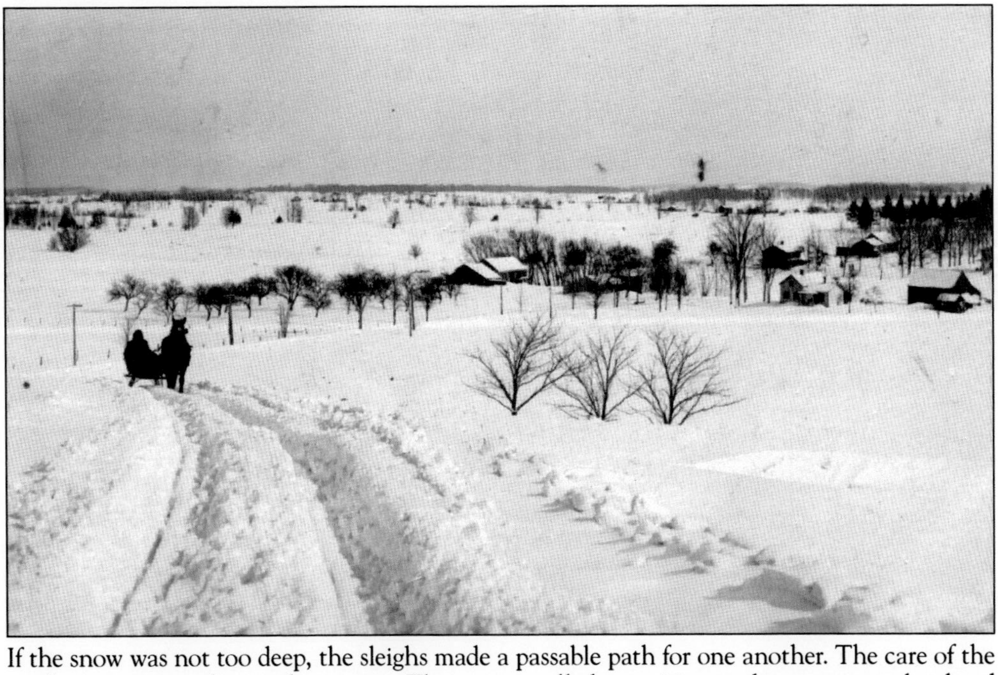

If the snow was not too deep, the sleighs made a passable path for one another. The care of the roads was entrusted to path masters. These men called out citizens whose property bordered the roads to keep snow cleared, allowing traffic to pass. This was a hopeless task during one of the famous snowstorms.

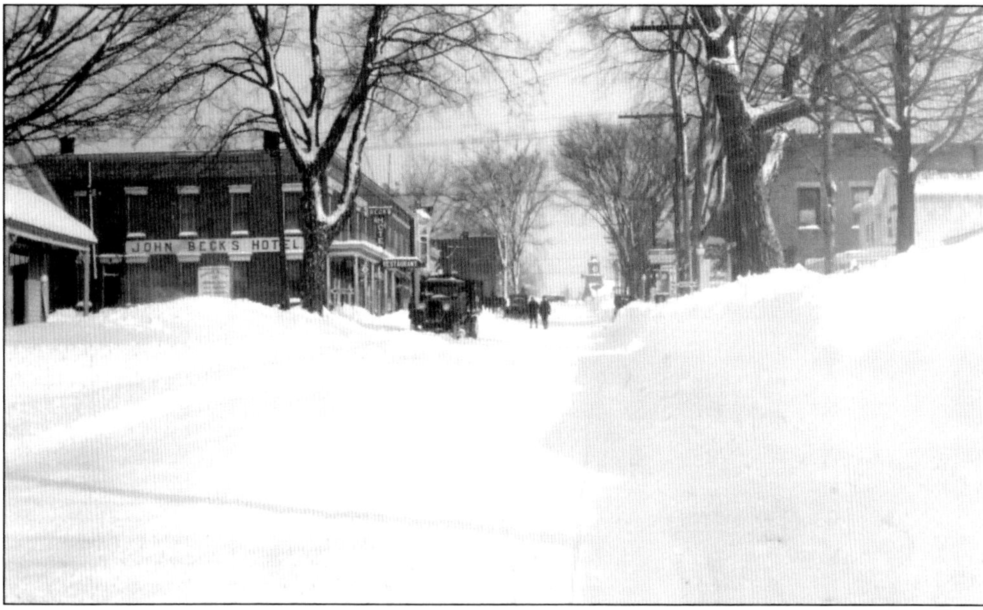

Snowplows quickly followed the development of the truck. It was not long before people learned the advantage of a V-shaped plow made of metal to make the roads passable. The plows became higher, and a wing was added so the work was easier. The people walking in the road seem to indicate the sidewalks did not fare as well. (Courtesy of the Barry Haynes collection.)

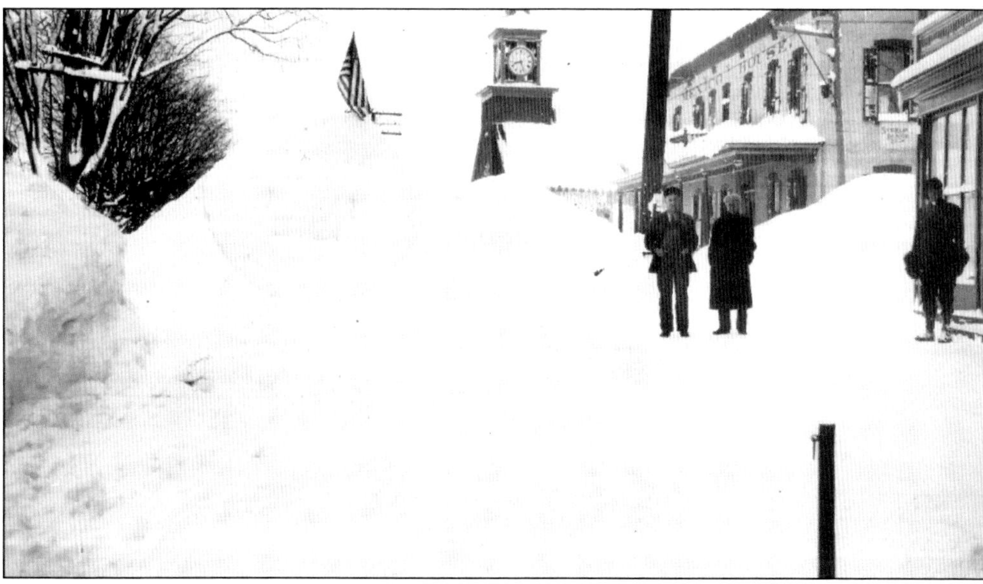

The snow piles on the corner of Main and Church Streets have filled the road with just a path to go around the highest point. The merchants shoveled the sidewalk and the road, but there is no place to put snow except up. Notice a brave adventurer has climbed the snow mountain and planted the flag to claim all the snow for America. (Courtesy of the John Castle collection.)

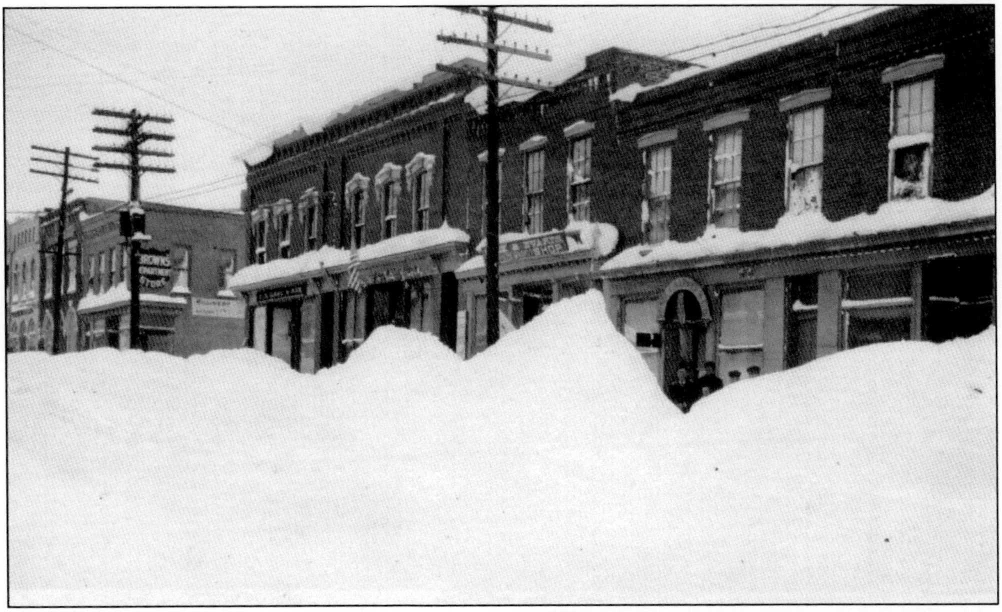

On the right, the people along the sidewalk found a place where they could see through the wall of snow. Keep in mind that under those high banks is a dirt road. The snow would melt slowly on the south side of the road, and by the middle of April, the people would be looking at mud several inches deep.

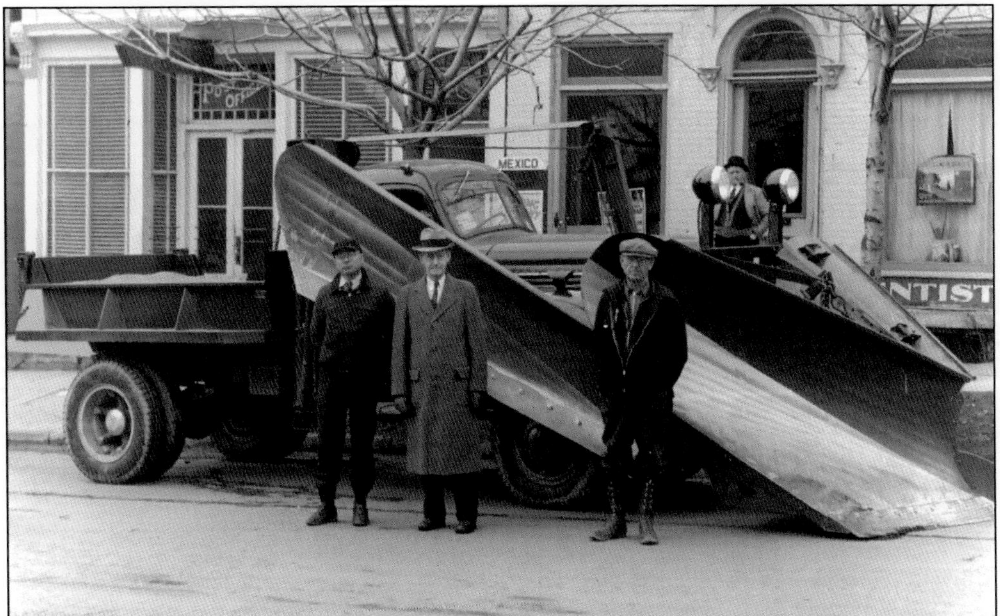

From left to right, Willard Fetcha, International Truck representative; Dr. Earle A. Mowry, Mexico mayor; and Sidney Cronk, Village of Mexico road commissioner, stand beside the new snowplow bought in 1941 for $3,695. The double plow was the very latest improvement in clearing the village streets during Mexico's famous winters. The 1895–1983 post office is seen on the left, and Dr. Herbert W. Whitney stands in front of his dental office on the right. (Courtesy of the Barry Haynes collection.)

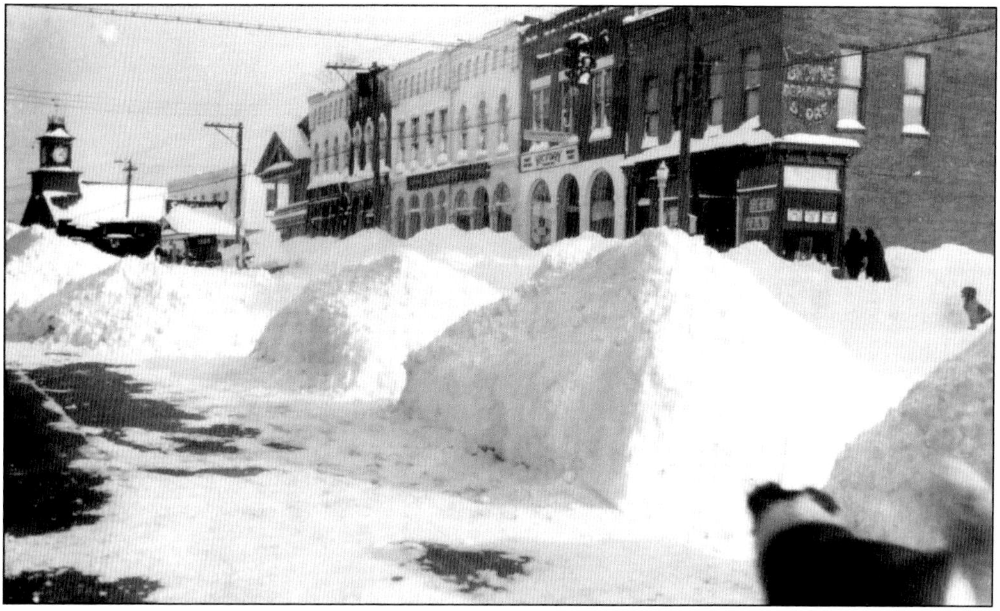

By February and March, even the dogs are happy to find a break in the snowbanks so they can see across the street. The merchants have shoveled the snow into the road to accommodate the ladies' long skirts and coats. A path from the road lets all prospective customers access the store.

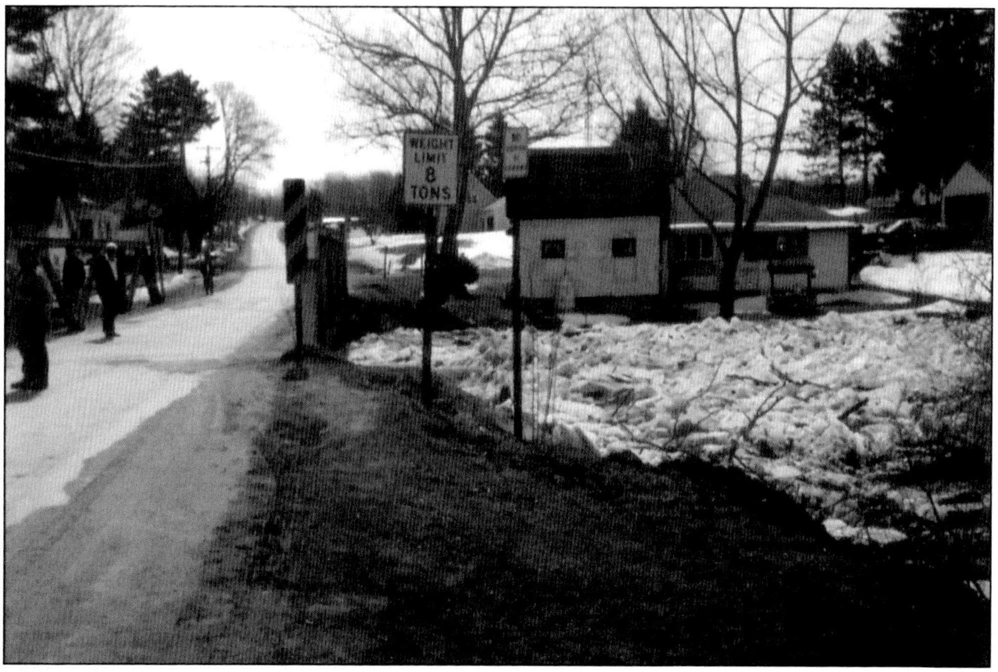

The Little Salmon River empties into Lake Ontario at Mexico Point. The ice breaks up, moves quickly over the rapids, and is met at the mouth of the river by large waves and strong winds. The ice is pushed from both ends and piles up so an ice jam is formed. The ice jam in 1993 was especially big. This is looking south from the bridge in Texas on County Route 16. (Courtesy of Melina Rurey.)

Six

NOTABLE PEOPLE AND NOTABLE HOMES

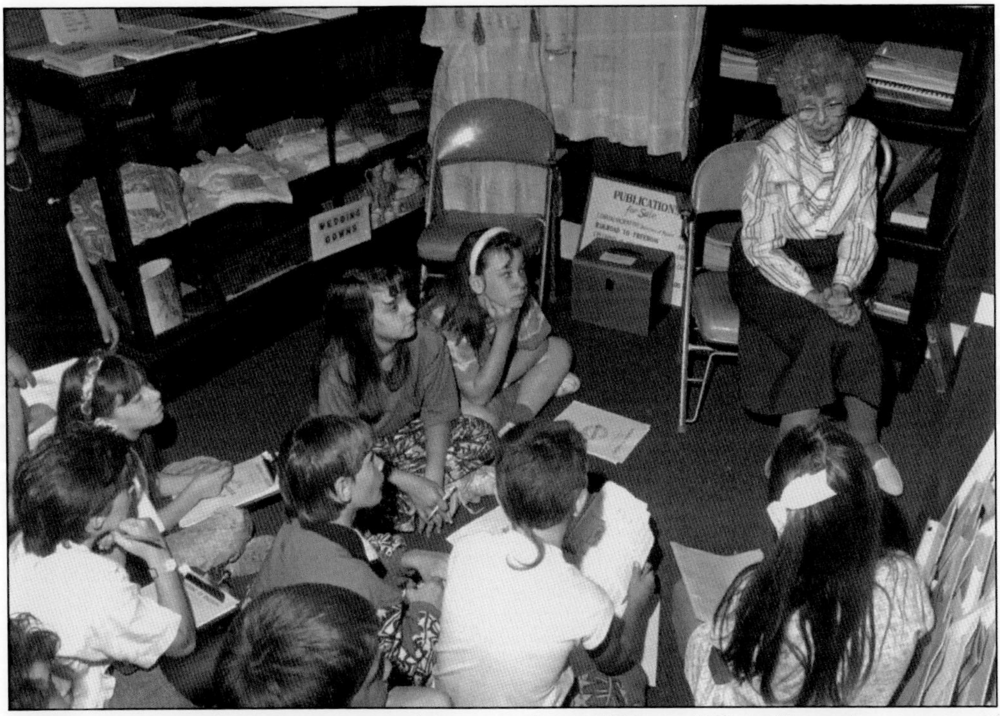

Euloda Keifer Fetcha, Mexico town historian from 1970 to 1992, talks with a group of schoolchildren. She was the leader in founding the Mexico Historical Society, and she gathered all the artifacts from the school attic for a museum and organized the Mexico Historical Museum in 1981. She also realized the goal of having a Mexico historic district in 1991. She will long be remembered for the outstanding historical legacy she left Mexico.

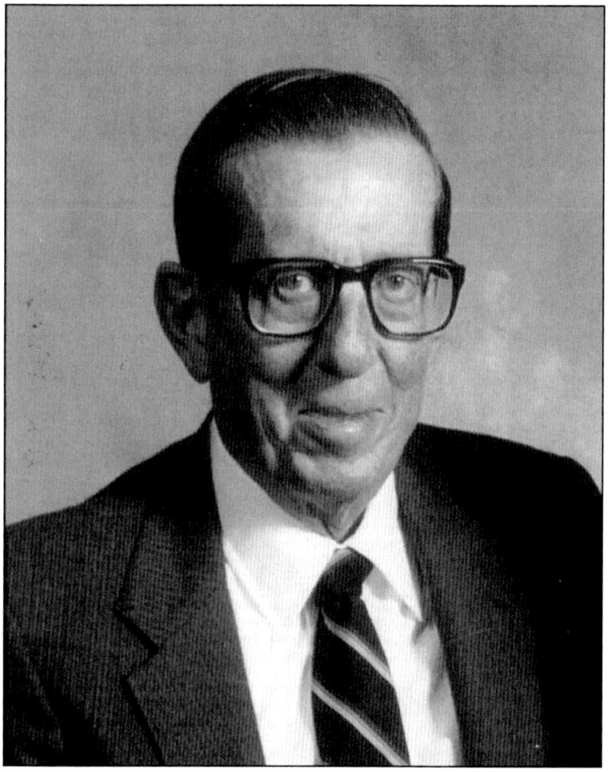

Dr. John Anderson finished his medical training and was in the service during the Korean War before returning to Mexico to start his practice in 1952. He was the last of the old-fashioned doctors who lived in the community, made house calls, knew his patients, and was available for emergencies anytime. Dr. Anderson and his wife lived here 33 years, raising a family of six boys and one girl. (Courtesy of Michael and Mary Mowry.)

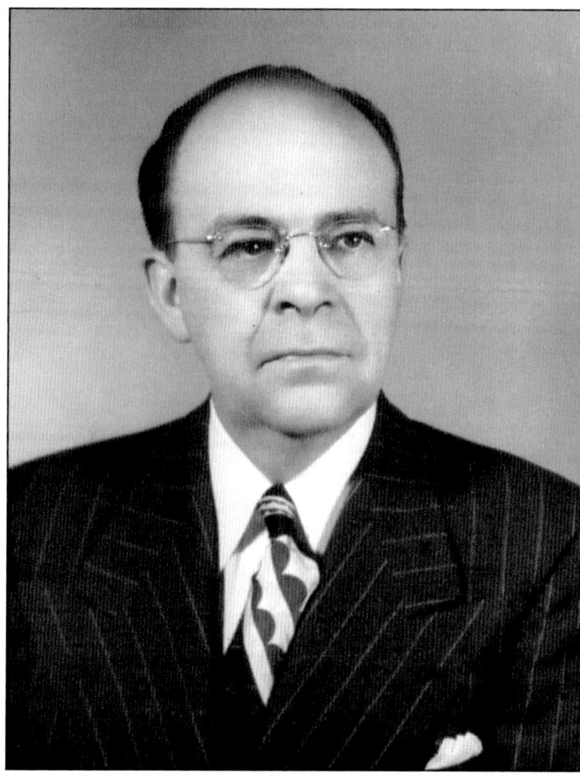

R. Austin Backus was a respected and influential citizen of Mexico. He began his career by founding the Backus Pedigree business. He was auctioneer at many of the most famous Holstein cattle sales throughout the nation from 1919 to 1953. He bought the *Mexico Independent* in 1924, was a member of the board of education, and was involved in the Presbyterian Church. As a good samaritan, he gave to many.

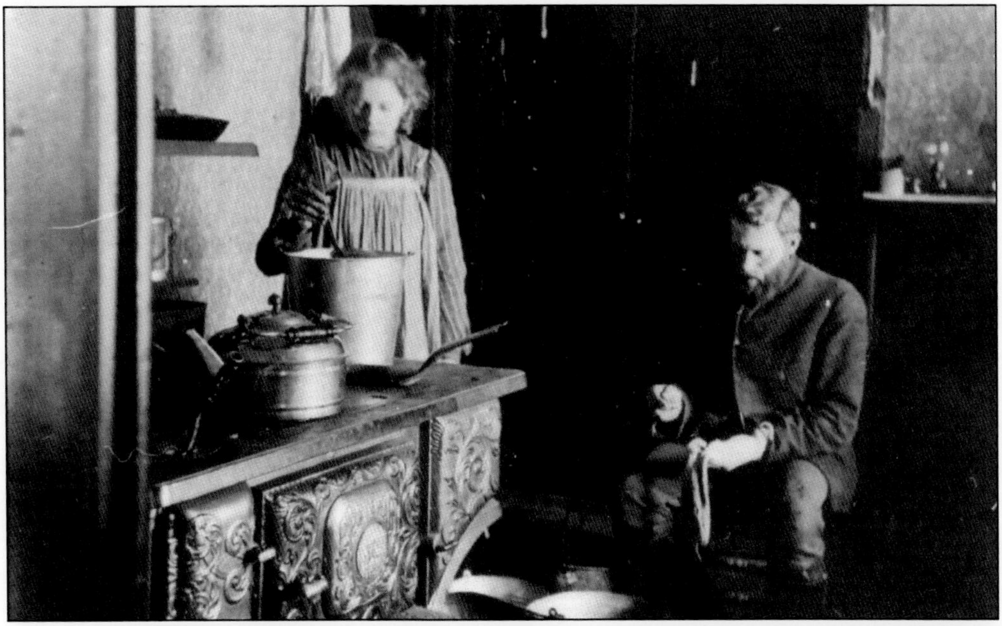

This photograph shows Eliza Emery Smith and her father, S. Foster Emery, in the kitchen of their home around 1905. The large cupboard in the background served as a place for dishes and cooking necessities. On the left of the stove is the lid lifter ready to remove the cover so more coal could be added. The center door is the oven, and the hot water tank is behind the door on the right.

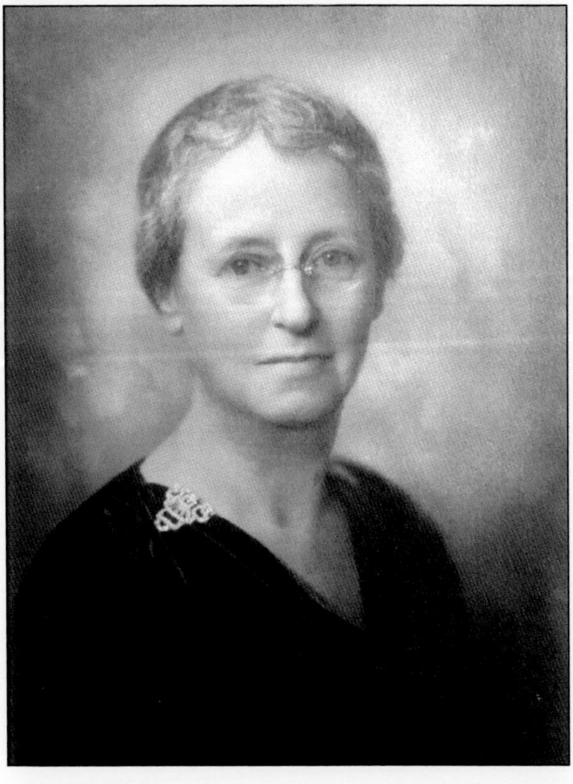

Elizabeth Simpson, a retired teacher, was Mexico town historian from 1940 to 1960. She spent over 12 years gathering material about the history of Mexico from old newspapers, town and village records, old publications, church records, and interviews with lifelong residents of Mexico. Her book *Mexico, Mother of Towns* became a definitive source used by all who are interested in local history.

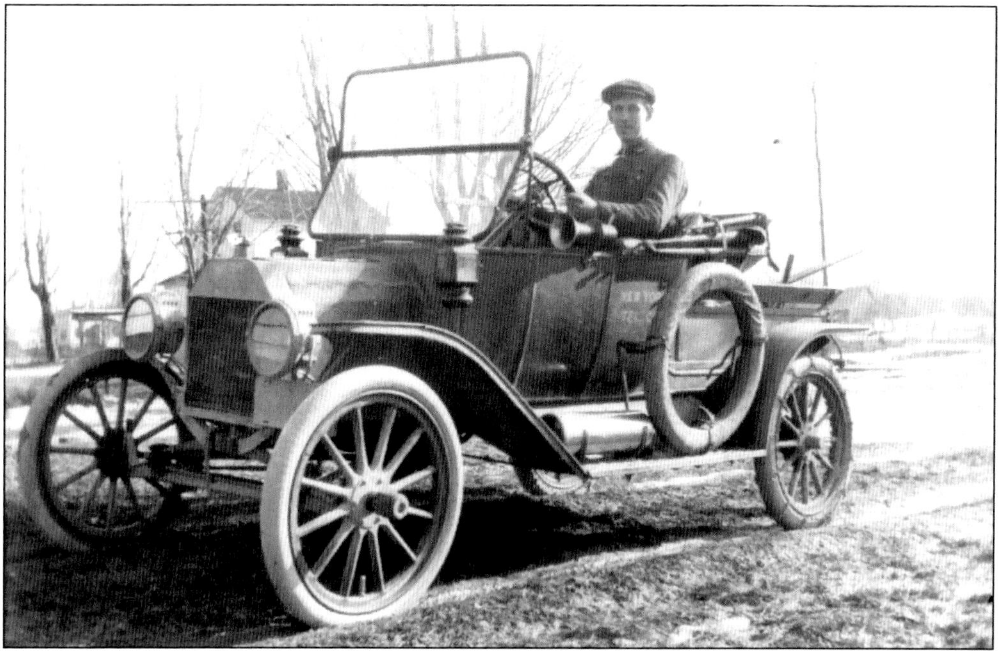

Charles Graves sits in the New York Telephone Company car in 1912. He worked as installer and repairman from age 16 to his retirement 49 years later. He was active in the Baptist Church for 68 years as teacher, deacon, and treasurer. He was a scoutmaster for 25 years. Typical of so many who live and work here, he contributed so much to the community.

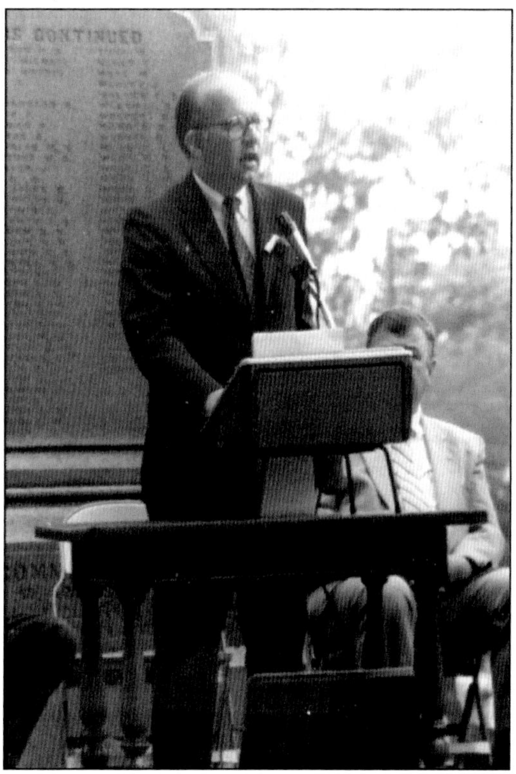

Michael Mowry gave the address at the cemetery on Memorial Day 1991. He welcomed the opportunity to honor all those who have been in the service of the country. Mowry had returned to Mexico in 1966 and joined his father, John B. Mowry, in his law practice. A year later, they moved their office to Main Street where Michael Mowry continues his practice in 2009.

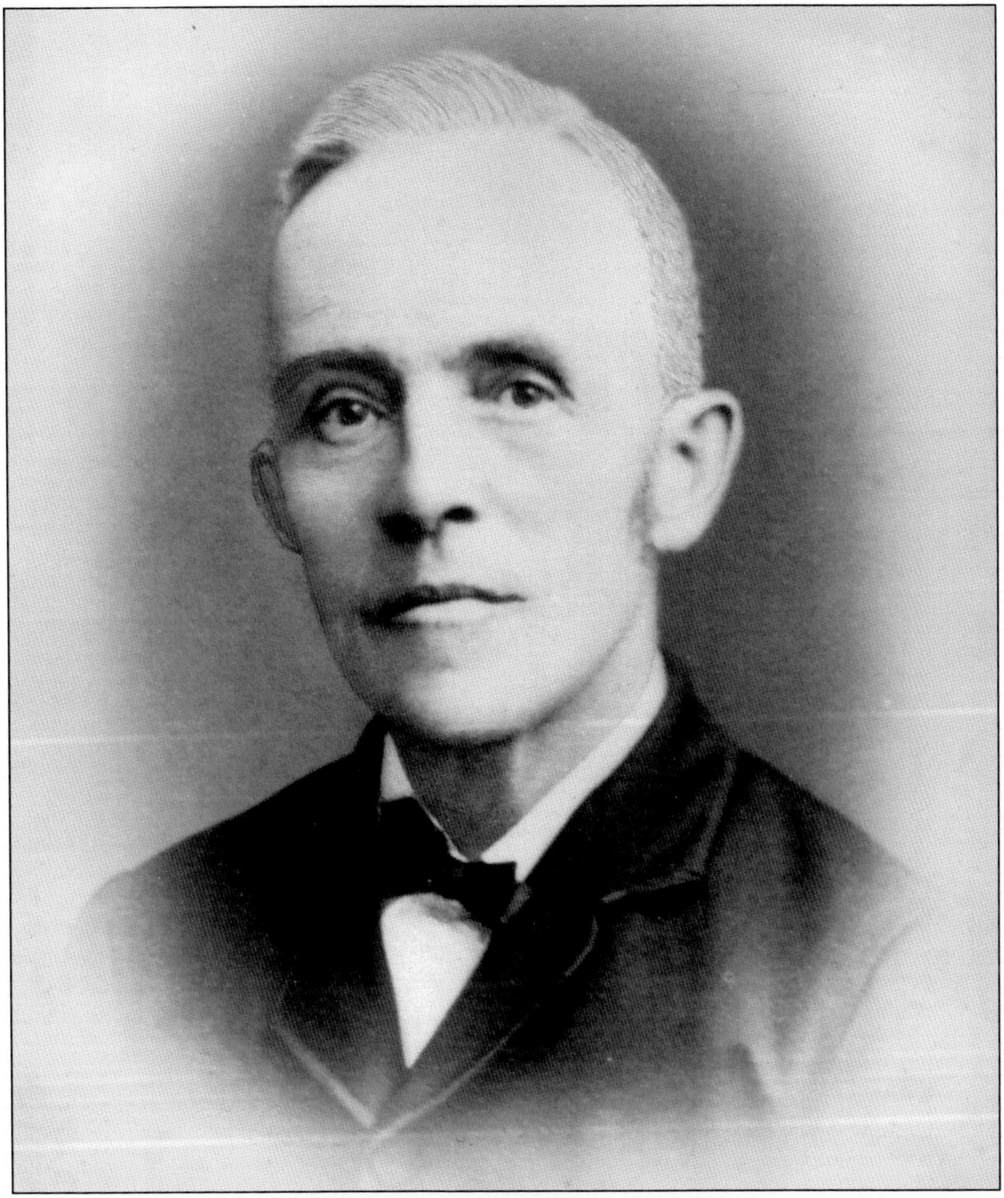

Henry Humphries and James M. Scarrit published the first issue of the first successful newspaper in Mexico on March 21, 1861. Humphries was editor for 56 years, 3 months, and 11 days. His goal was to print "a local newspaper devoted to the interest and welfare of this place and adjacent towns." The two partners began their modest enterprise over the store on the northwest corner of Main and Jefferson Streets. They began with a secondhand outfit given to them by their former employer in lieu of wages due them, consisting of a hand press, which took two men to operate. The office moved twice before ending in 1869 on the second floor over what is now the public library. It remained there until R. Austin Backus built an office on North Jefferson Street. Humphries became sole owner of the newspaper in 1865. He interested himself in all that concerned the good of the community and especially of the children. He died in England in 1924 at the age of 90. Memorial services were held in Mexico and a stone placed in the village cemetery.

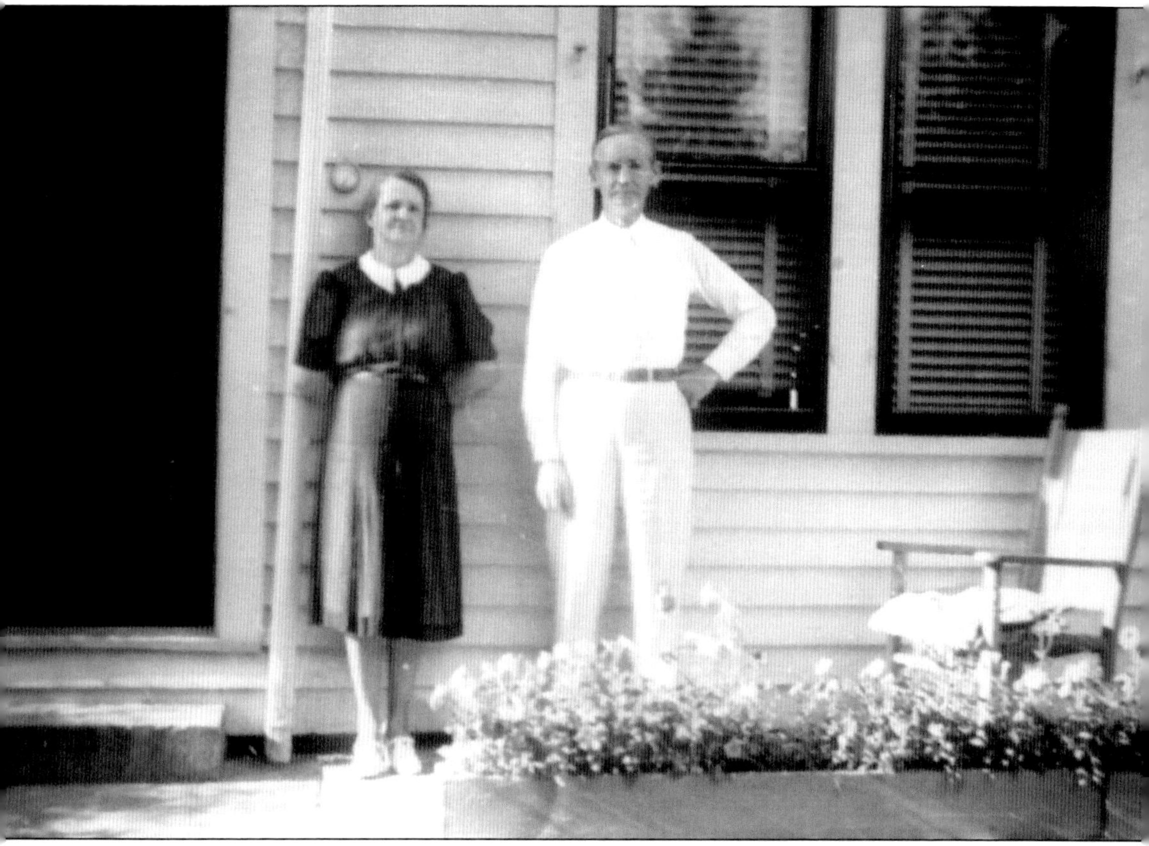

Dr. Earle A. Mowry came back to Mexico to start his practice in 1904. Those were the days when the doctor went to the patient's home. He was a familiar figure as he drove his horse and buggy to make house calls. A year later, he married Margaret Brennan, the head surgical nurse at University Hospital in Syracuse. She took care of the home situations and office calls while her husband was making the house calls. In 1910, the family bought its first automobile for summer use only. The doctor was often paid with a chicken, ham, or eggs. In an emergency situation, home surgery was performed on the kitchen table at the patient's home; a surgeon from Crouse-Erving Hospital and a nurse would come to Mexico and assist. Dr. Mowry contributed much to the community. He was president of the school board and mayor of the village. He was instrumental in getting the village to purchase land with pure never-ending springs on it, thus giving Mexico one of the best water systems in the state. (Courtesy of Michael and Mary Mowry.)

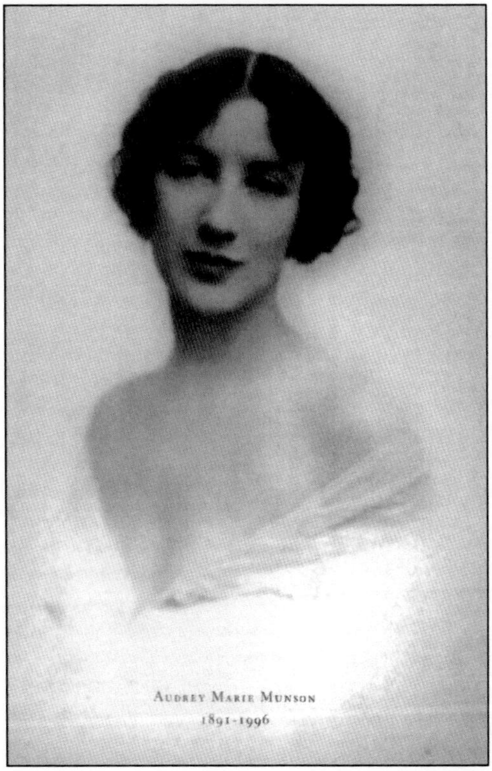

Audrey Munson spent most of her early years in the Mexico/New Haven area. She was 15 years old when she posed for a photographer in New York City, which began her career as a well-known nude model. She was selected as the primary model for sculptures and murals for the Panama Pacific Exposition, and she posed for many statues found around New York City. Her image is found on the Walking Liberty half-dollar and on the Mercury Head dime. She did four silent films between 1915 and 1921, but society was not ready for nude movies. Munson and her mother returned to the Mexico area in 1922. She was committed to Ogdensburg Psychiatric Institution where she lived as a favorite of the staff until her death in 1996.

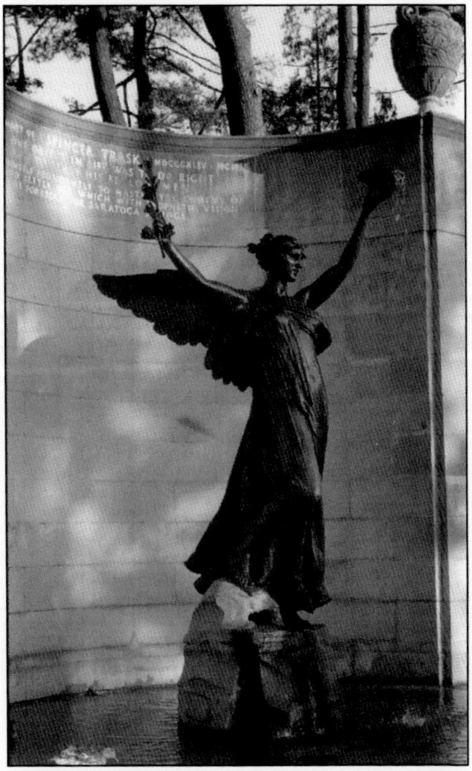

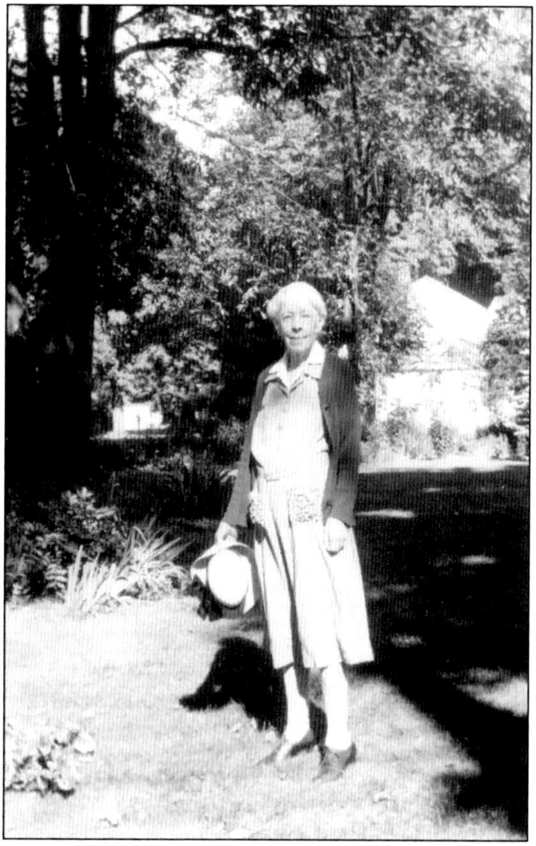

Irene Hungerford lived a life that was an inspiration and blessing to all those whose lives she touched, earning her the title "a woman to warm your heart by." She attended Mexico Academy, beginning her teaching career in the local district schools. She taught at Cornwall-on-Hudson for 10 years before returning to Mexico in 1909 to teach French and German. In 1918, Hungerford became the first permanent librarian in Mexico High School and set about cataloging the books. She continued this position until she retired in 1936. One of her outstanding contributions was assisting in the designing and setting up of the library in the high school. The bronze plaque on the door reads in part, "In appreciation of her fineness of charter, devotion to her work and the lasting impression she has made upon the faculty and students of Mexico Academy."

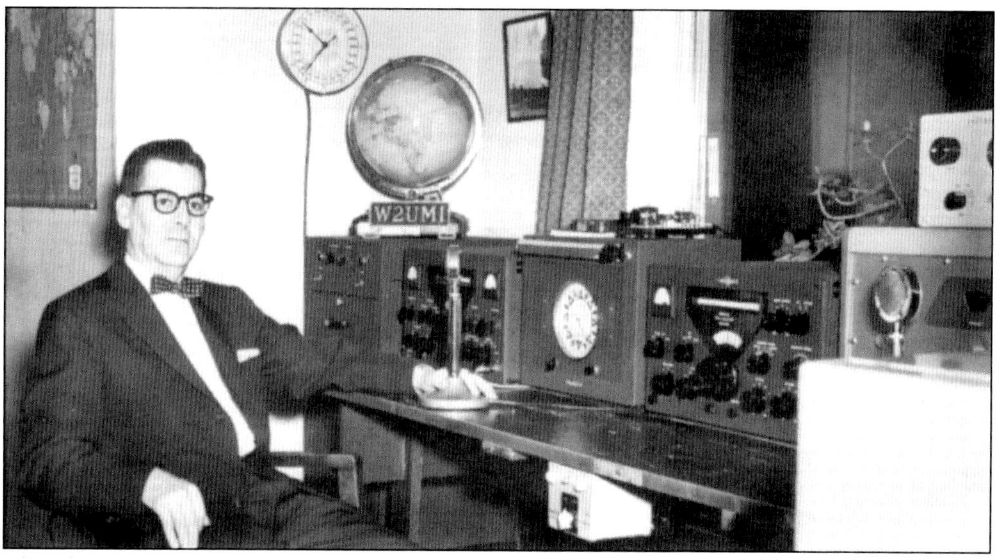

This photograph of Richard Whitney was taken in 1957. There were several ham radio operators in Mexico, of which Whitney was one. He received several commendations for his radio work after hurricanes and the Alaskan earthquake in the 1950s. In 1937, he began working with Robert and Lulu Brown and was one of the cofounders of Brown-Whitney-Brown Food, now known as Grandma Brown's Beans.

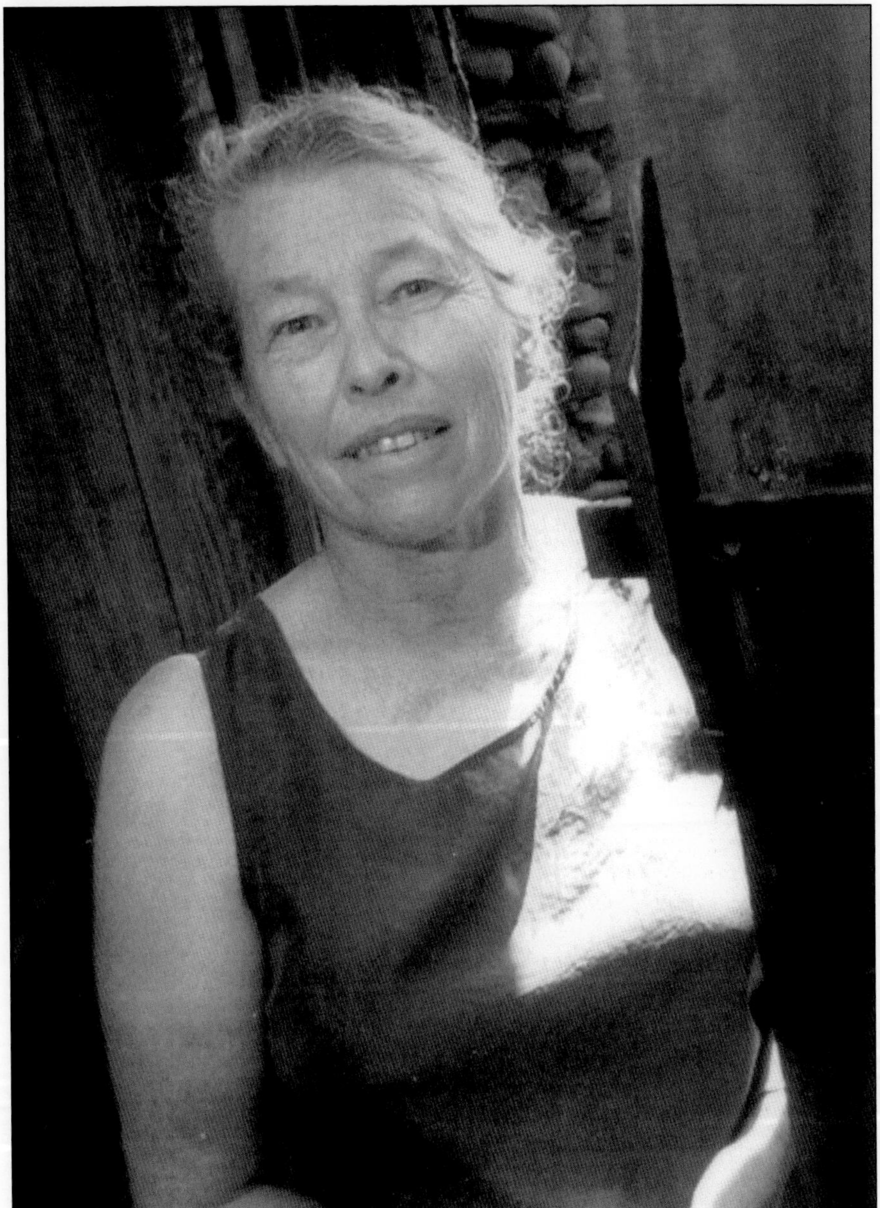

Grace Partrick Roop grew up in Elizabeth, New Jersey, but her parents were from Mexico, and they returned every summer to stay at Mexico Point. New York State bought the land on the east side of the Little Salmon River to use as a boat launch in 1978. It also bought the west side of the river to control the entry into Lake Ontario. But the west side was neglected, and the unique Casey's Cottage was being destroyed by vandals. Roop was very disturbed by the rundown cottage and the useless area where a resort once stood. She organized a group of people who shared her interest in 1989. Then she began years of talking and writing to the New York State Department of Parks and Recreation, state representatives, and the Mexico Town Board. Finally the state agreed to lease the land to the town, and the town agreed to help care for the park. Roop's dream continues to move forward. A board now oversees Mexico Point Park. The community once again enjoys the lake.

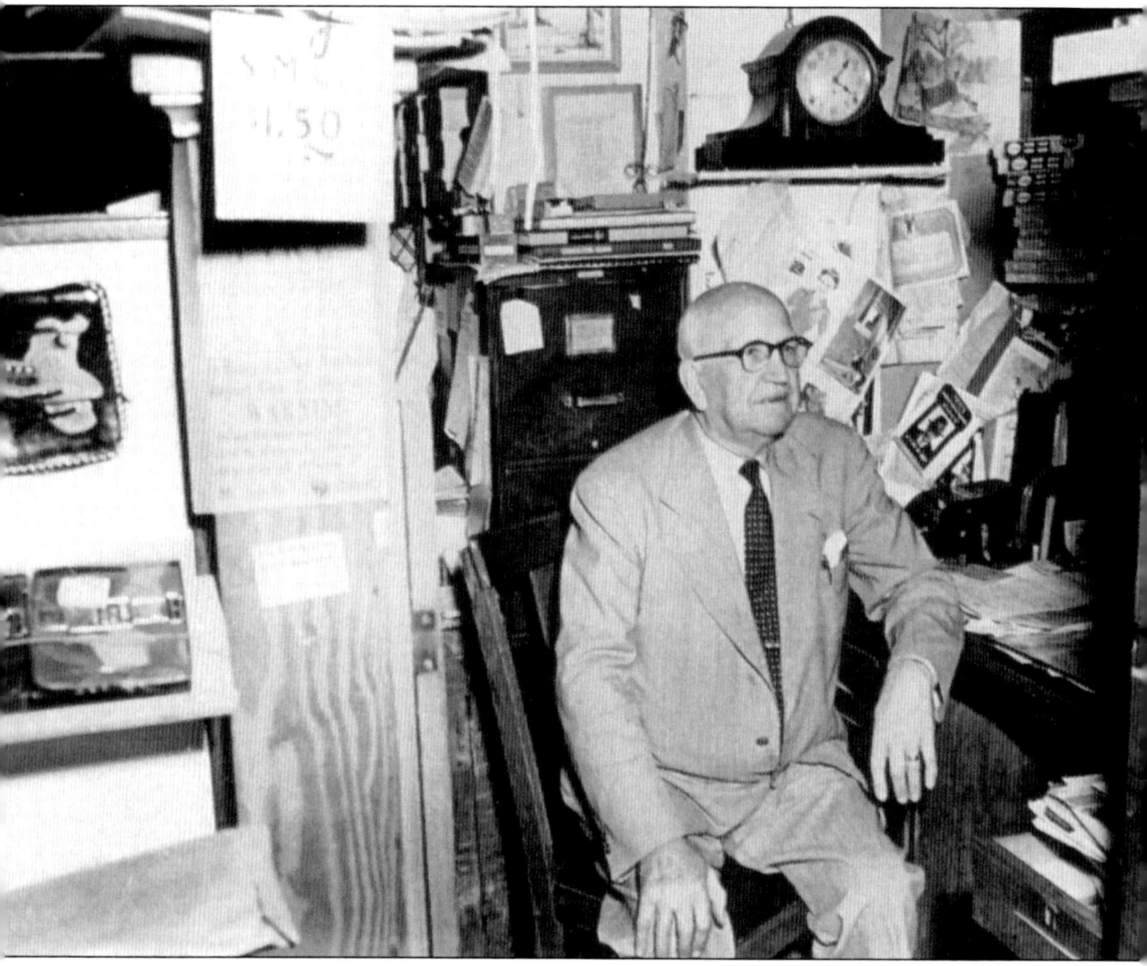

Spencer J. Ramsey was born on a farm in Texas, New York, in 1873. His first job was for a business in the village of Mexico. He did the delivery, using a wheelbarrow in the summer and a sled in the winter to trudge all around the village. He left Mexico to work for a short time as a traveling salesman in the Camden and Albany areas. He later returned and became a partner in the store with Cook and Jordan in 1905. He soon became the sole owner. John Ramsey joined his father in the business in 1933 and his grandson John (Jack) Ramsey joined the firm in 1958. Changes in the way of life in small communities led to a decline in local shopping, and after 96 years in business, the store closed its doors in 1989. Spencer J. Ramsey was a kind man and often helped those in need. He was a quiet man who loved his church, his family, and the community. (Courtesy of Nancy Ramsey Murray.)

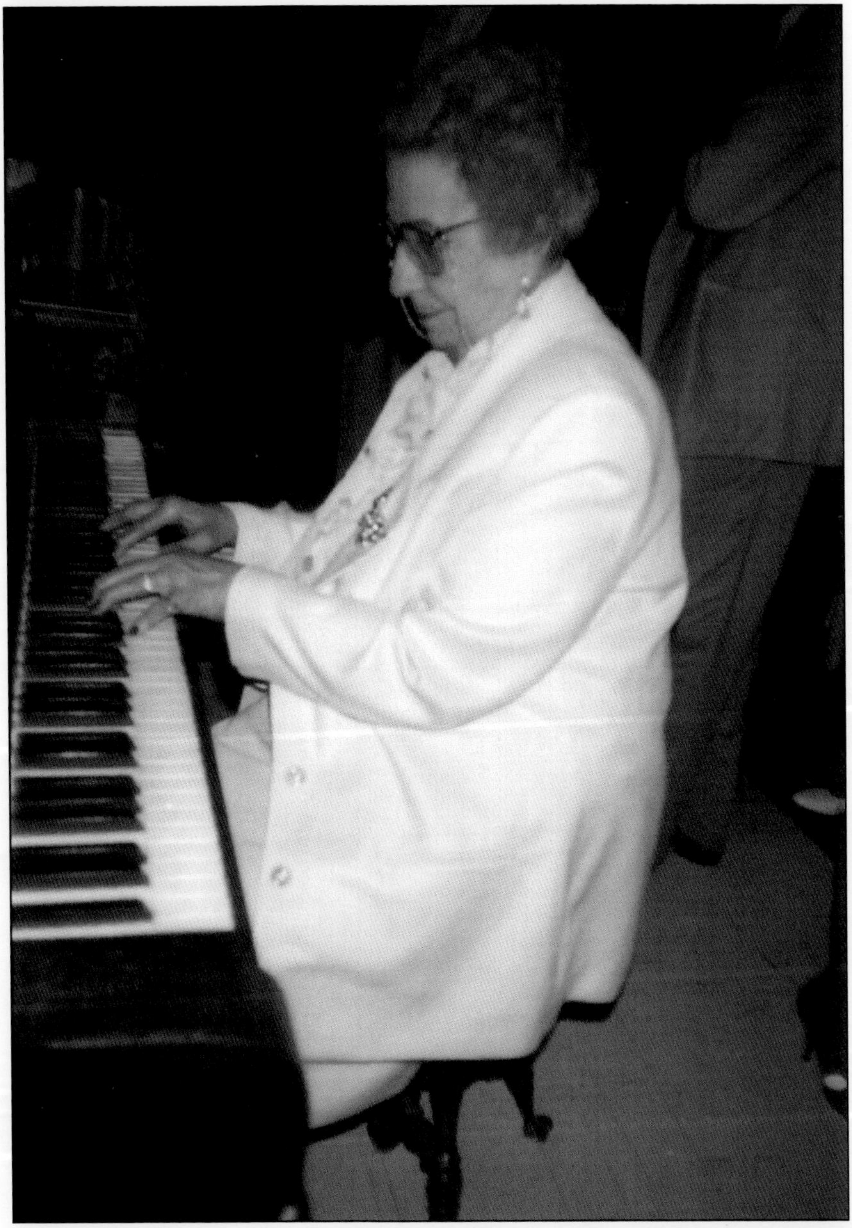

Grace E. Moore was born in 1917, the daughter of Earl and Ethel Moore. She graduated from Mexico Academy and worked 10 years for Backus Pedigree and then 20 years for Oswego County Social Service. Since the age of six, music has been her life. She began taking piano lessons as a little girl and later took organ lessons. Music is instinctive for her and she can play for hours without sheets of music. She can play anything from honky-tonk to hymns and from show tunes to classical music. She loves to share her gift and bring happiness to others. She also has a lovely soprano voice and has sung in the Methodist Church choir since she was a young girl. In 2001, she retired after more than 50 years as the choir director. The Methodist Church has honored her years of service by creating the Grace E. Moore Music Scholarship for a Mexico Academy and Central School graduate who is pursuing further study in music. Moore is lovingly called "Mexico's first lady of music."

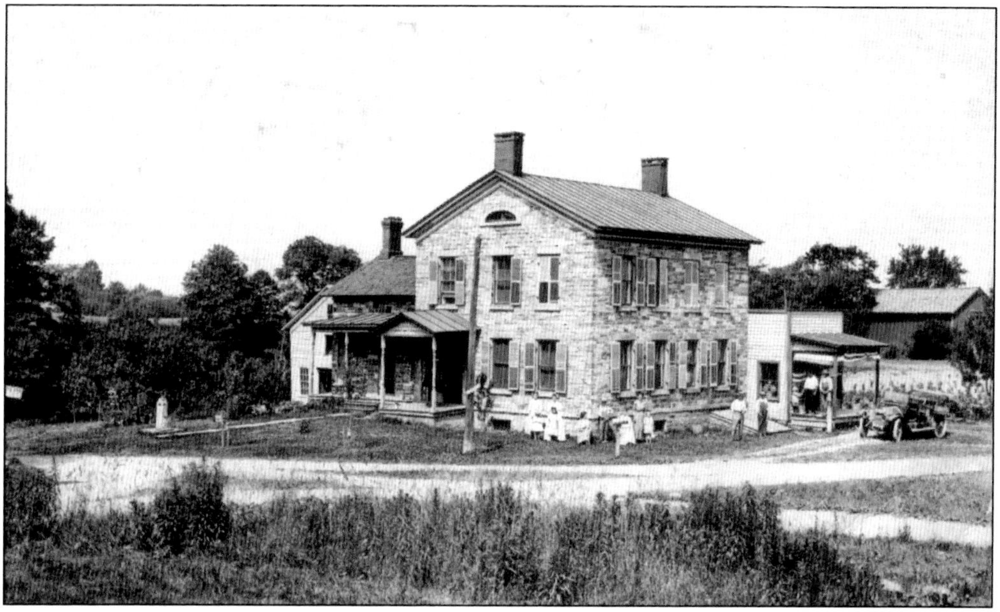

The beautiful home of John and Jane Brunson in Arthur was built as a tavern in 1838. The entrance of the wing is marked with the words *Bar Room* carved in the lintel over the door. The main section of the house is made of stone from the Arthur quarry. By early 1900, the building had become a private residence, and a store was located on the back. (Courtesy of John and Jane Brunson.)

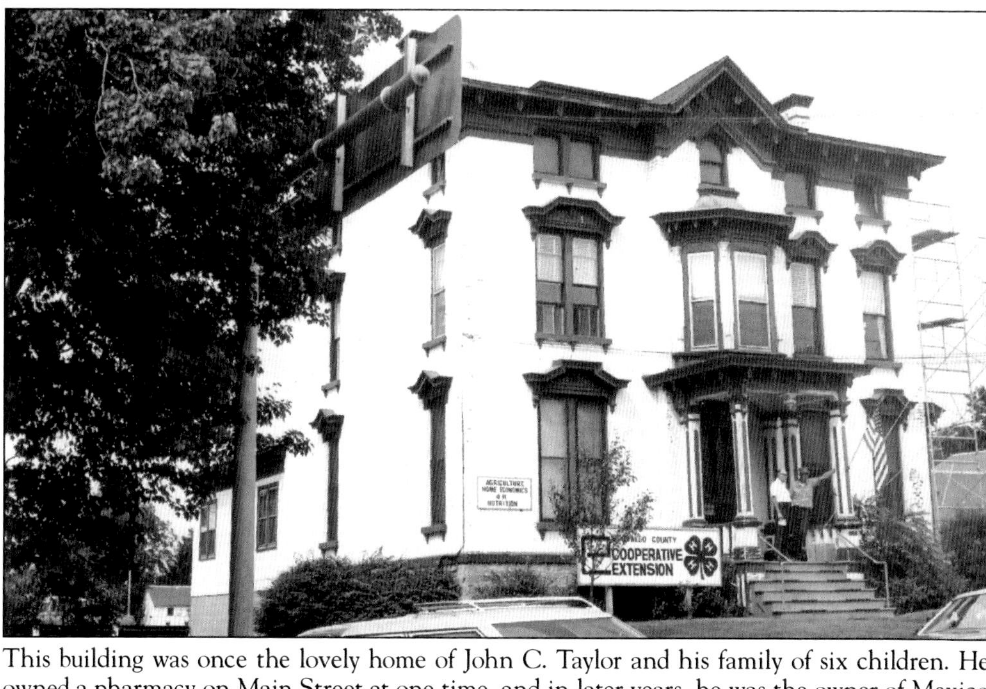

This building was once the lovely home of John C. Taylor and his family of six children. He owned a pharmacy on Main Street at one time, and in later years, he was the owner of Mexico Motor Car Company. The home was later sold and became the welfare office. When welfare grew to include many social services, the office moved out to a new location, and Cornell Corporative Extension moved in.

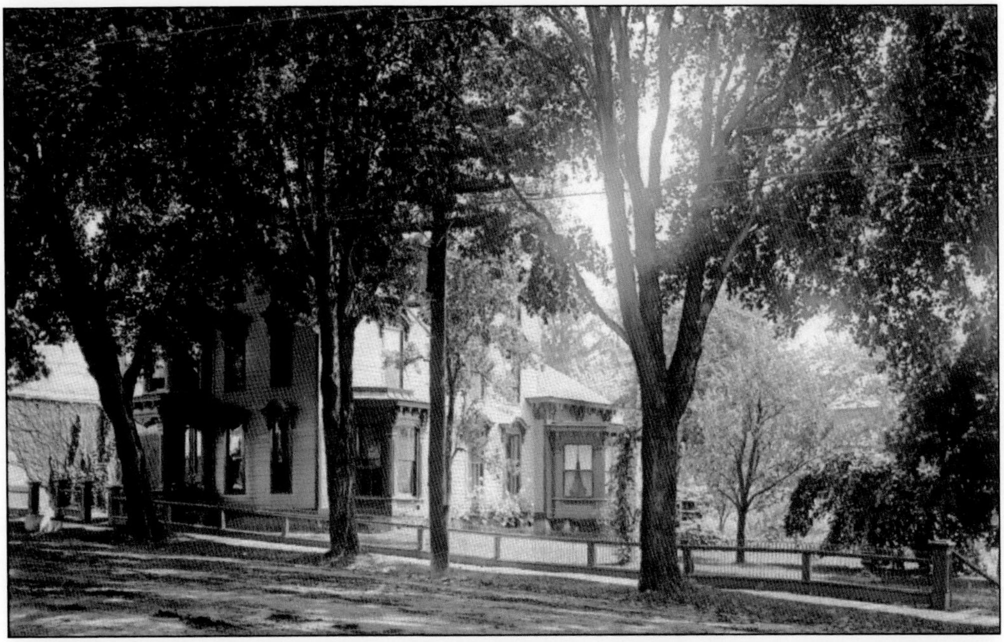

Key Bank now stands on the site of this lovely home of Fanny Thomas, who lived in it for 98 of her 100 years. She was the daughter of Amos C. Thomas, owner of Toronto Mill and the Thomas block of stores (from Jefferson Street to Giovo's). During the summer months, she enjoyed serving tea to a group of little girls or to her friends under the tree in the side lawn.

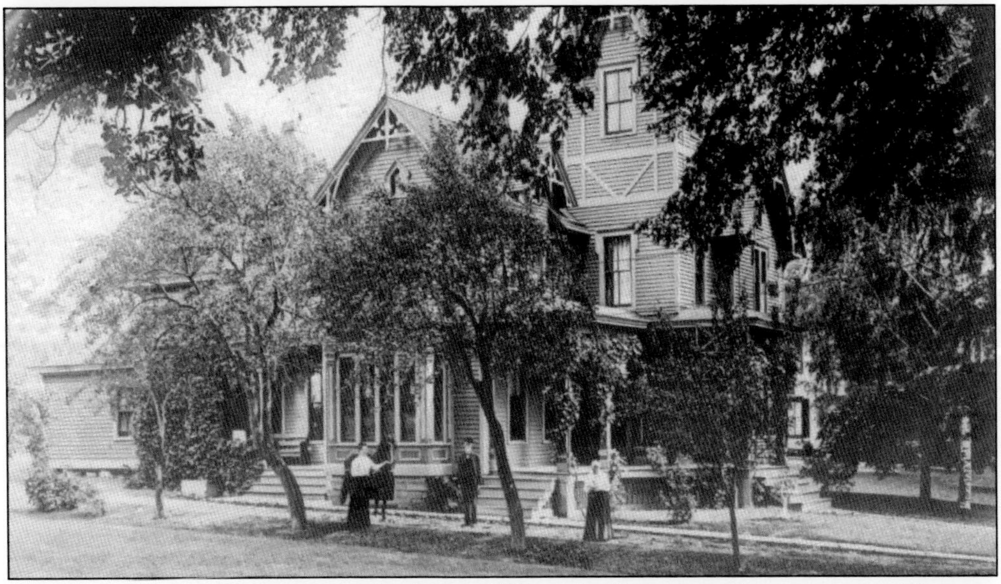

This home on Church Street was the home of Edwin L. Huntington for many years. He was a Civil War veteran who was discharged in 1865 as a captain and came home to open a drugstore. He served the community as sheriff in 1894. When electricity came to Mexico, 20 streetlights were installed and were run 20 nights a month (not necessary when there was a full moon) and were turned off at midnight when all citizens were in bed. Early in 1891, the Mexico Electric Light, Heat, and Power Company, with Huntington as president, was able to furnish full service. Leonard Lawton and his family live in the house now.

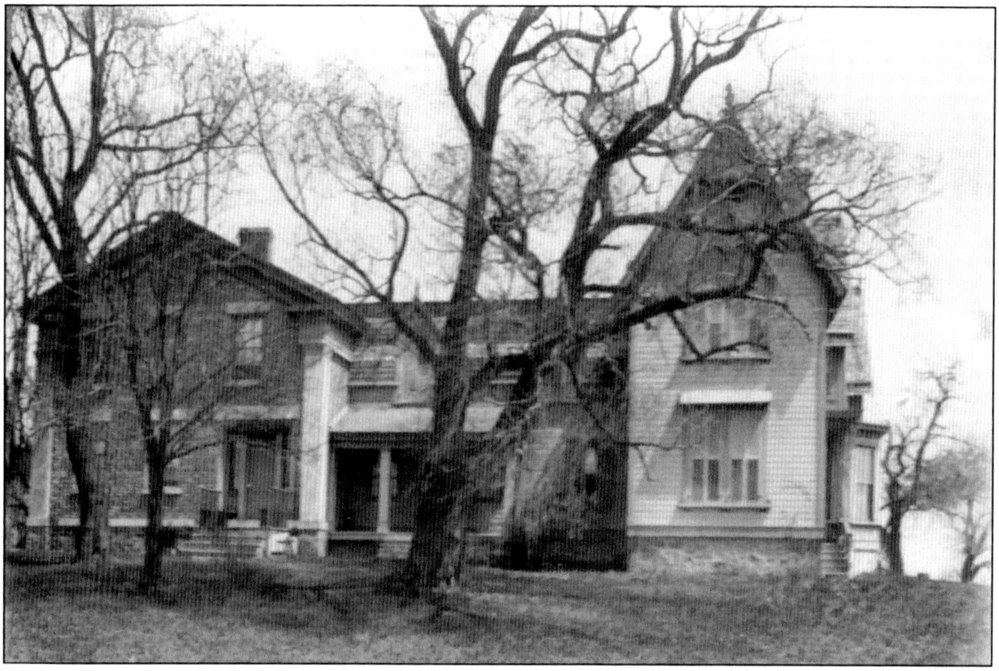

Richard Hamilton built the wood-frame section of this house in 1824 and the cobblestone wing in 1848. His son-in-law added the Gothic wing in 1879. If a train got held up in Mexico because of snow-blocked tracks, the passengers were taken here for a warm meal. The home became known as "the Beanery." The house, now greatly remodeled, is the home of the David Brooks family.

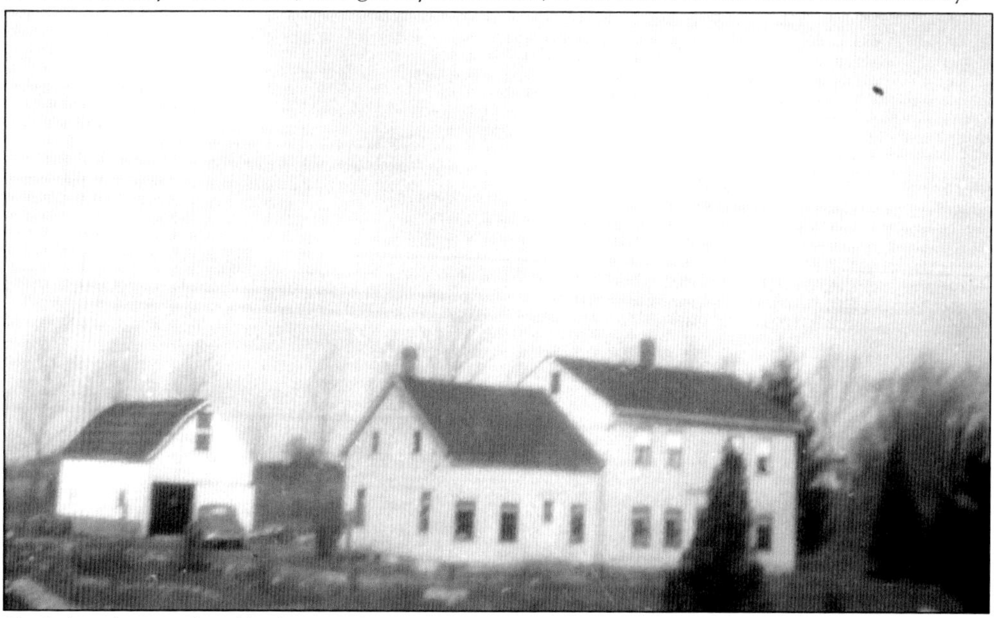

Shubal and Lucinda Alfred arrived in Mexico in 1807. He built the first frame and plank house in the village. The Master Masons organized a lodge chapter and began meeting in the home in 1808. Seven women began meeting there in 1810, forming a congregation that became the Presbyterian Church. A school was opened in the barn in 1811. The home was also known for sheltering runaway slaves. (Courtesy of the Barry Haynes collection.)

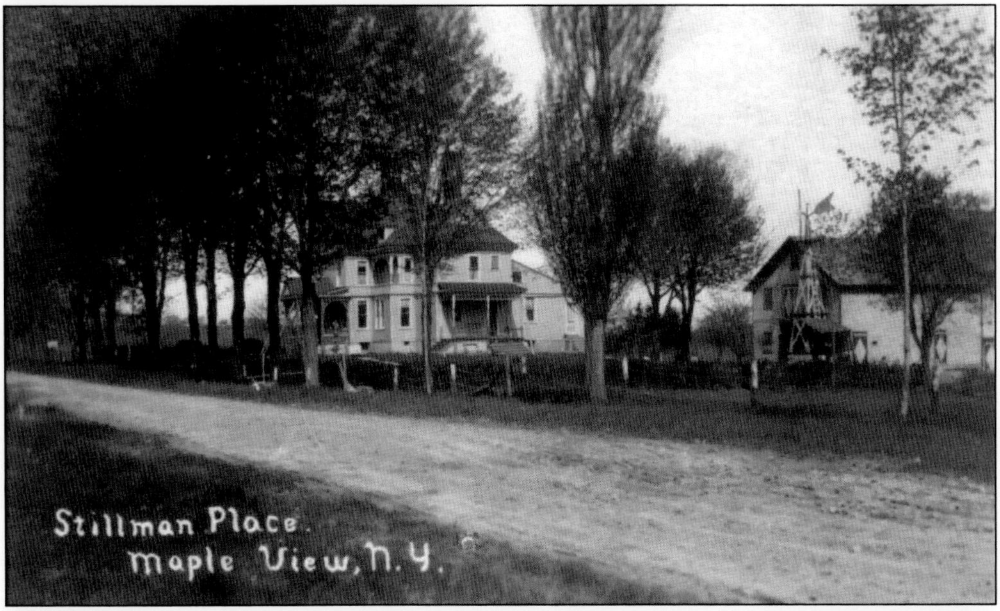

The Stillman farmstead is on State Route 104 west of Maple View. In 1899, Charles Stillman had the large Queen Anne–style home built on the family property. A mill house was built on the southeast corner of the barn over a well. A windmill pumped water into a small concrete tank that would hold two or three 40-quart milk cans. The property passed out of the Stillman family in 1913.

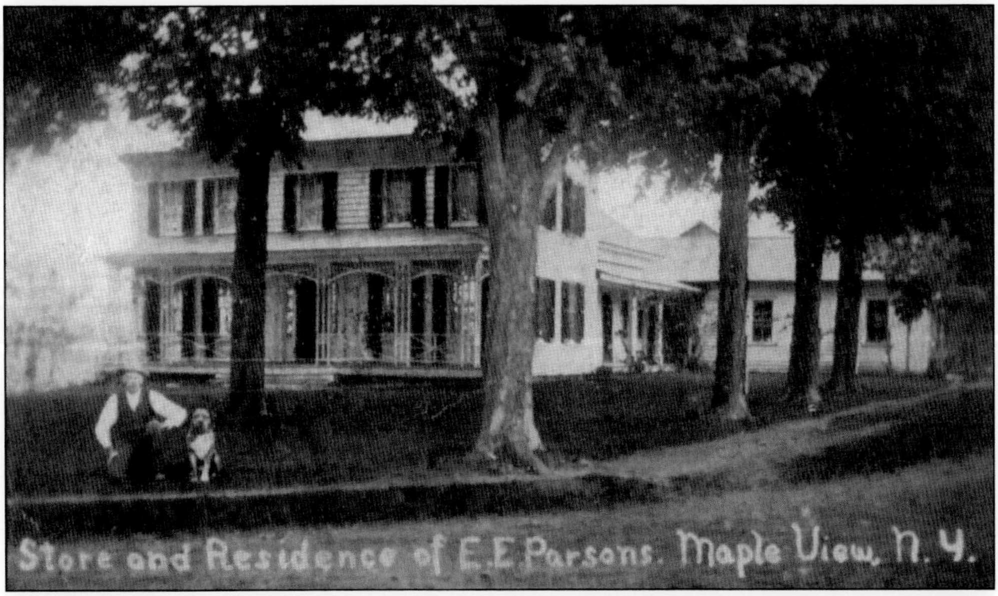

The Skinner Parsons home is on the northeast corner of State Routes 11 and 104. Avery Skinner married Elizabeth Huntington in 1821 and settled at the crossroads he named Union Square. He secured a post office in 1826 and was appointed postmaster, he developed the plank road companies, and he strongly advocated the building of Syracuse Northern Railroad in the 1870s. He was active politically, serving as county treasurer, county judge, and in the state assembly and state senate. E. E. Parsons lived here 80 years later.

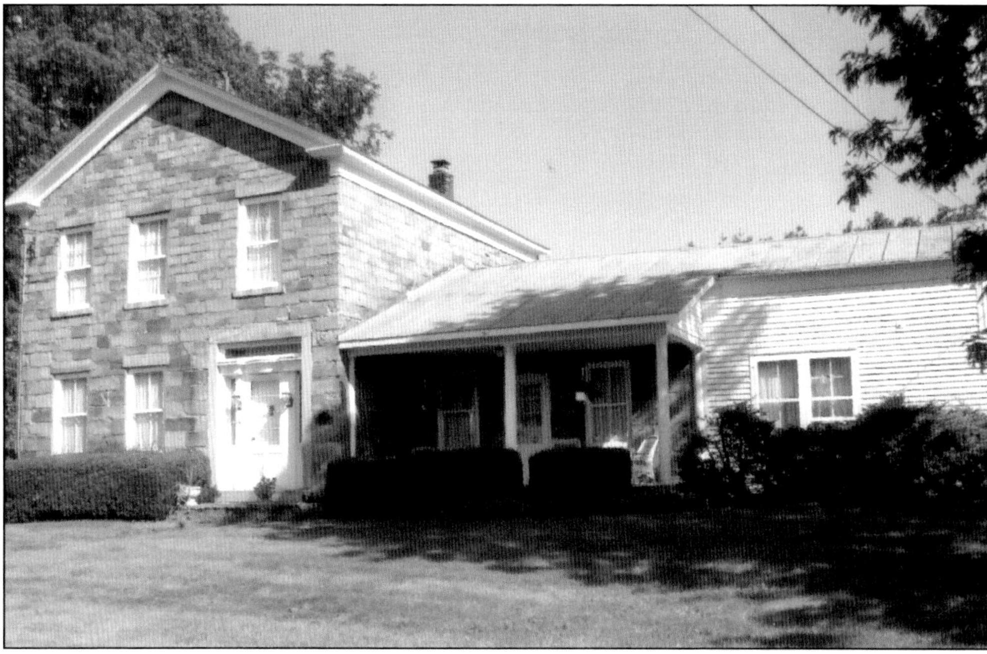

When Leonard and Minerva Ames came to Mexico in 1804, they built a log cabin with a sheepfold on the north side, which was used by the itinerant minister of the Methodist Church as a place to hold services as early as 1808. The log cabin was replaced by the wood-frame wing on the right in 1815, and the two-story stone wing was built in 1835. (Courtesy of Sandra Scott.)

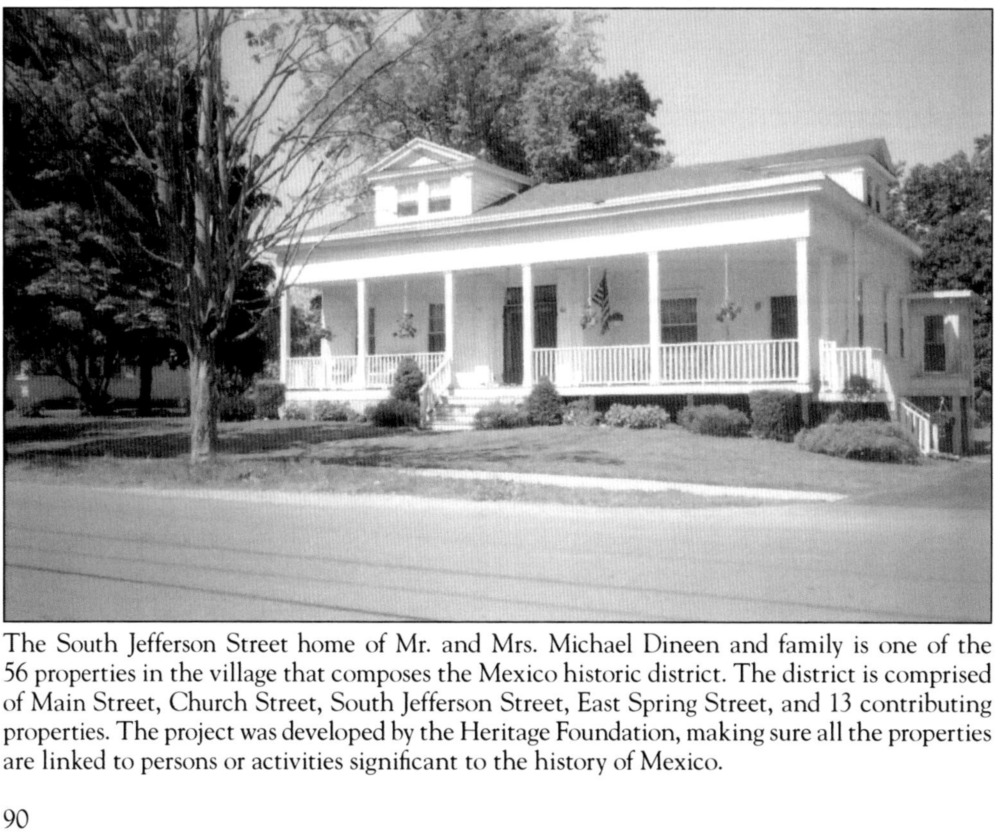

The South Jefferson Street home of Mr. and Mrs. Michael Dineen and family is one of the 56 properties in the village that composes the Mexico historic district. The district is comprised of Main Street, Church Street, South Jefferson Street, East Spring Street, and 13 contributing properties. The project was developed by the Heritage Foundation, making sure all the properties are linked to persons or activities significant to the history of Mexico.

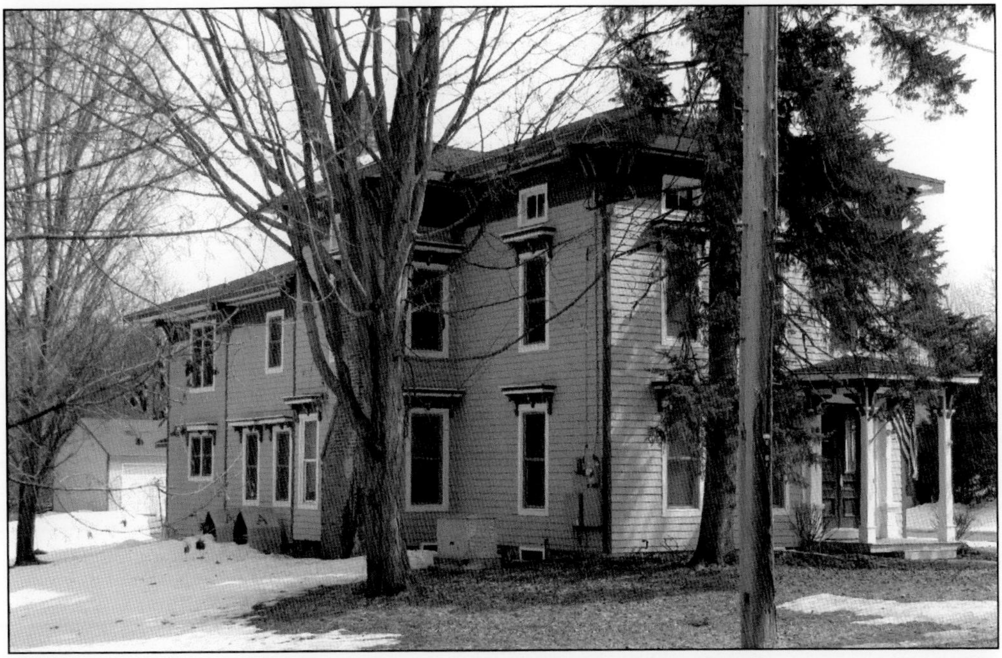

William H. Osborn bought this house on Lincoln Avenue 1898 when he came to Mexico. He also bought Toronto Mill and State Mill from Almeron Thomas. Osborn was a great admirer of fine houses and owned several. There was a large stable behind his home. The home is now owned by David and Sharon Anderson and has been carefully restored.

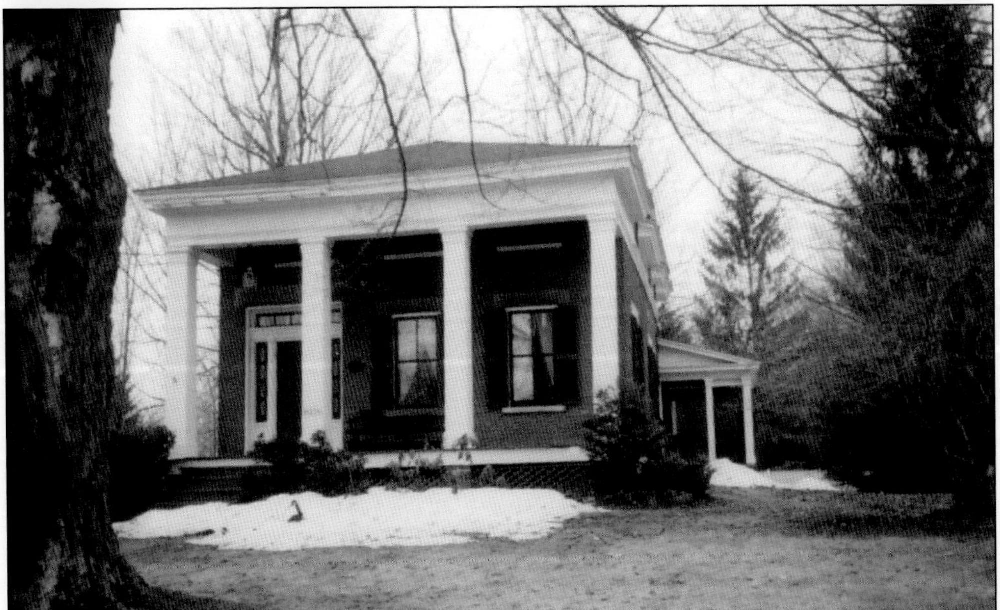

For many years, this lovely house was the home of Charles Webb. He served the community as town clerk, and around 1850, he was a trustee of school No. 8. During the 1860 election campaign of Abraham Lincoln, Webb was captain of the marching club called the Wide Awakes. An excellent example of a Greek Revival building, this home is lovingly cared for by Ron and Rita Jardin. (Author's collection.)

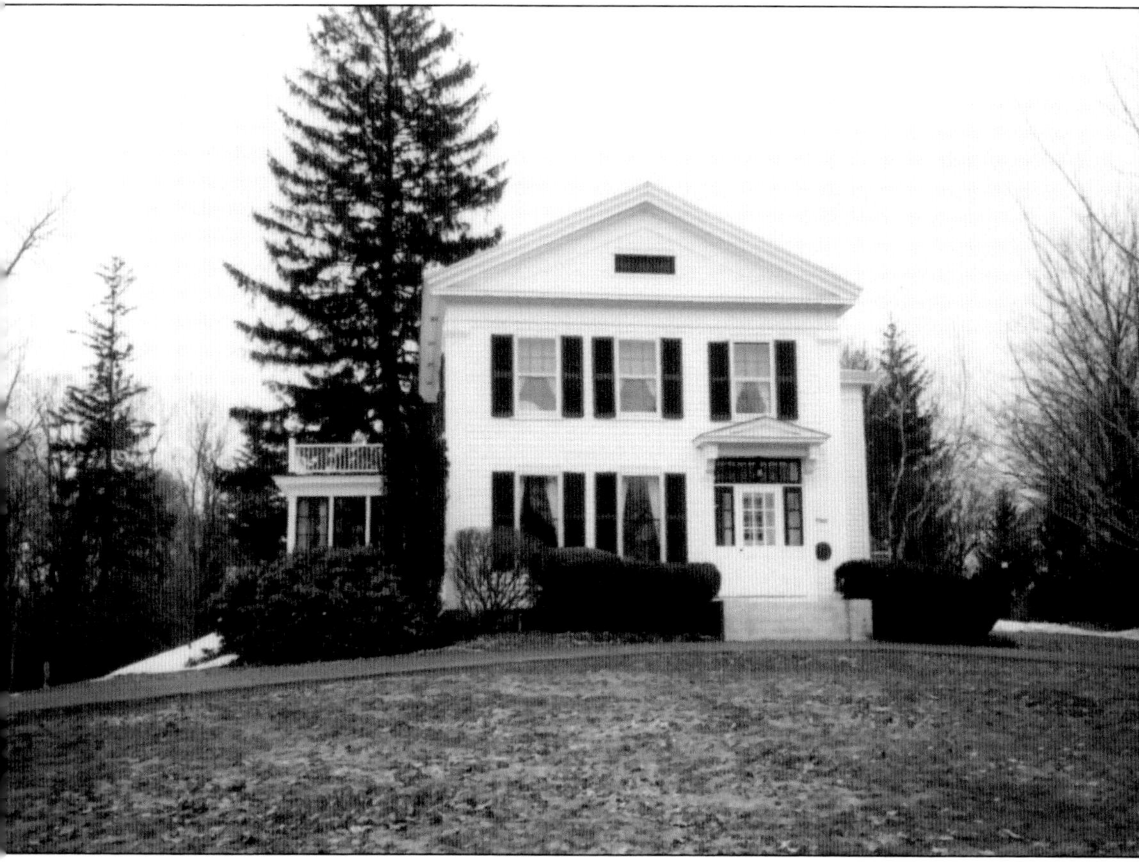

The house on the corner of Spring and Church Streets was built about 1843 by Warren Allen. He was raised on a farm but followed the carpenter's trade for 20 years. He was also a cabinetmaker, an ordained Methodist minister, an undertaker, a dentist, and a physician. He sold the house to Luther Conklin in 1859. Conklin was a leading citizen in the community until 1878, when the residents of Mexico were appalled to learn he had embezzled money from Oswego County for over 21 years. Harriet Ames Rundell, a homeopathic doctor, and her husband lived here. She was loved by the community, and it was said the patient felt better as soon as "Auntie" Rundell walked into the room. Dr. Tobias Green was the next owner, followed by Lee Houghton. The present owners are John and Katherine Mowry. This beautiful home and the people who lived here have contributed much to the community.

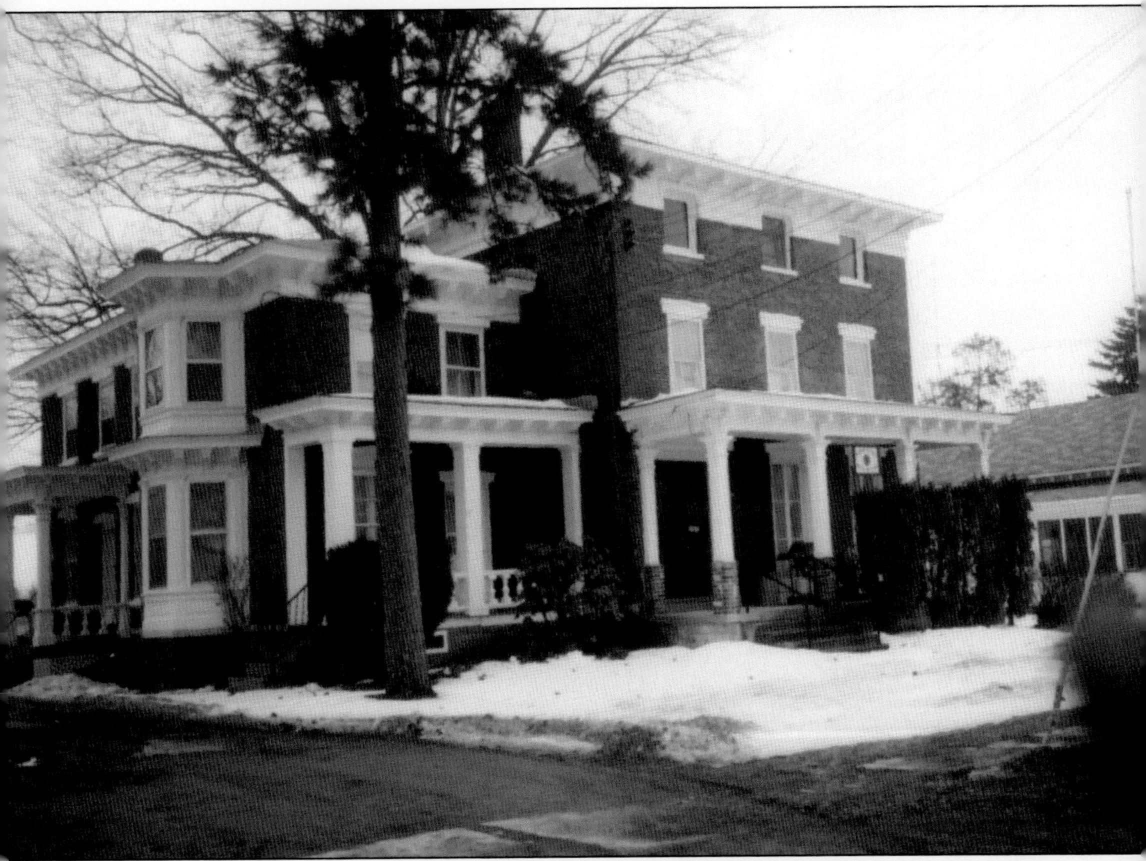

The Timothy Skinner home is located on Scenic Avenue. Built about 1865, it is an outstanding example of the Italianate style. He was the son of Avery and Elizabeth Huntington Skinner and raised in Maple View. Skinner came to Mexico in 1853 and studied law. He joined with Judge Cyrus Whitney in the law and banking firm of Whitney and Skinner. He practiced law the remainder of his life. He served the community as surrogate for 20 years, was village president (mayor), was a trustee of Mexico Academy, and was an active member of the Masons. His son Avery W. Skinner was principal of Mexico Academy, superintendent of Oneida Schools, director of examination at the University of the State of New York, and held other educational positions. The auditorium of the present-day school building commemorates his memory. The Skinner family sold the property to the American Legion in 1946. The house was sold to Quniton Bentley, who is restoring it.

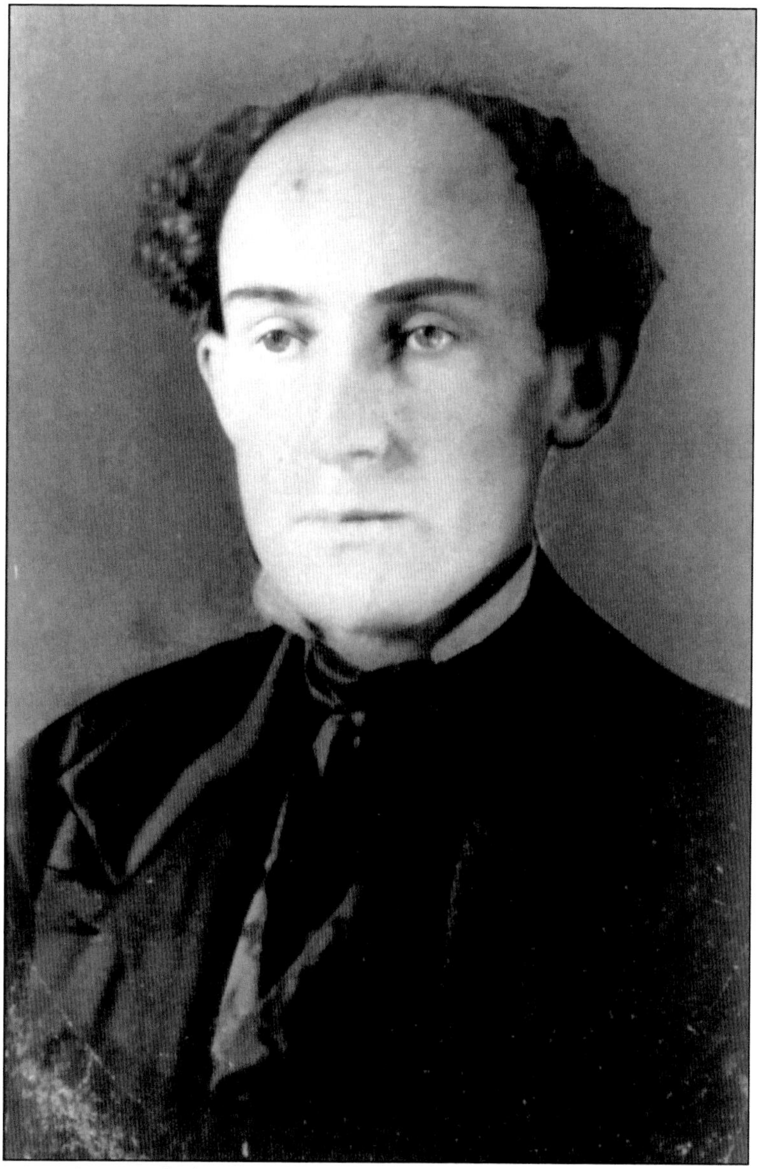

Asa Wing was a famous abolitionist. Mary Smith Mack wrote about her ancestor in 1992, described here: It was the 11th of September 1855. The large assemblage had gathered from near and far, and so many had come from round about that their vehicles almost barricaded the village streets. What was it all about? It was to honor the memory of Asa Wing, who devoted his life to freeing the slaves. In the village cemetery near the grove, a monument was unveiled, reading upon its base, "Asa S. Wing, died March 8th, 1854, aged 38 years. He trusted in God and loved his neighbors. Erected by the Friends of Freedom." Frederick Douglass, famous ex-slave, journalist, and lecturer, gave the eulogy that day. In his address he said, "The crime of slavery deeply disturbed him. Night after night, and day after day, in wet or dry, in heat or cold, he poured out his life for perishing slaves." Asa Wing went to his early death speaking through this state and New England. He was identified with the first-class antislavery orators in the state. On September 11, 1855, the first monument in the Mexico Village Cemetery was dedicated to Asa Wing. Between 2,000 and 3,000 people attended the service.

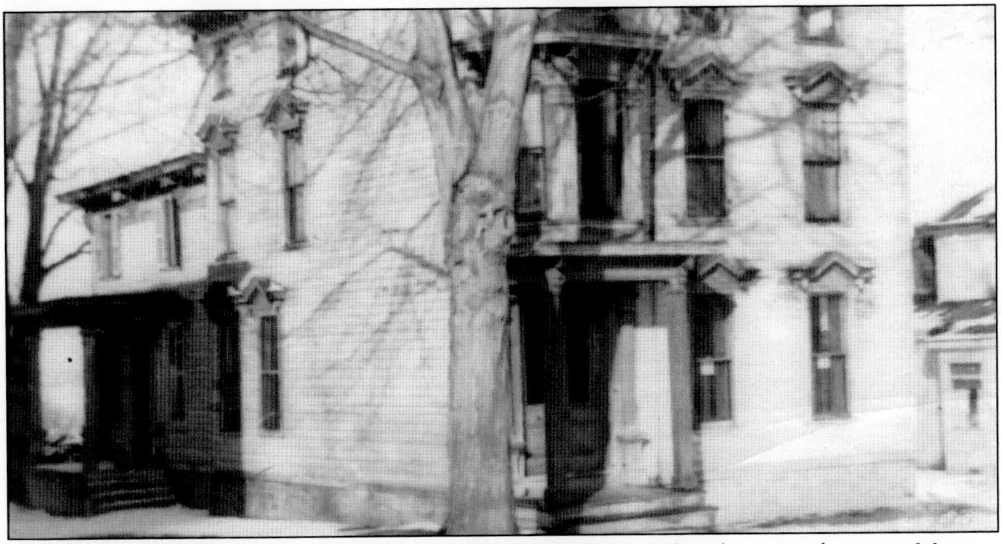

In 1832, Starr Clark exchanged his home and business in Utica for a house and store in Mexico. Through the years, he became active in the Whig Party and the Underground Railroad. Passengers of the Underground Railroad were hidden in a dark tank room over the kitchen in his home. The house was just east of the tin shop, and to avoid detection in case of a search, a tunnel was constructed between the cellar of the shop and house. Clark's obituary in 1866 spoke of him as one of the oldest, earliest, and most prominent citizens and a zealous member of the Whig Party. Many in Mexico today will remember the house as Fred Peterson's jewelry store of the mid-1900s. The only change is a picture window in the front on the right.

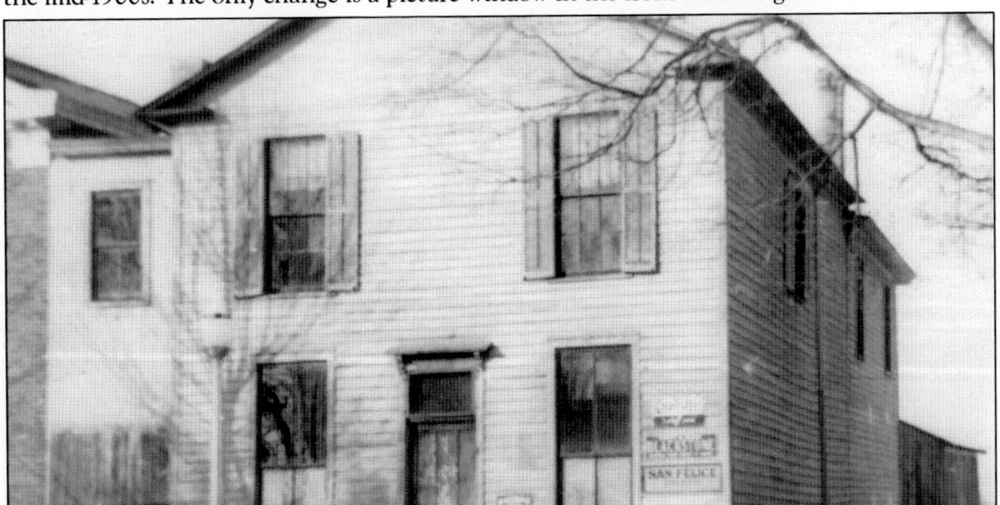

When Clark came to Mexico, he sold dry goods and groceries in the store. In later years, he sold stoves, stovepipes, and tinware of all kinds. He was widely known as an abolitionist and as the stationmaster of Mexico's Underground Railroad. Grants from New York State and the federal government have been set aside for the Mexico Historical Society to restore the tin shop as an Underground Railroad site.

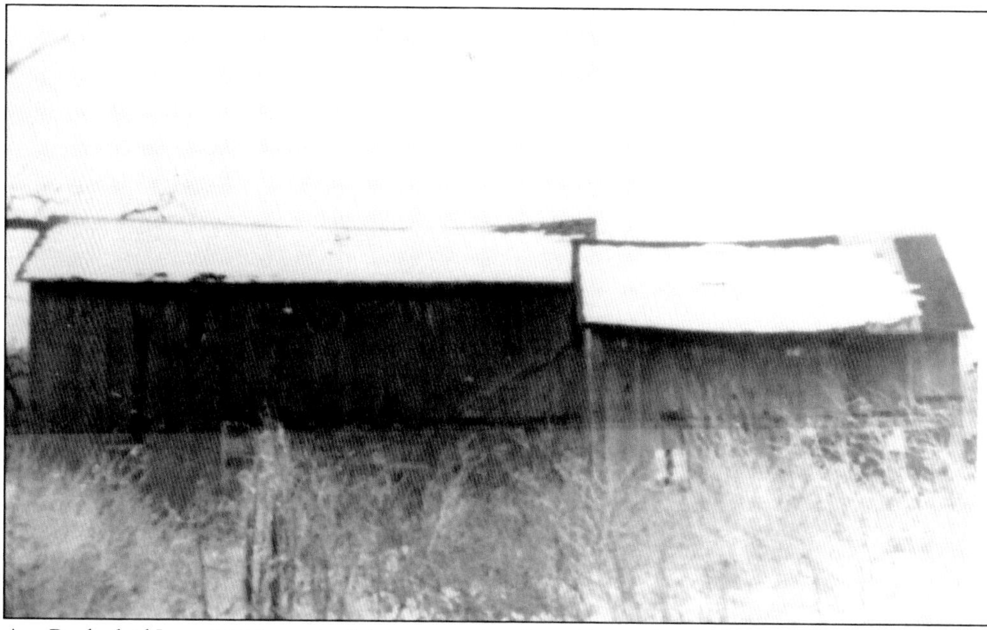

Asa Beebe hid Jerry McHenry in this barn on Academy Street during the famous escape in 1851. McHenry, a former slave, had been arrested by U.S. marshals in Syracuse, as they enforced the fugitive slave law. The abolitionists fought the law with an event known as the Jerry Rescue. McHenry was brought to Mexico and hidden here before being moved to Oswego and then freedom in Canada.

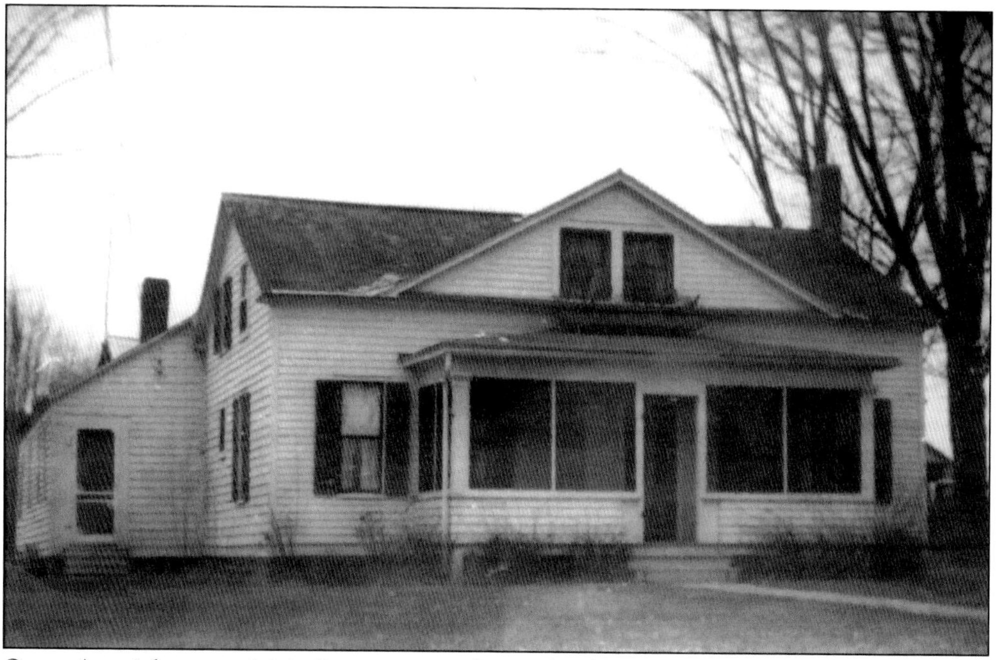

Orson Ames's home on Main Street was a safe stop for slaves on the Underground Railroad to freedom. The most famous event was Ames's part in the famous Jerry Rescue. The abolitionists, testing the fugitive slave law, freed McHenry from jail in Syracuse and eventually brought him to Mexico. He was hidden at the home of Ames the first night and then moved to Beebe's barn.

Seven

Open for Business

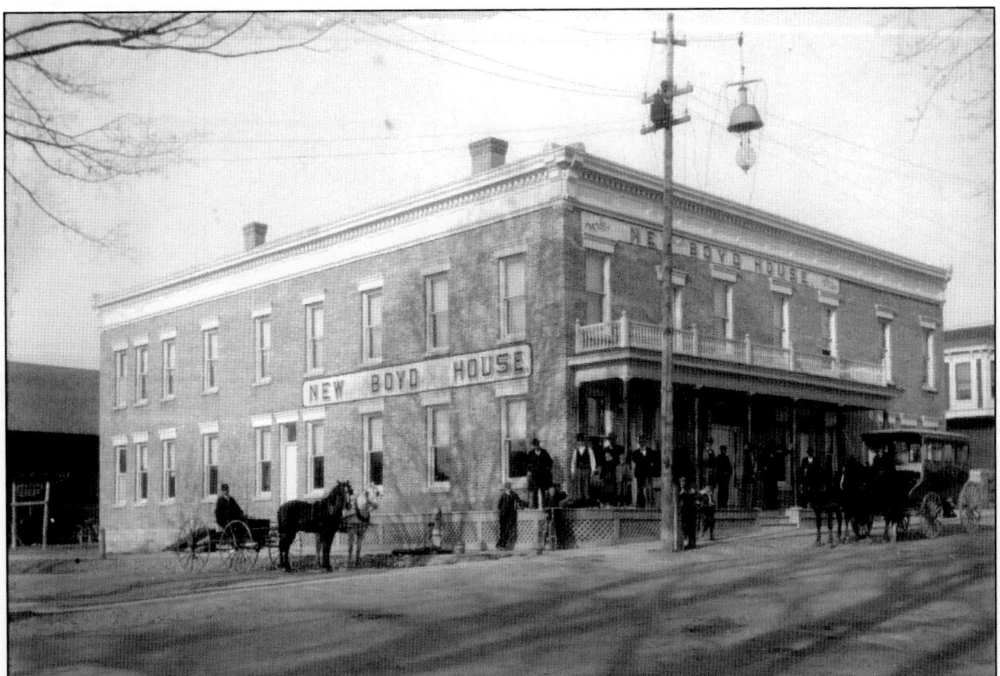

Capt. David Boyd bought the three-story hotel on the corner of Main Street and Scenic Avenue. When it burned in 1898, he rebuilt it as a two-story structure and named it New Boyd House. John Beck bought the popular landmark in 1912, and it continued to be known as Beck's, with his children John, Catherine, and Isabelle as proprietors until it was sold in 1980. (Courtesy of the Barry Haynes collection.)

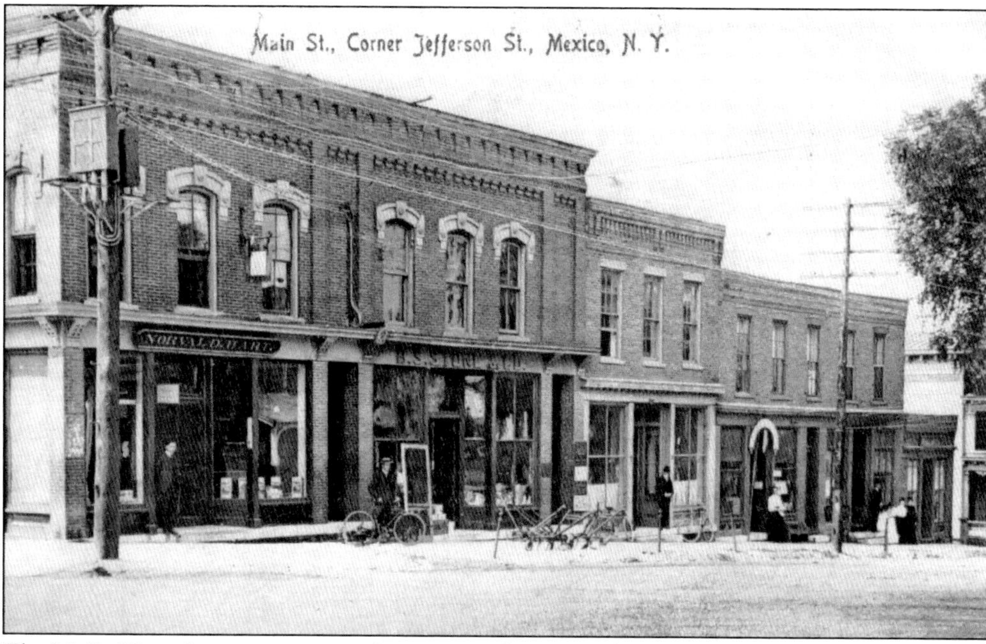

The N. B. Hart drugstore was on the corner of Main and South Jefferson Streets. The B. S. Stone hardware store was next to it. Douglas and Edward Crandall bought both stores and took out the adjoining wall to make their pharmacy larger. It is now the home of Hart and Stone Store. (Author's collection.)

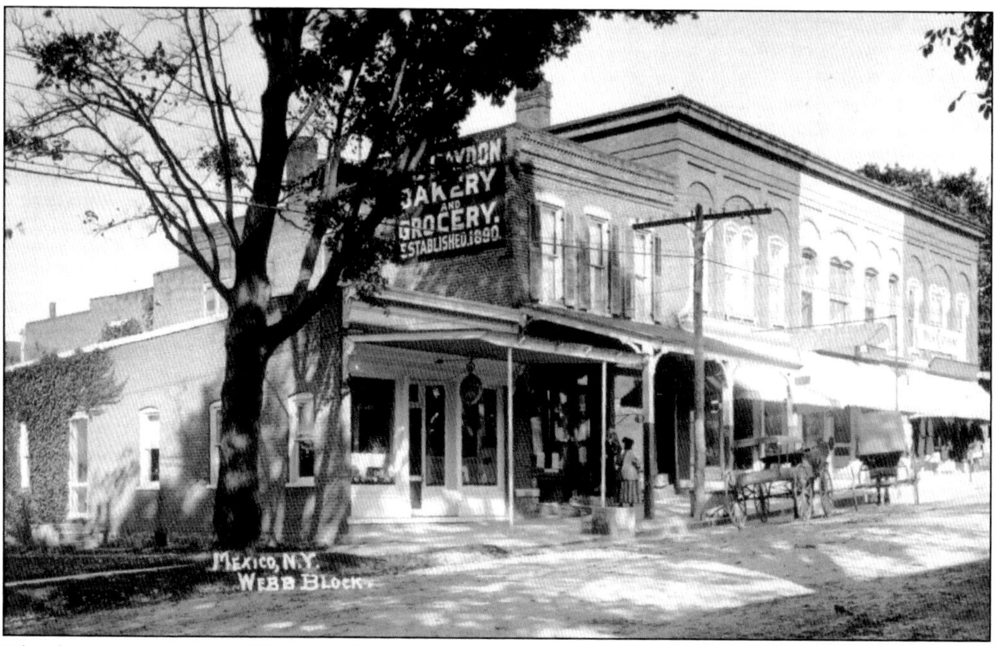

The former wooden buildings on the north side of Main Street going west from Jefferson Street burned in 1854. Henry Webb rebuilt three solid brick buildings on the site. Through the years, the buildings have housed the Mexico newspaper, a bank, a drugstore, markets, a flower shop, a hardware store, a hairdresser, and other businesses. The two smaller stores on the left were added before 1900. (Courtesy of the Barry Haynes collection.)

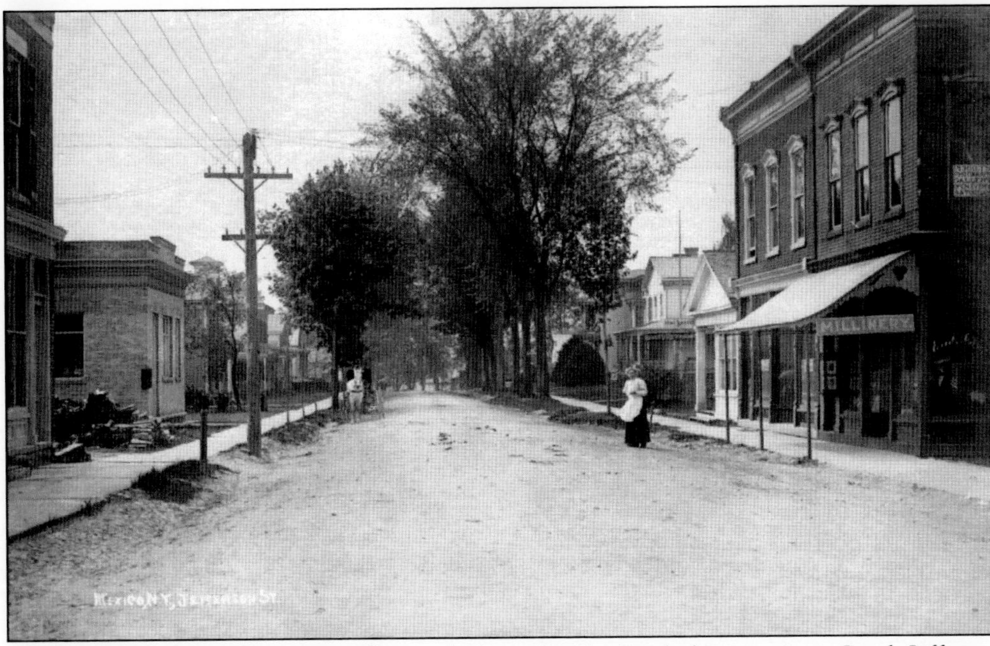

The two brick buildings on the right stood where the Key Bank driveway is on South Jefferson Street. Earl and Lulu Brown rented the first building in 1920 where the Browns had living quarters, and Lulu Brown had a millenary and dress shop. It was in their kitchen where she began making baked beans to sell. The next building was rented by Clarence Smith, a master mechanic. The little building is the museum. (Courtesy of the Barry Haynes collection.)

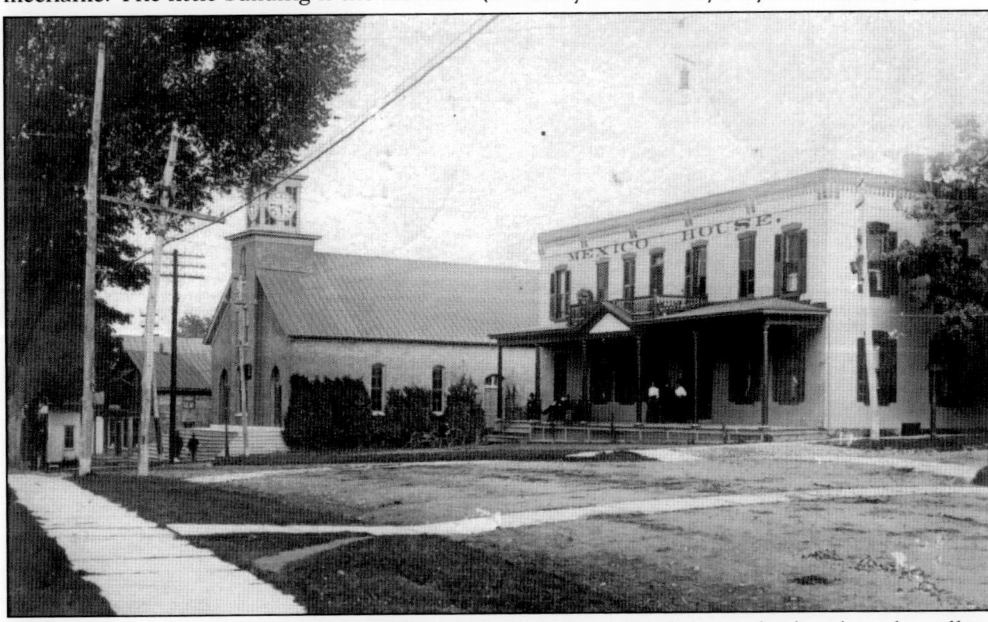

Mexico House Hotel was built in 1865 on the lot where the first regular hotel in the village had been built in 1823. C. S. Mayo bought the hotel and put an addition along Church Street, which added rooms to the first floor and a 30-foot-by-60-foot public hall on the second floor. The hotel burned in 1937 and was replaced by a Sinclair gasoline station and garage. (Author's collection.)

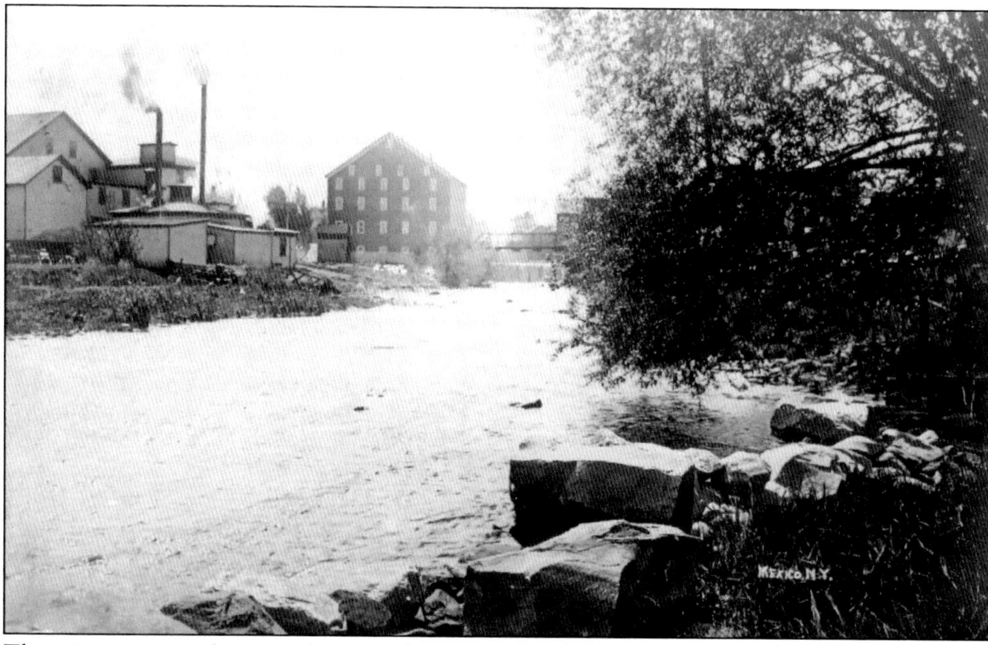

This picture was taken standing on the west side of the Little Salmon River looking south toward Main Street. On the left is the back of Rosemary Creamery, which was on North Street. The tall building is the Osborn-Dexter feed mill. The falls can be seen in the middle. (Courtesy of the Barry Haynes collection.)

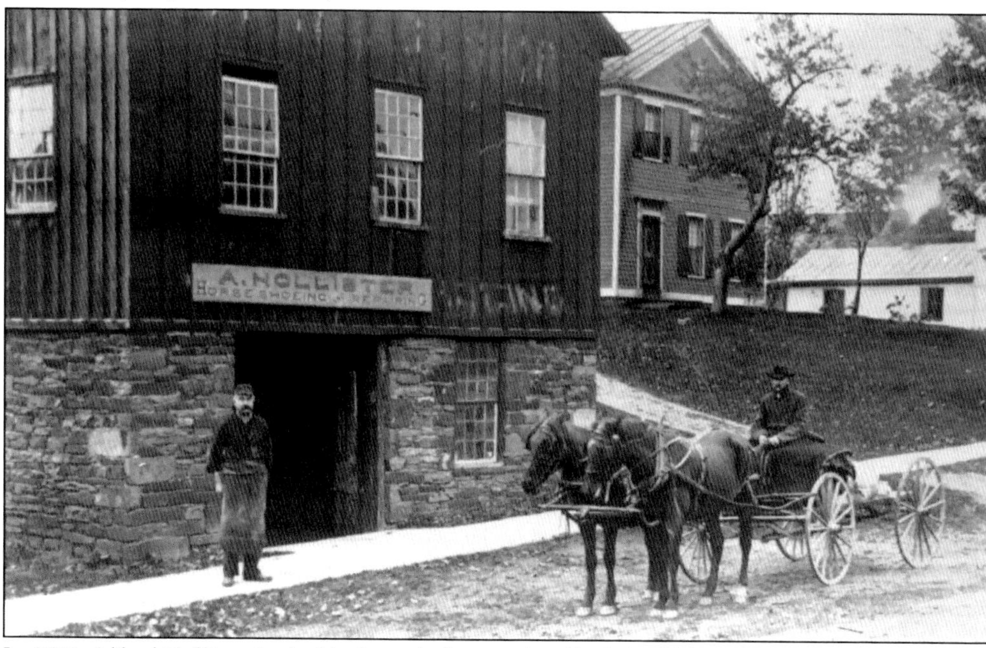

In 1910, Alfred Hollister had a blacksmith shop in Asa Beebe's old foundry on the southwest side of Black Creek. By 1930, the building had been replaced by a small gasoline station and garage, and that was replaced by Mimi's Restaurant in 1963. The Robinson-Adams house on the hill was designated a historical landmark. The home was built about 1826. (Courtesy of the Barry Haynes collection.)

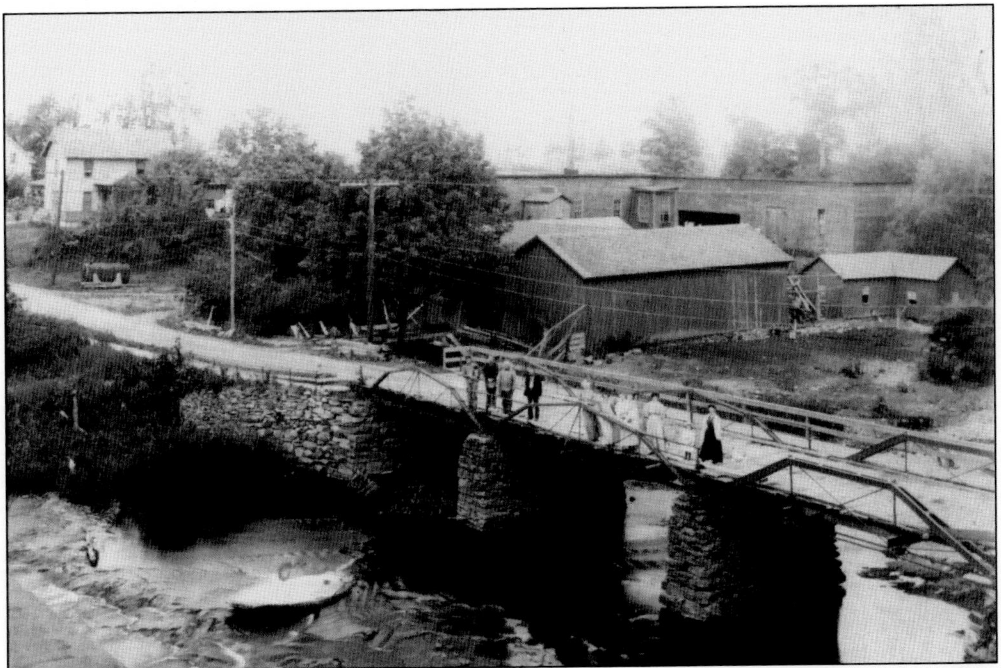

Toad Hollow was the milling area at the northwest corner of the village. The planing mill of Edwin Ames Jr. and Frank Penfield is seen just north of the bridge that crosses the Little Salmon River on Academy Street. Other milling businesses at Toad Hollow included a door, sash, and blind factory, a gristmill, a sawmill specializing in barrel hoops, and the animal poke factory.

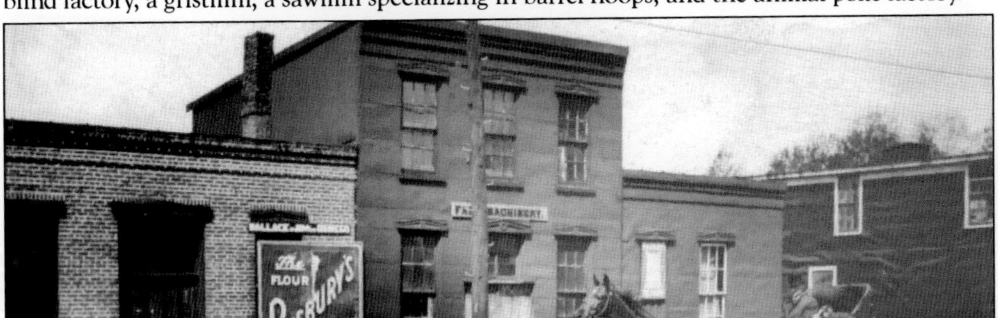

Clark Foundry and Machine Shop was west of Black Creek on the north side of Main Street. Luther Jay Clark bought the Beebe foundry in 1879 and established a business of manufacturing boilers and portable engines that continued for more than 25 years. In 1939, the untiring efforts of Dr. L. D. Pulsifer secured the land on both sides of Black Creek to add to the school campus. (Courtesy of the Barry Haynes collection.)

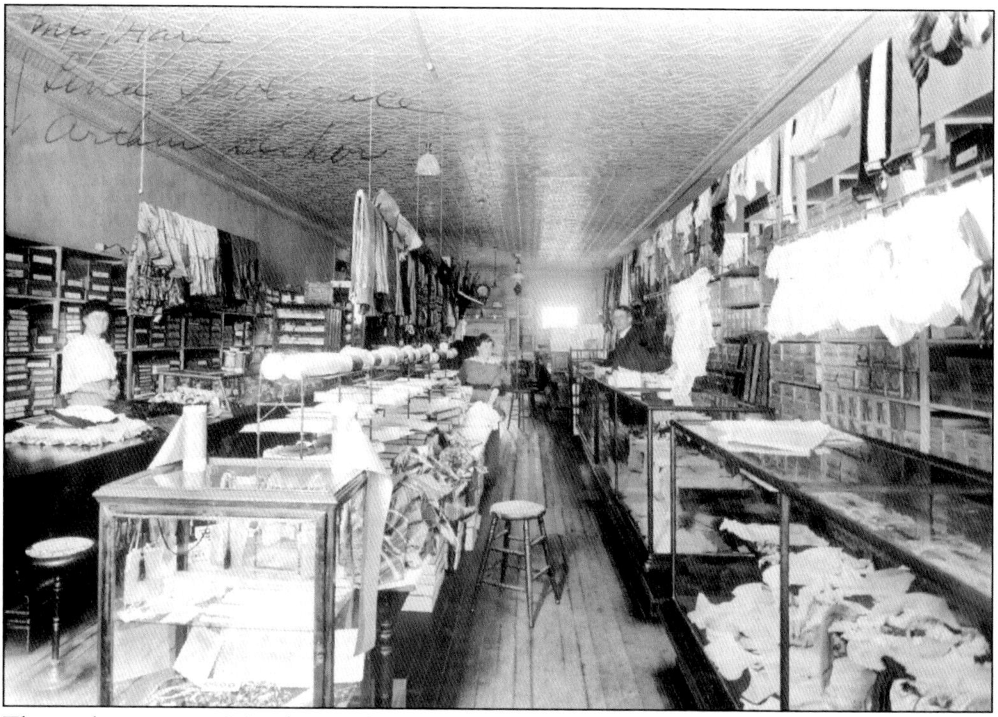

This is the interior of the dry goods store of C. E. Hare and Company in 1915. The store was located at the corner of Main and North Jefferson Streets. Marie Hare stands with bolts of material, a Mr. Becker is by the shoe boxes, and Lean Severance is by the center island where there are rolls of lace and other trimmings.

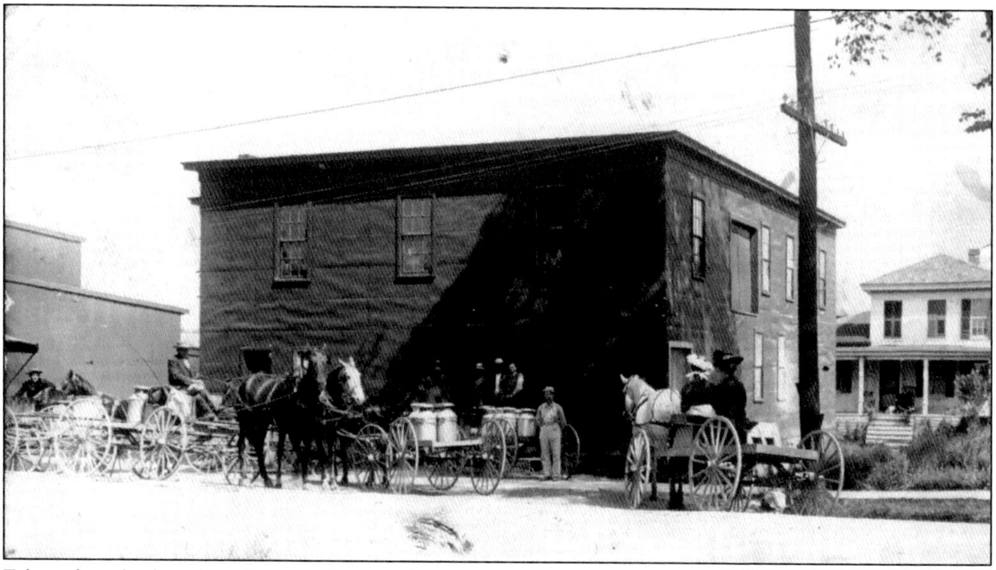

Edward and Theodore Stevens had a planing business in this building around 1903. The shop was on Main Street on the east side of Black Creek close to the dam where the school park has been for many years. "The shop made doors, windows, boards and moldings so common and necessary in the early homes." Clark Foundry and Machine Shop was close to the falls on the west side of Black Creek. (Author's collection.)

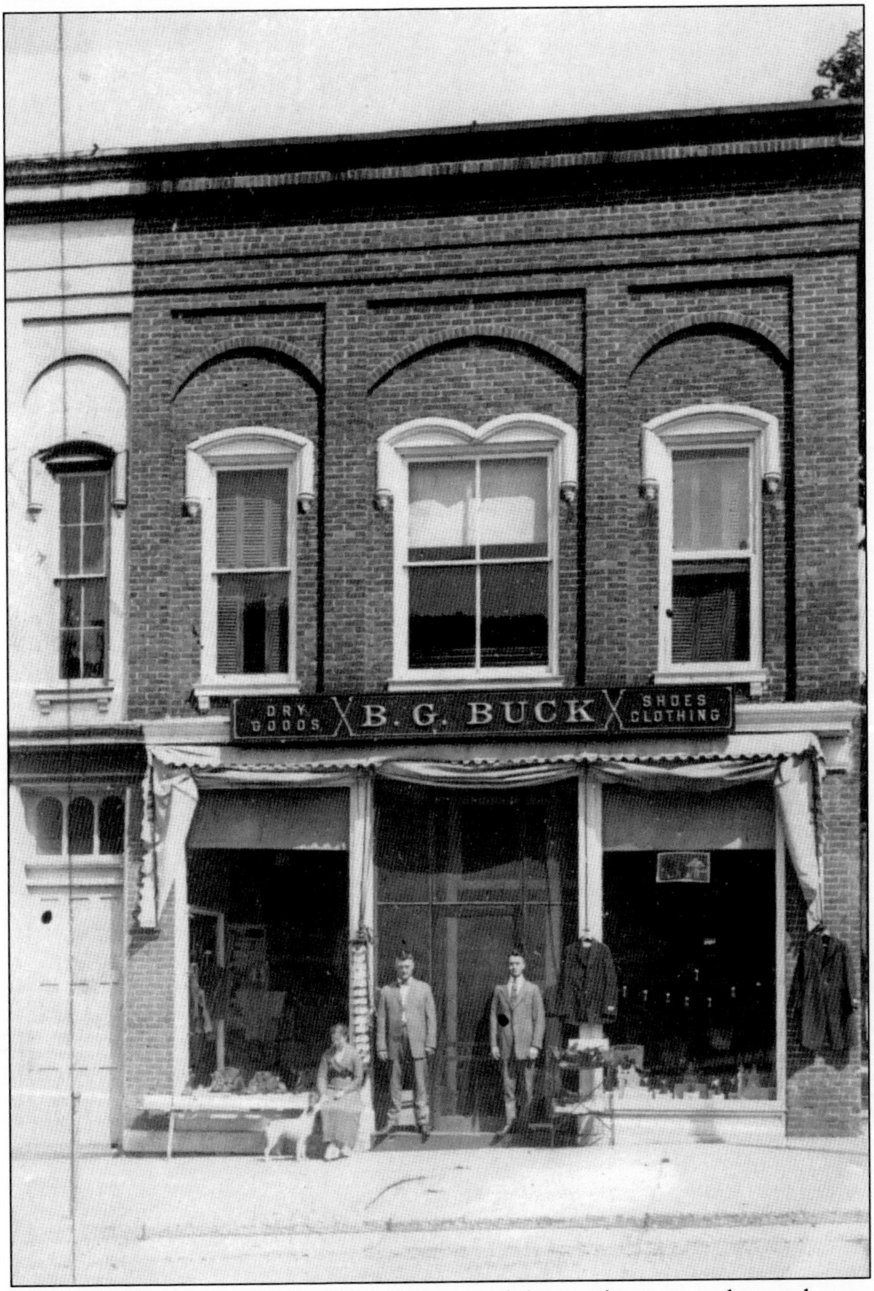

Bert S. Buck stands in front of his gents' clothing and dry goods store on the northwest corner of Main Street and North Jefferson Street. The lady seated on the left and the clerk standing on the right are unidentified. Buck started his career as a barber and had his own shop until about 1910 when he went into the clothing business. After a few years, he moved his business to the Ramsey Block. Here he continued business until a fire wiped out his stock. He left Mexico for a few years but returned in 1928 and did some barbering until his death in 1934. The store saw many businesses. The second floor was the first home of the *Mexico Independent* in 1861, and the first floor was a bank, a dry goods store, a hardware store, a jewelry store, and a restaurant. (Courtesy of the Barry Haynes collection.)

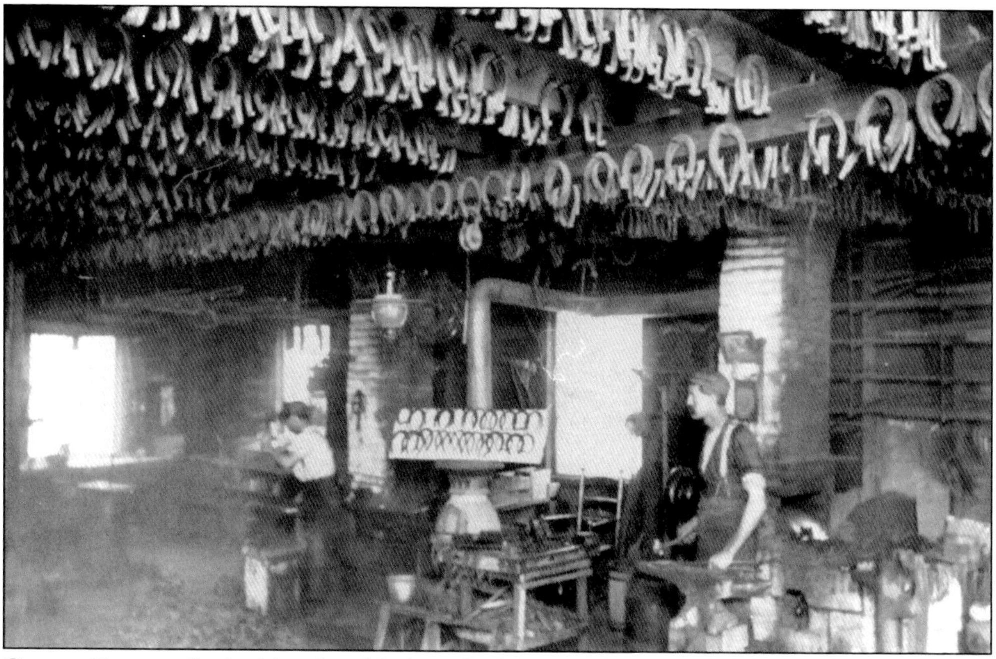

George Consene Sr. had his first blacksmith shop on Main Street just west of Ames Street around 1885. Charlie Sharp was his blacksmith apprentice. They continued working together when the shop was moved to Scenic Avenue. In 1923, Consene moved again to West Main Street into a shop across from his home.

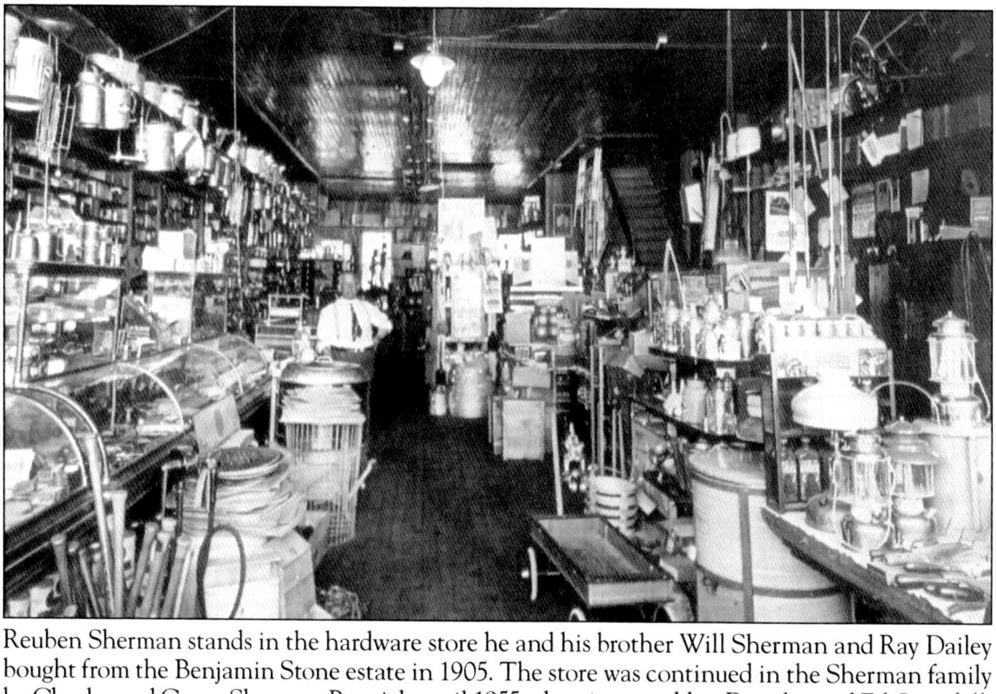

Reuben Sherman stands in the hardware store he and his brother Will Sherman and Ray Dailey bought from the Benjamin Stone estate in 1905. The store was continued in the Sherman family by Charles and Grace Sherman Partrick until 1955 when it was sold to Douglas and Ed Crandall. It was said that customers could buy anything there they might ever want if they could wait for them to find it.

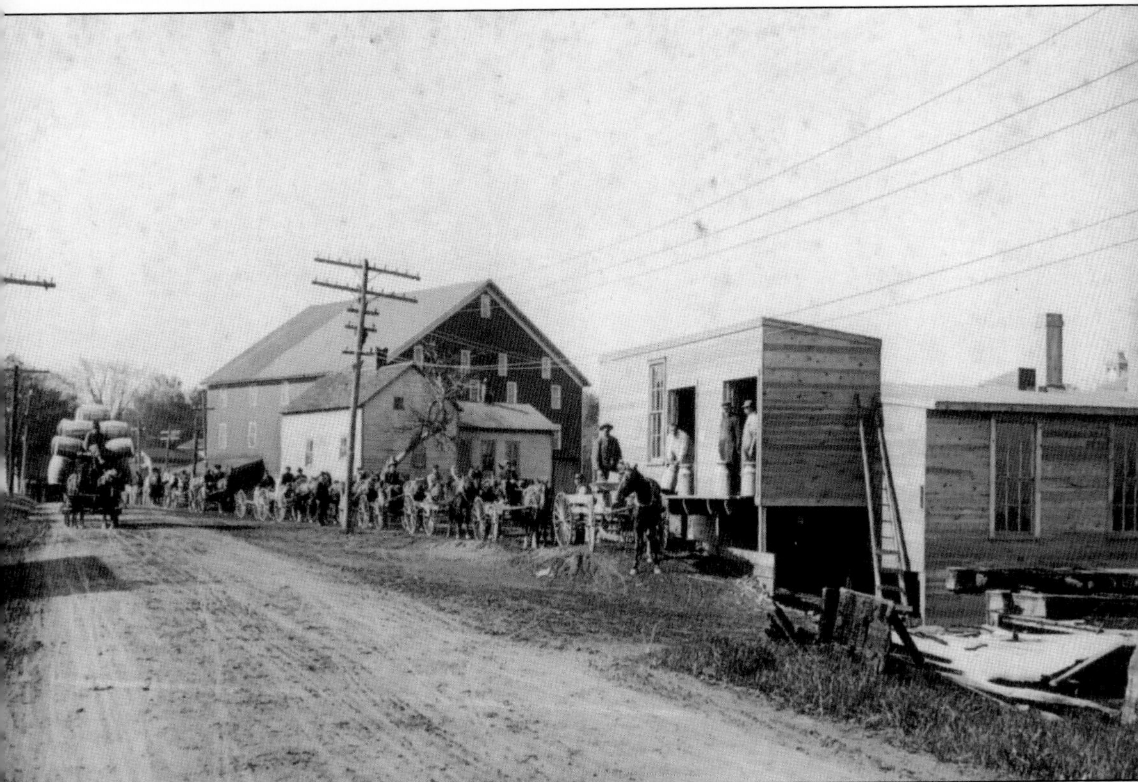

The farmers line up at Rosemary Creamery on North Street waiting their turn to have their cans of fresh milk emptied. The plant opened in 1903 and was welcomed by the farmers. Their crops were seasonal and were dependent on the weather for quantity and quality. The farmer could have more cows and a good steady income by selling his milk year-round. The plant successfully made powdered milk until it was destroyed by fire 10 years later. The large building in the center of the picture is Osborn's Mill, where the farmer could stop for feed if he needed it. The wagon on the left is loaded with barrels of flour from Osborn's Mill. It is headed for delivery in Fernwood and Pulaski.

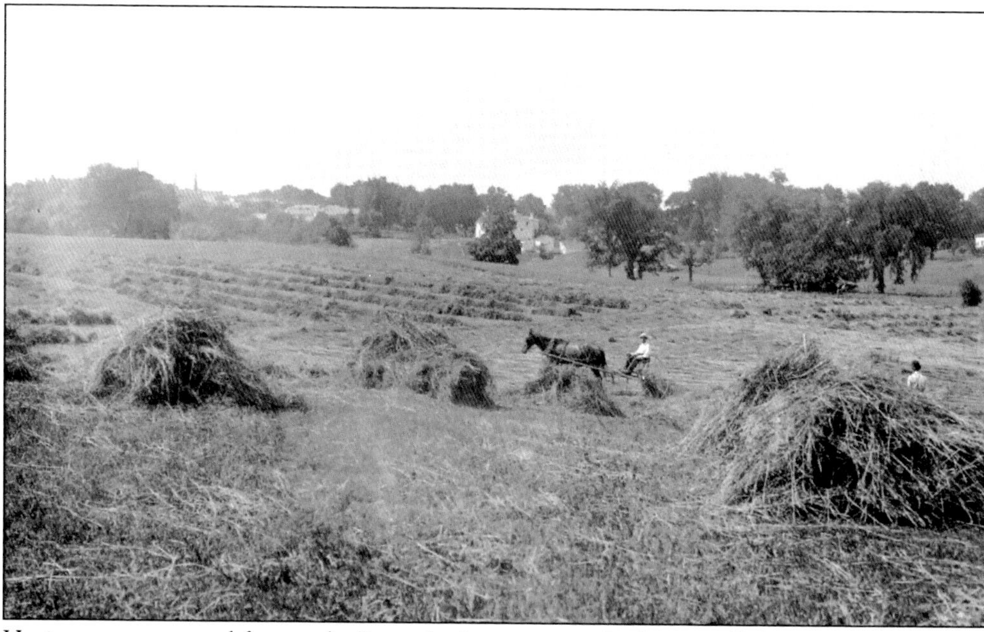

Haying was an annual farm task. Once the hay was cut, the horse pulled a rake to make rows. When the farmer was sure the hay was dry, it was collected on a horse-drawn loader and wagon and stored in a loft in the barn. Less than two acres would have been cut by hand using a scythe. (Courtesy of the Barry Haynes collection.)

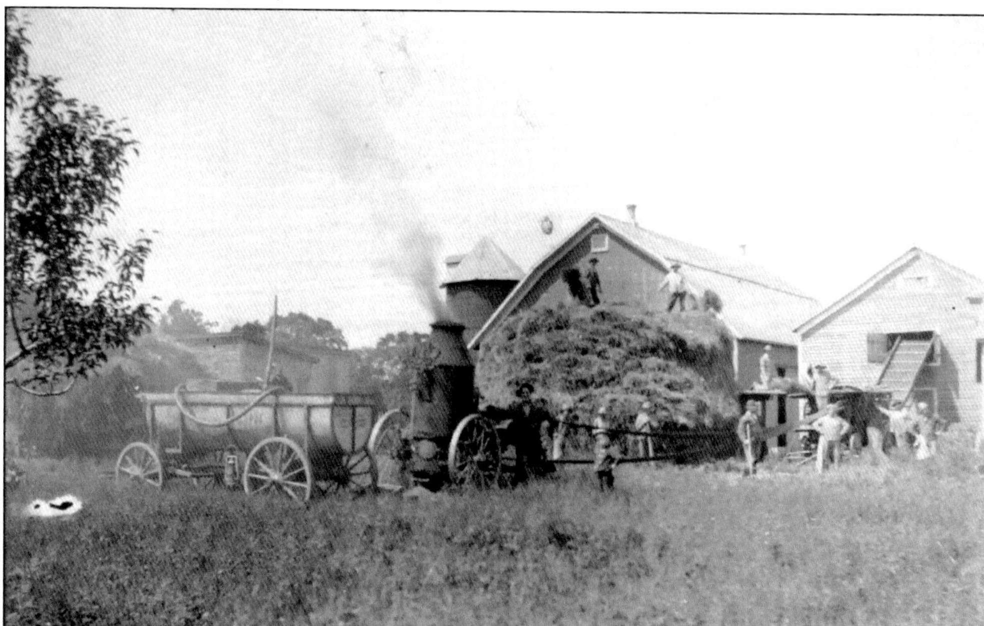

The farmers helped one another at threshing time. Here an early steam-powered threshing machine is at the Buck farm, and all the neighboring farmers have come to help get the grain in the granary. The straw was saved for bedding for the animals. When they were finished here, they moved the thresher to the next farm and began all over again with the neighbor's crop of wheat or oats. (Courtesy of the Barry Haynes collection.)

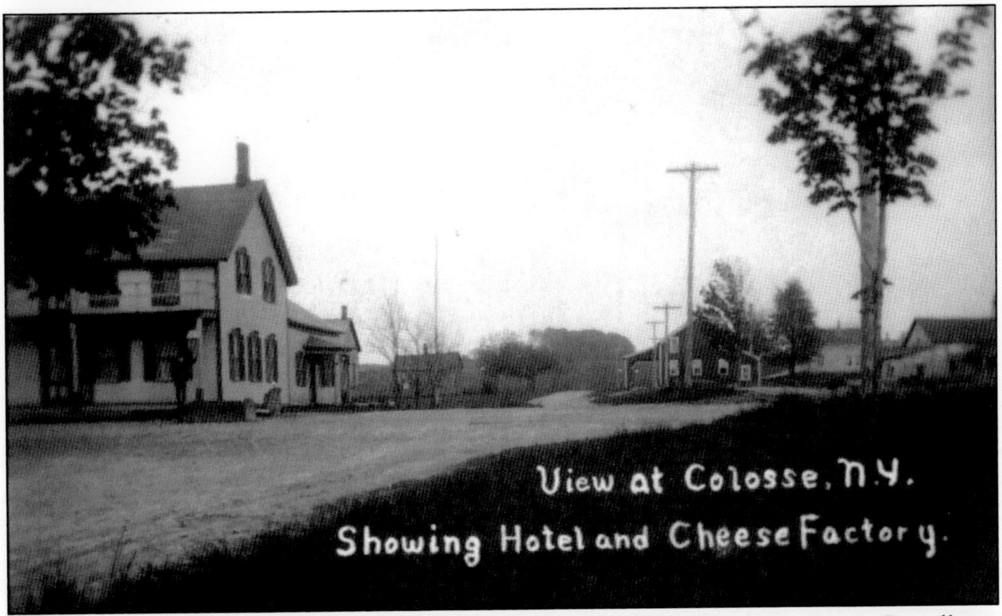

The hotel at Colosse, shown on the left, faced what is now State Route 11. Grover Bartell was the owner for the 30 years before his death in 1950. The family continued the business a few more years. It was demolished in 1982. The Colosse cheese factory is shown on the right. John R. O'Mara was the owner for many years, and his cheese often won awards for excellence.

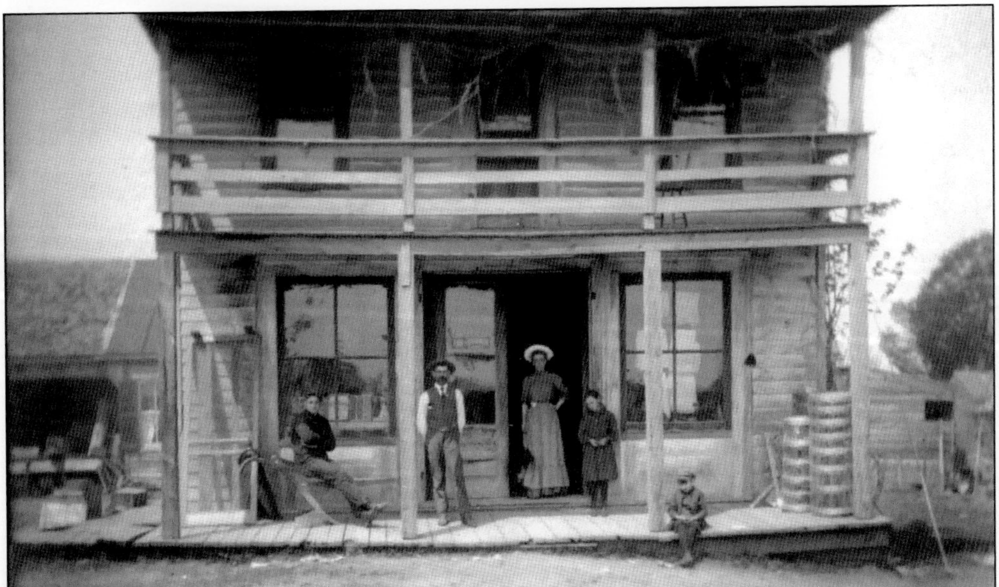

The settlement of Colosse at the intersection of State Routes 11 and 69 was an active community. It was the location of the first school, first church, and first cheese factory in the town of Mexico. In this 1906 photograph, Celeste Henry's general store on the southeast corner is shown. Later Arthur and Larine Goodno operated the store for 27 years. The business closed in the 1970s, and the building was razed in 1992.

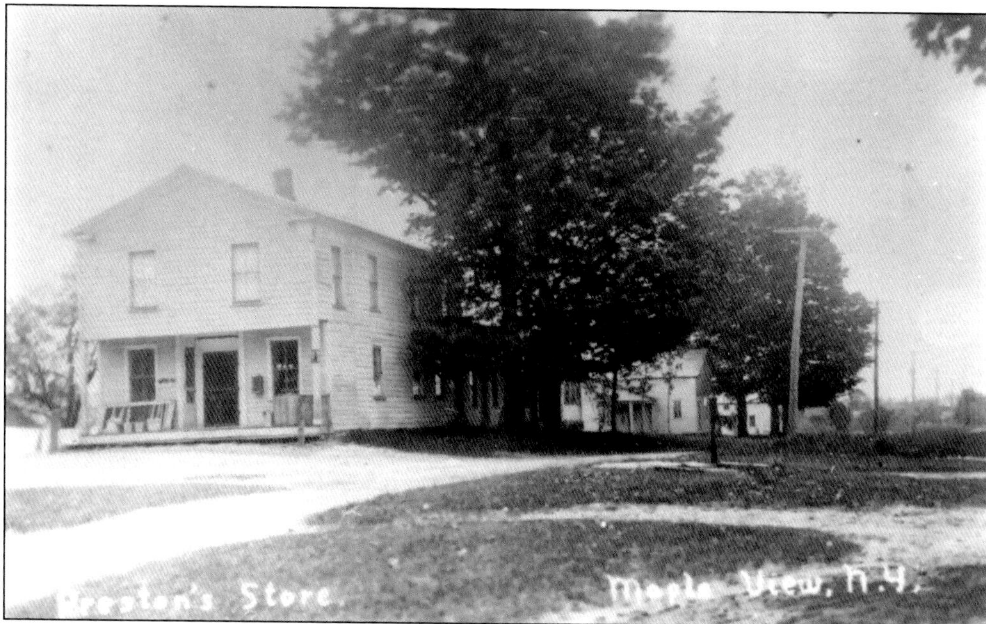

Walter E. Preston ran a small grocery store on the southeast corner of State Route 11 in Maple View in the early 1900s. He was followed by Frank Smedly and George Dimon, who ran feed stores. Later Manley Wilmer had a grocery store with gasoline pumps in front. Charles and Rose Cutuli bought the business in 1947. The business continued to grow and expand for two generations. It became Ostranders in 1992. (Author's collection.)

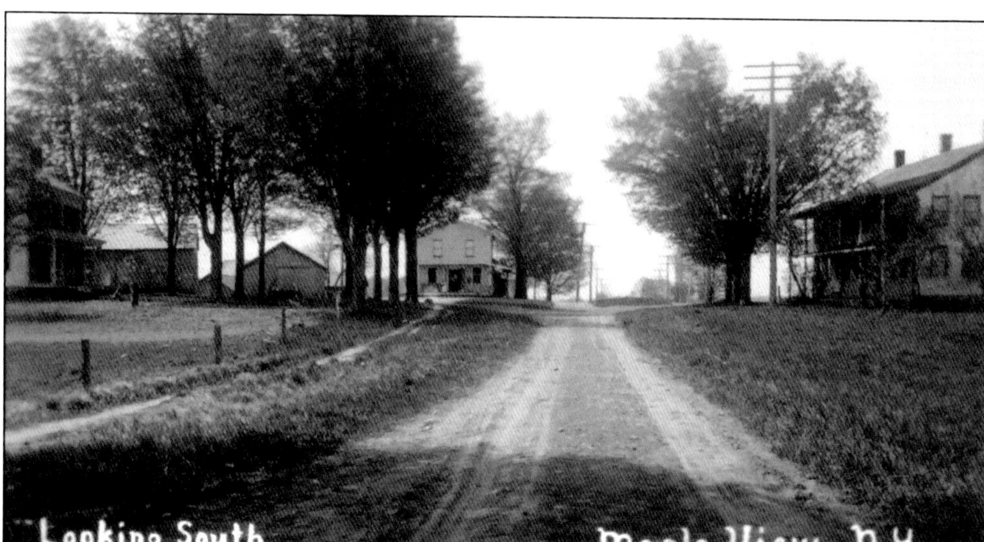

The only north–south road from Watertown to Salt City (Syracuse) passed through Union Square (Maple View). The Union Square Inn, right, was a very popular stopping point for travelers using this route. One night, 300 teams stayed over as they traveled to the city for a year's supply of salt. (Author's collection.)

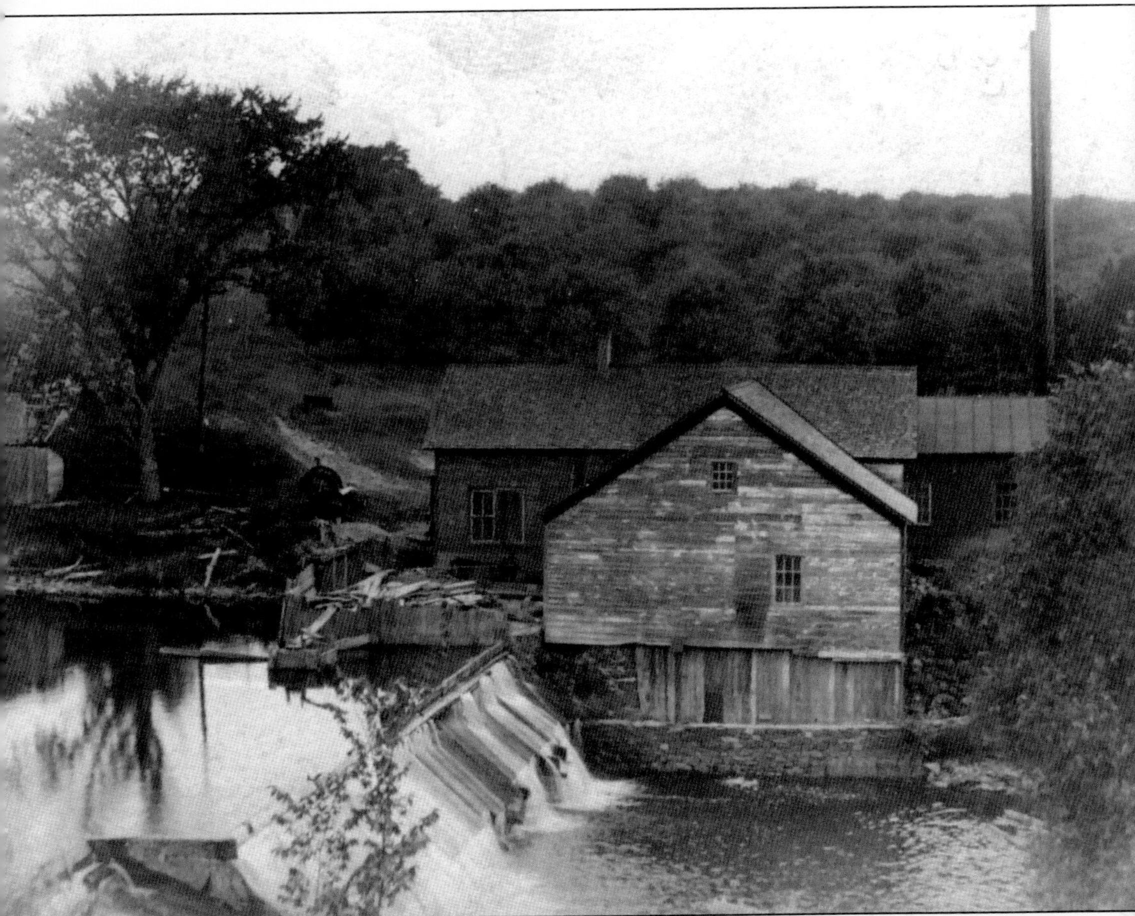

In 1890 the Schuyler Electric Company bought the Hendrickson mill dam in Little Salmon Creek south of the village. The purchase of the dam gave the company excellent waterpower to generate electricity. Two hundred incandescent lamps were wired, and new orders were coming in daily, including half a dozen residences. At first, the streetlight service was to be given until midnight on 20 nights in the month. All good people were supposed to be off the streets by midnight, and the moonlight shown on the streets on the other 10 nights. In 1891, Mexico Electric Light, Heat, and Power Company was able to furnish full service. The crab apple orchard behind the plant was one of several in the area. Before the use of the commercial product Certo, the pectin in crab apples was necessary to set jams and jellies. The crab apple, like all fruit, grew well in the Mexico area and was shipped as far away as Michigan. (Author's collection.)

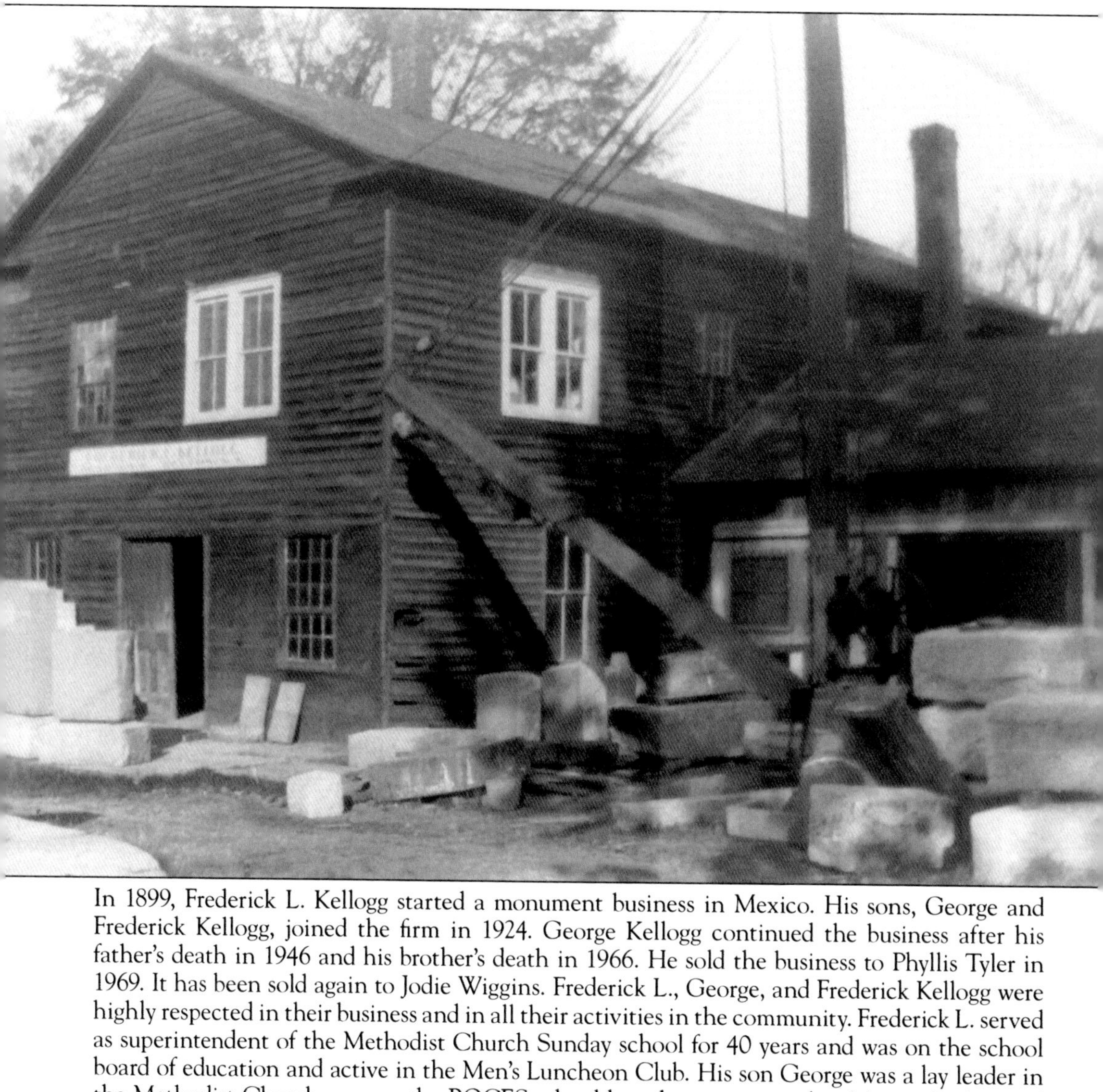

In 1899, Frederick L. Kellogg started a monument business in Mexico. His sons, George and Frederick Kellogg, joined the firm in 1924. George Kellogg continued the business after his father's death in 1946 and his brother's death in 1966. He sold the business to Phyllis Tyler in 1969. It has been sold again to Jodie Wiggins. Frederick L., George, and Frederick Kellogg were highly respected in their business and in all their activities in the community. Frederick L. served as superintendent of the Methodist Church Sunday school for 40 years and was on the school board of education and active in the Men's Luncheon Club. His son George was a lay leader in the Methodist Church, was on the BOCES school board, a mason, and in Mexico Lodge, and served as supervisor of the Town of Mexico. His son Frederick was a veteran of World War II, a member of the American Legion, and a 29-year member of the fire department.

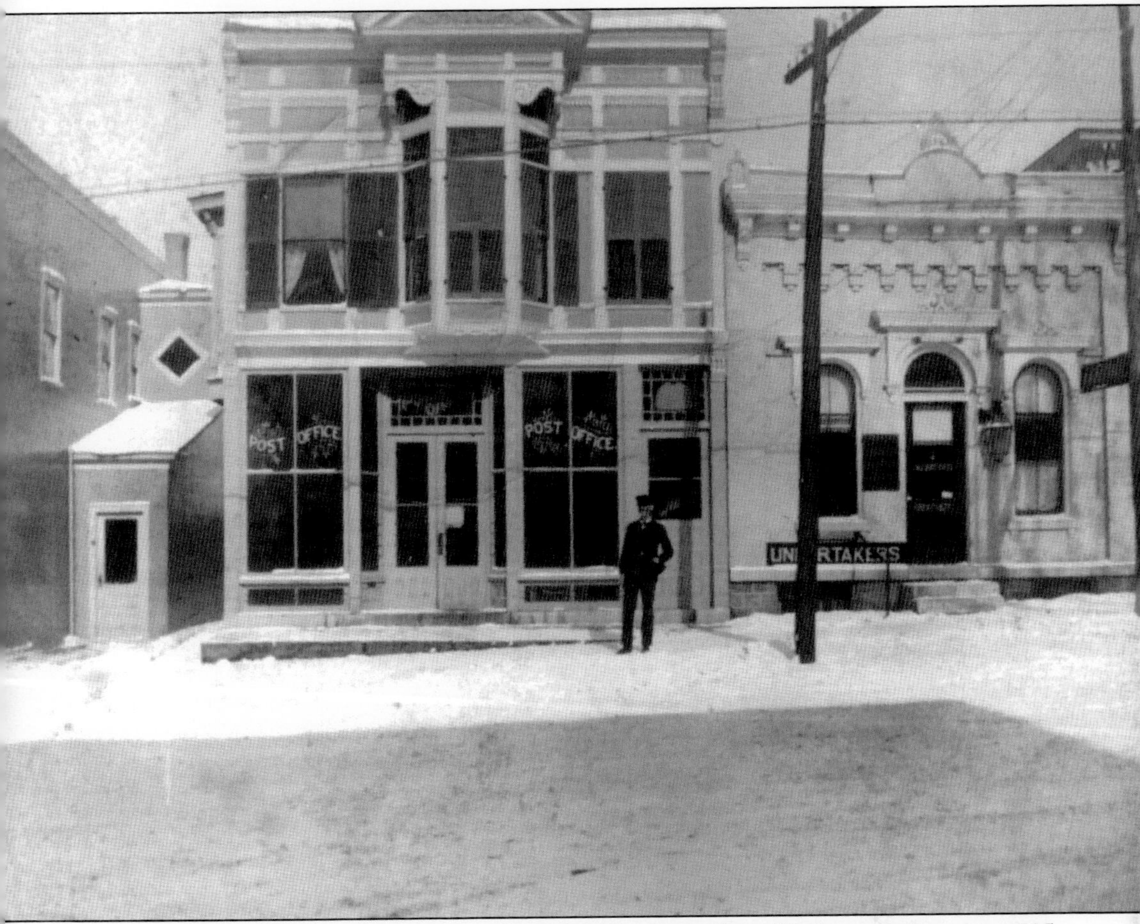

The Mexico Post Office found a home on Main Street across from Washington Street in 1895 in this building owned by postmaster Jerome Baker. The postmaster was a political appointment that depended on the party of the current president, so as new presidents were elected, the postmaster changed and so did the post office. In 1813, Calvin Tiffany was postmaster with mail delivered once a week to his tavern east of the village. In 1815, the post office was moved into the village. From 1830 to 1895, there were 15 postmasters and different post offices, including Starr Clark's tin shop and Rawson Butler's store. After 1895, the postmaster changed less often, and the post office stayed in the same building, rented first from Jerome Baker and later from Glen Smith. The post office thus remained in the building until 1983 when the federal government erected a post office on the corner of Main Street and Norman Avenue. (Author's collection.)

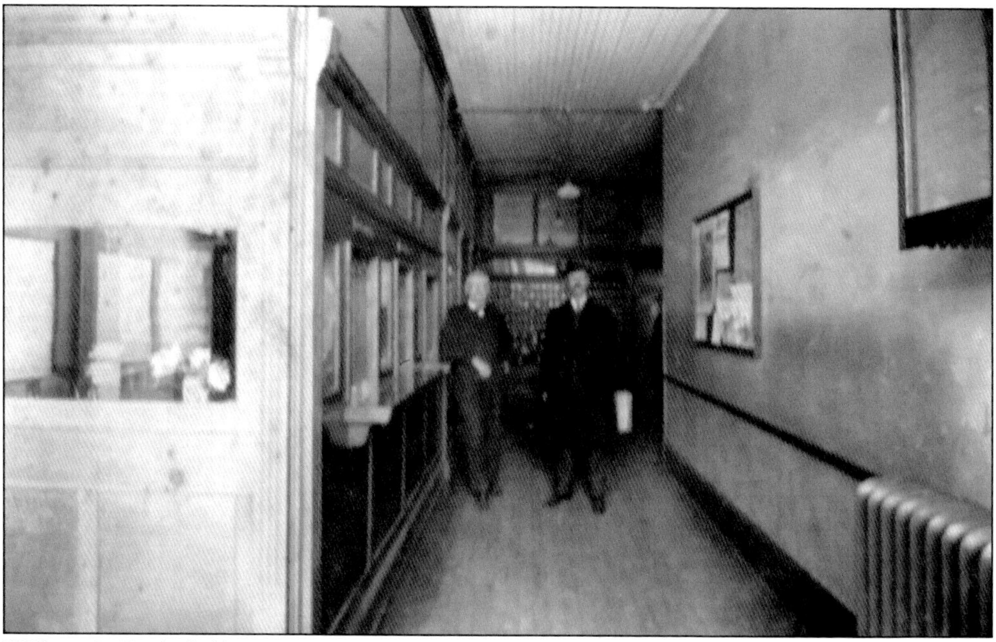

William L. Buck (left), postmaster, and Henry D. Nicholas pause in the lobby of the post office in 1924. The Mexico Post Office does not meet population requirements for home delivery. However, if a rural mail route goes past a home in the village, that person may take advantage of rural free delivery. The boxes seen behind the men were for those who got their mail at the post office. (Courtesy of the Barry Haynes collection.)

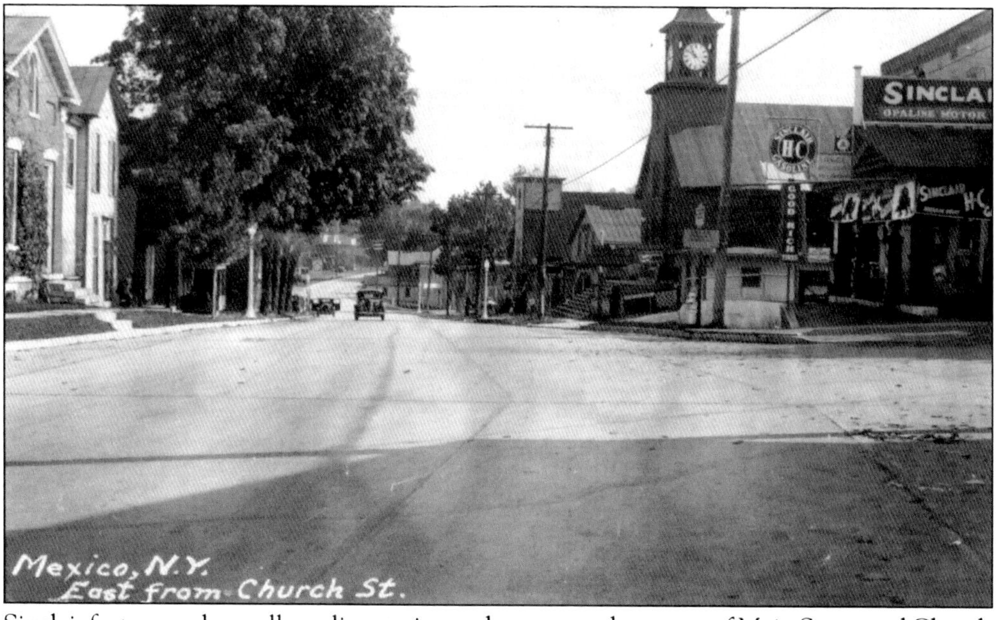

Sinclair first opened a small gasoline station and garage on the corner of Main Street and Church Street. The roof of Mexico House can be seen over the Sinclair sign. Mexico House burned in 1937, and Sinclair moved back from the road and built a new, bigger gasoline station with three pumps. It had two bays where workers could change oil and make other repairs to the popular automobile. (Author's collection.)

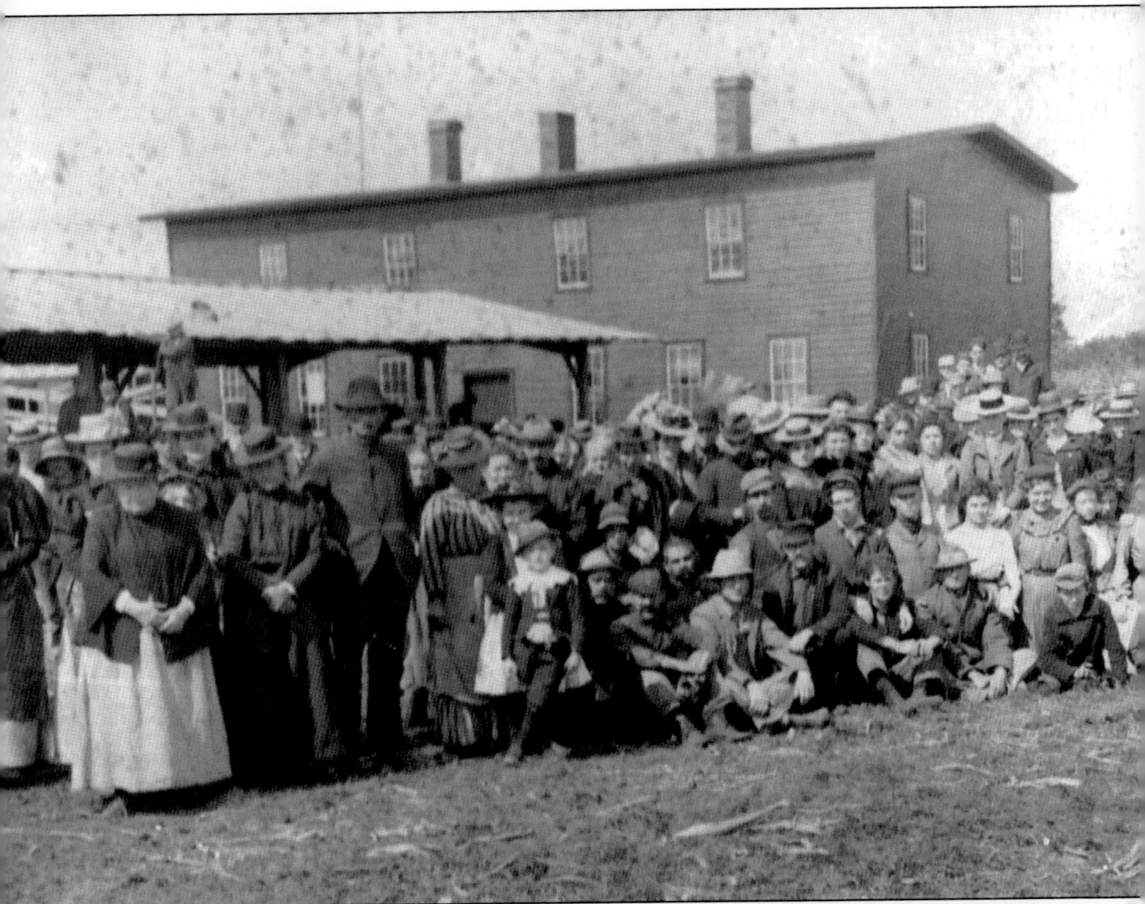

The workers at Wilson's Canning Factory pose for a picture around 1903. George H. Wilson built the factory next to the railroad in 1885, and during the canning season, thousands of cans of corn and string beans were shipped to markets in the cities all over New York. Apples and pumpkins were also shipped in season. This business was a great benefit to the village and the town, furnishing employment to both men and women and paying the farmers for their produce. The women and children did the tedious jobs, such as husking corn. Wilson moved to Mexico in 1892 from Taberg, where he had also had a canning business. He was active in the Methodist Church and served the community as mayor. He died in 1920, and the business was continued by Jerome Baker until his death in 1930 when it closed.

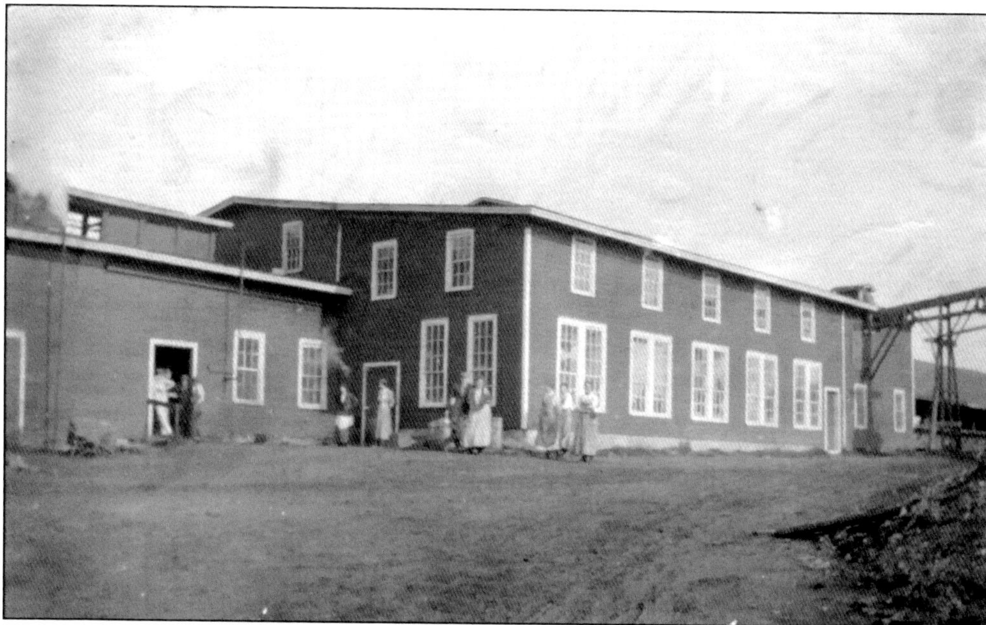

This unusual photograph shows Wilson's Canning Factory up close, as a few of the workers pause during a long day of work. The factory was built on the railroad line from which canned corn, beans, and pumpkins could conveniently be shipped to market. The work was seasonal, and an average of two million cans per season were shipped when there was a good harvest. (Courtesy of the Barry Haynes collection.)

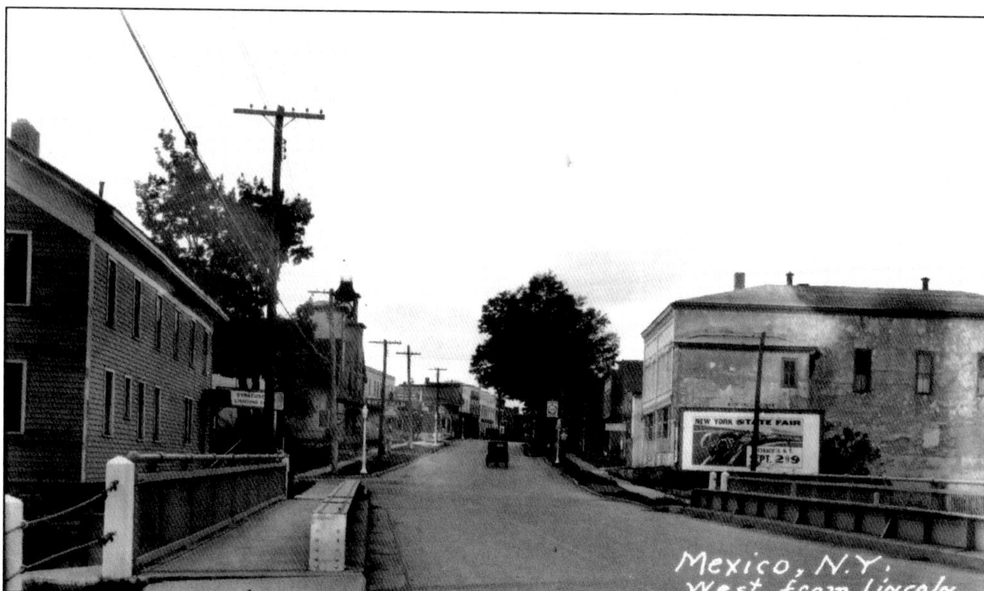

The Penfield Wagon Shop is shown on the left in this photograph. In 1891, it was purchased by Edwin L. Huntington, head of Mexico Electric Light, Heat, and Power Company, for company headquarters. The building was destroyed in 1927 to make room for an electric substation. The building on the right was long known as Fraternity Hall. The Odd Fellows held their meetings on the first floor, and Masonic organizations used the second floor. The building burned in 1980. (Author's collection.)

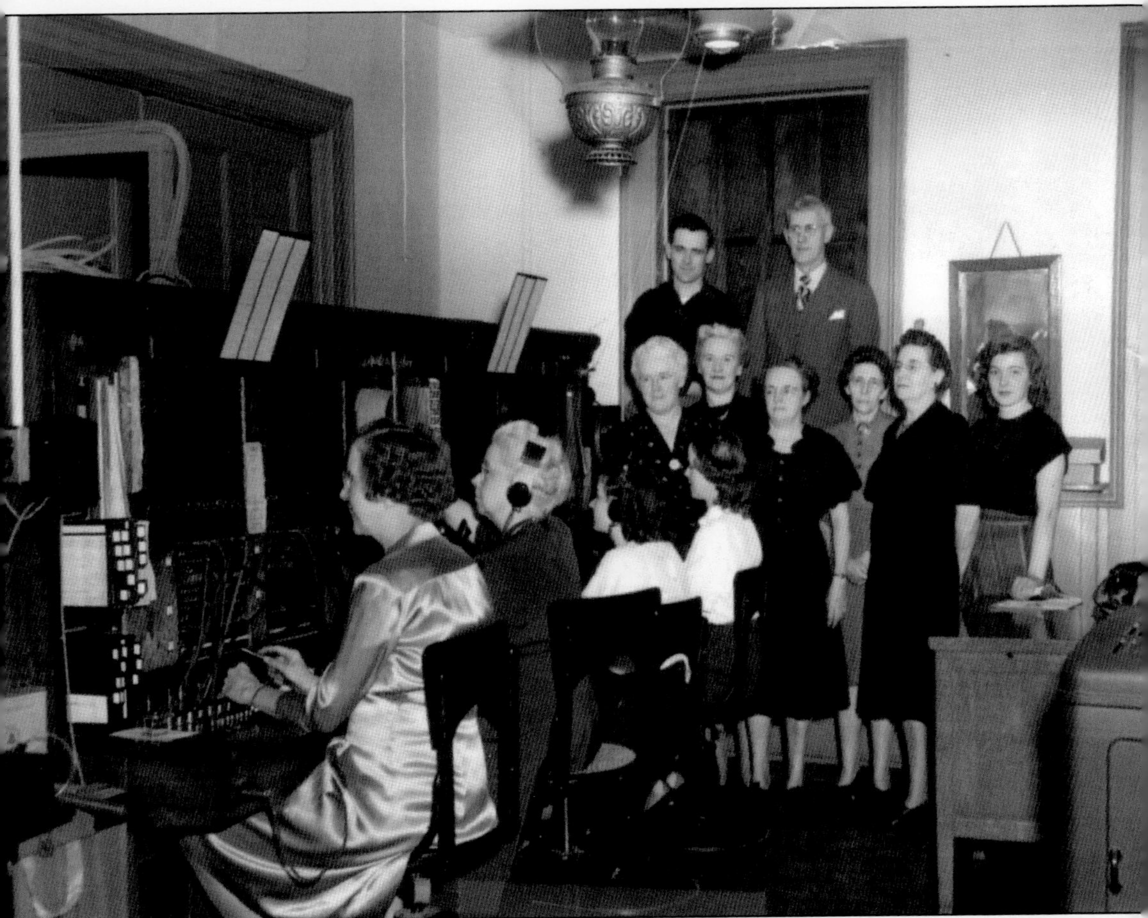

In 1881, there were a few telephones between homes and places of business. In 1884, one could telephone to the lake and to Pulaski from one of the four telephones in the village. In 1887, a line was installed to Parish, Central Square, Brewerton, and eventually Syracuse. In 1904, the Ontario Telephone Company had 51 subscribers and the great convenience of all-night service. The New York Telephone Company was established in Mexico in 1906 and bought out the two other telephone companies that were here. The switchboard was located over the store on the southwest corner of Main and Jefferson Streets. Around 1912, the company had grown, and a four-position switchboard was installed, as shown in this 1940 picture. This board was used until 1949 when the dial system was installed. Pictured are, from left to right, (seated) operators Kathleen Brown, Maybelle Kenyon, Fern Cone, and Anne Ballard; (standing) Louisa Willis, Anne Benz, Irene Buck, Mary Boyd, Rebecca Trowbridge, and Pat Parker. Behind them are repairmen Kenneth Willis (left) and Charles Graves. (Courtesy of the Barry Haynes collection.)

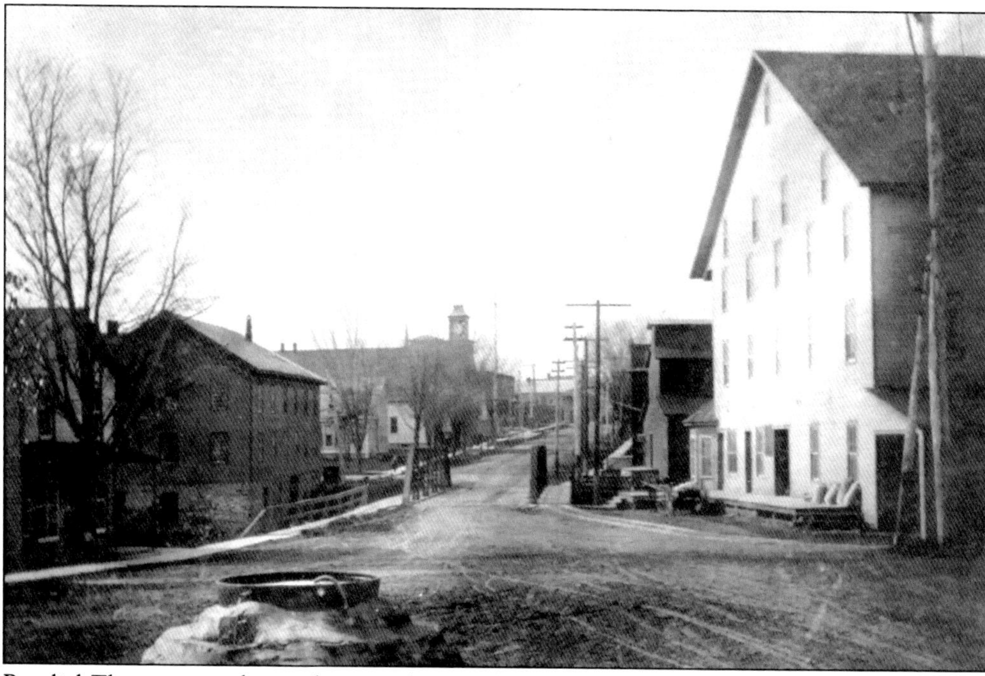

Bezaliel Thayer erected a carding machine and clothing factory on the east side of the Little Salmon River in 1825. Almeron Thomas converted the property into a gristmill prior to 1861. He named it Toronto Mill, which resulted in the part of the village east of the river being called Canada. He also purchased the mill on the west side of the water and named it State Mill. Toronto Mill did custom grinding and cold barrels of flour, graham flours, buckwheat flower, oats, corn, and meal. The business passed to his sons Amos C. and Frederick Thomas, and it was run by the Thomas family for 40 years. William H. Osborn bought the mill in 1898, and F. G. Ludington bought it in 1910. Earl C. Dexter bought the mill in 1919 and sold his own blend of feed. When lightning struck Dexter's mill in 1942, it burned to the ground. The Thayer corner was vacant after 177 years.

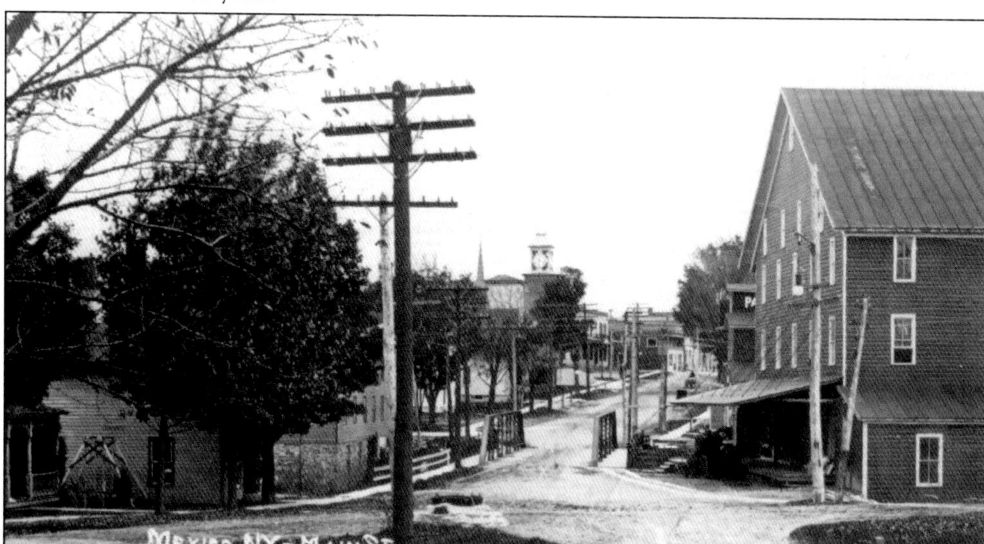

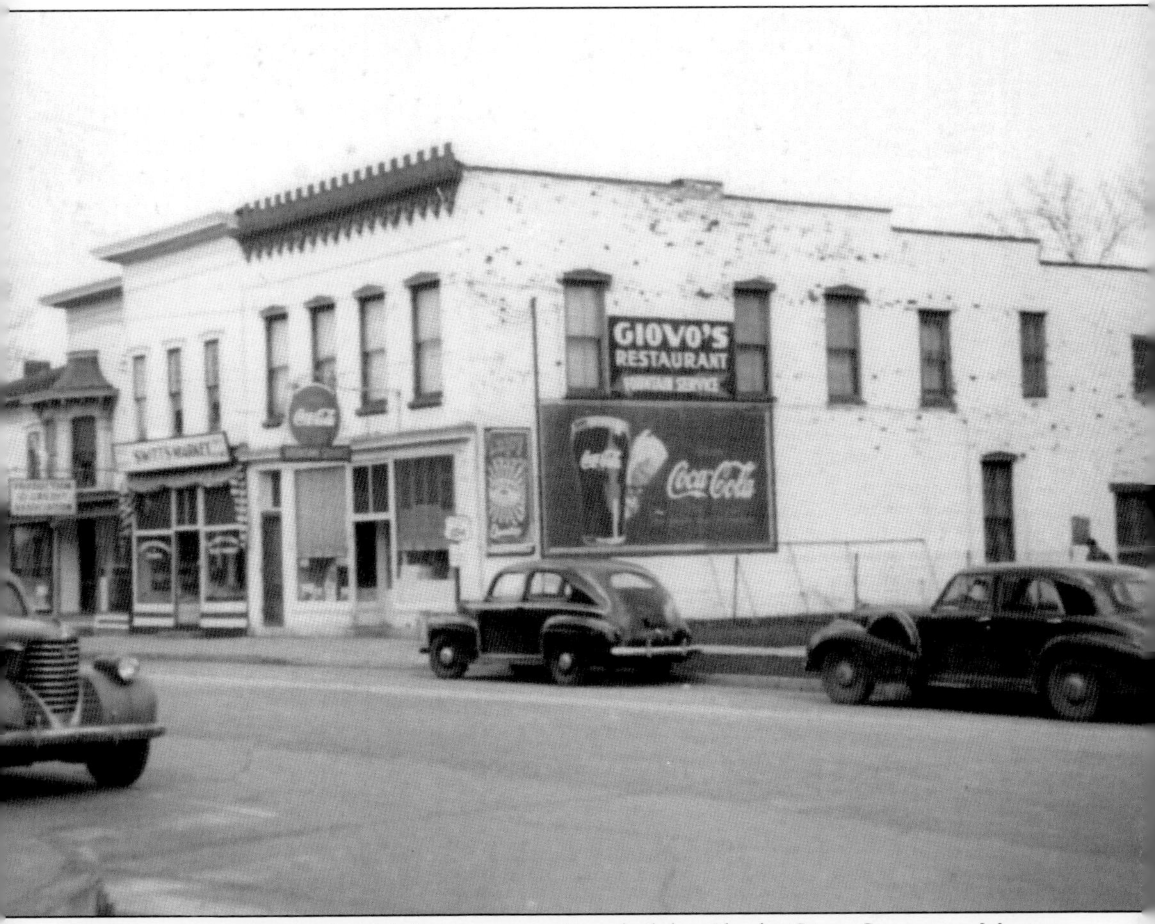

Giovo's was a business and a club for young people and adults. Charles Giovo Sr. came to Mexico in 1909 and located in this store, selling fruit, homemade candy, and homemade ice cream. The business grew and lunches were served. When he died, the other stores in the village closed from 9:00 to 10:00 a.m. out of respect for their fellow businessman. His son Charles Giovo Jr. took over the business. Charles Giovo Jr. loved his family, his work, the community, and most of all the young people. Giovo's was a place where friends gathered or where a young man took his girl for a cherry phosphate. His calm, friendly, caring manner was respected by the kids, and if he saw someone headed for trouble, he gave them advice and they would listen. Giovo's stayed open many nights as one of the kids waited for a ride home after a school activity. Adults stopped in too for a Coke, coffee, or ice cream and good conversation. Mexico has always been a nice place to live because of people like the Giovos.

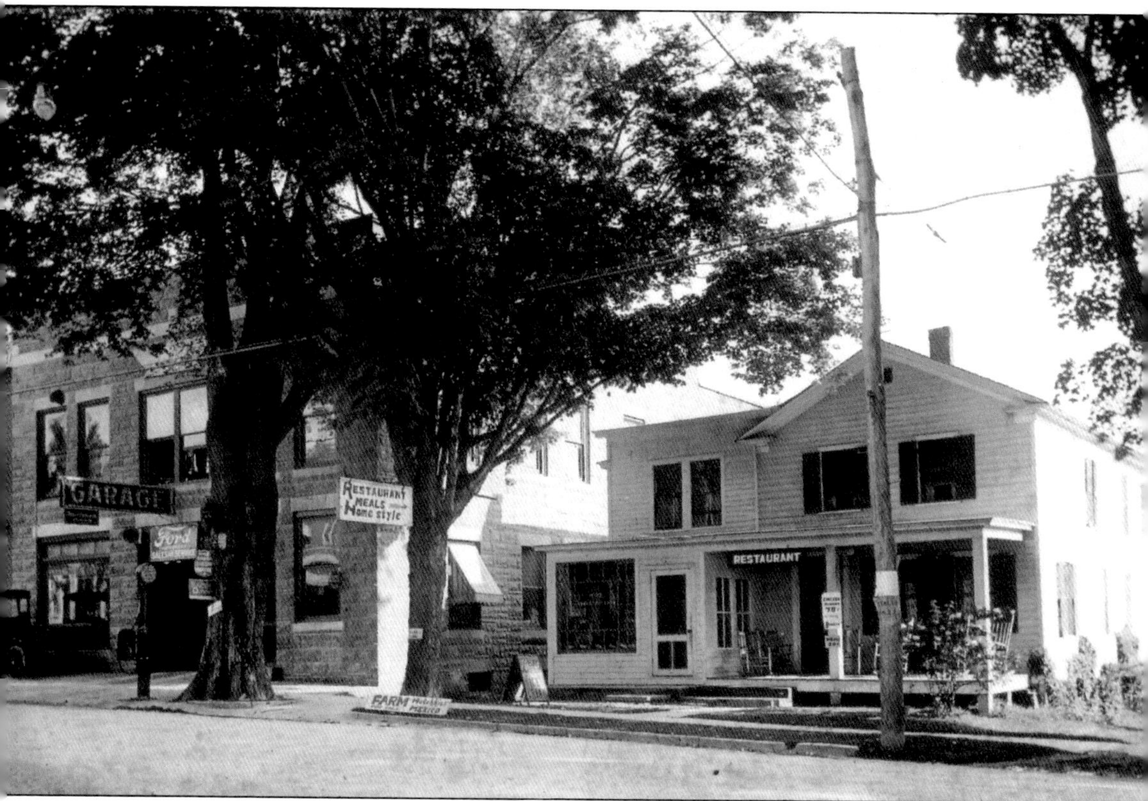

Frank and Hattie Hotchkiss owned the Hotchkiss Restaurant and Tourist Home in Mexico across from Beck's Hotel in 1920. When Frank died in 1926, the business was passed to his son and daughter-in-law, Glenn and Elva Hotchkiss. Glenn Hotchkiss was an automobile mechanic so Elva ran the business. A sign in front read, "Hotchkiss Restaurant, Mother Does the Cooking." The Sunday chicken dinners were most popular with the locals. In 1931, the Hotchkisses advertised a complete Thanksgiving dinner from soup to nuts for $1. The tourist home attracted travelers and salesmen who needed a good meal and a bed. In the early 1940s, the restaurant closed and the business eventually became a home to those who needed room and board for extended periods, like teachers or the engineers supervising the paving of State Route 104. Elva Hotchkiss married Harold Fish in 1957. She continued to live in her home until her death in 1959 and the business closed.

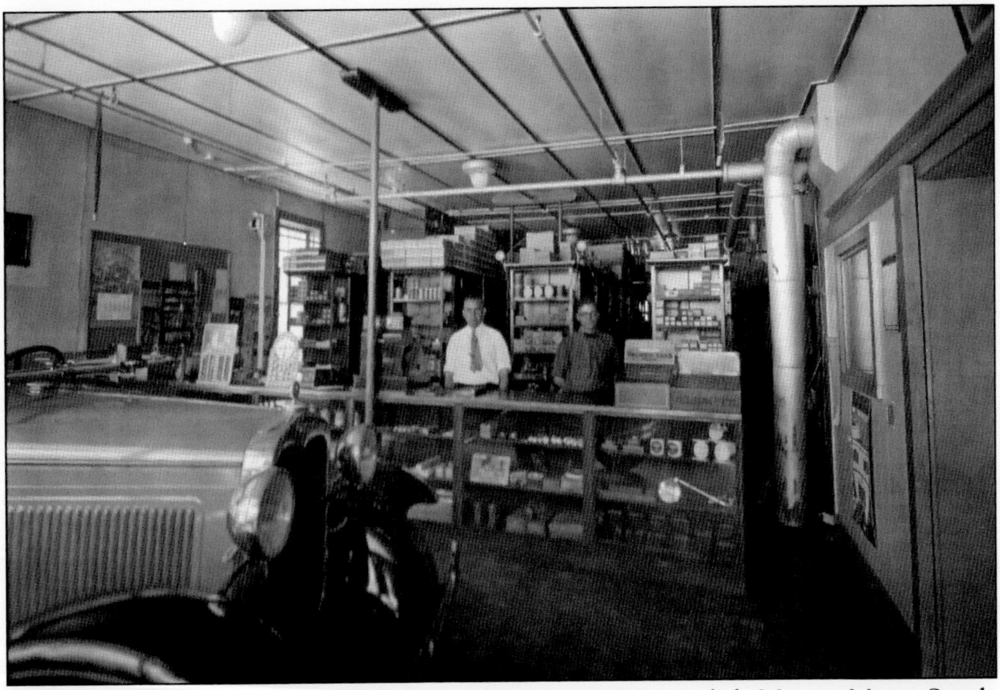

As the automobile became common, new businesses were needed. Mexico Motor Supply Company and Garage opened in 1911. Dean Buck and Willard Fetcha stand in the supply area of the business in this photograph from about 1930. The variety of supplies was very limited, so only a small portion of the building was needed for this department. The building also served as a repair garage and a sales room.

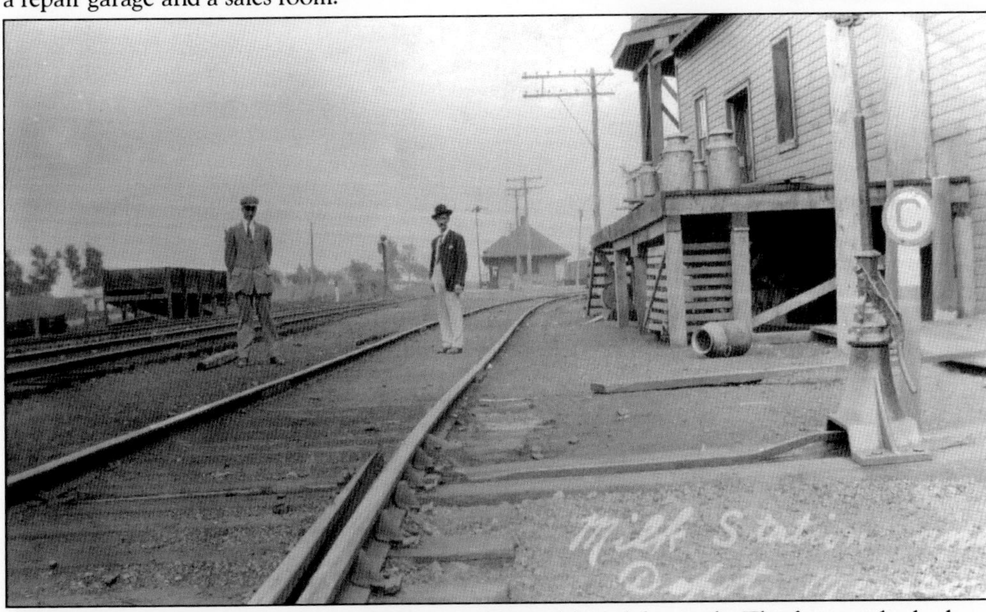

The coming of train service through Mexico changed farm life greatly. The farmer who had one or two cows to supply his family could now own several cows. He added to his income by selling the extra milk. The milk was taken to the milk station in large cans and shipped to the city dairies to be put in bottles for delivery. (Courtesy of the Barry Haynes collection.)

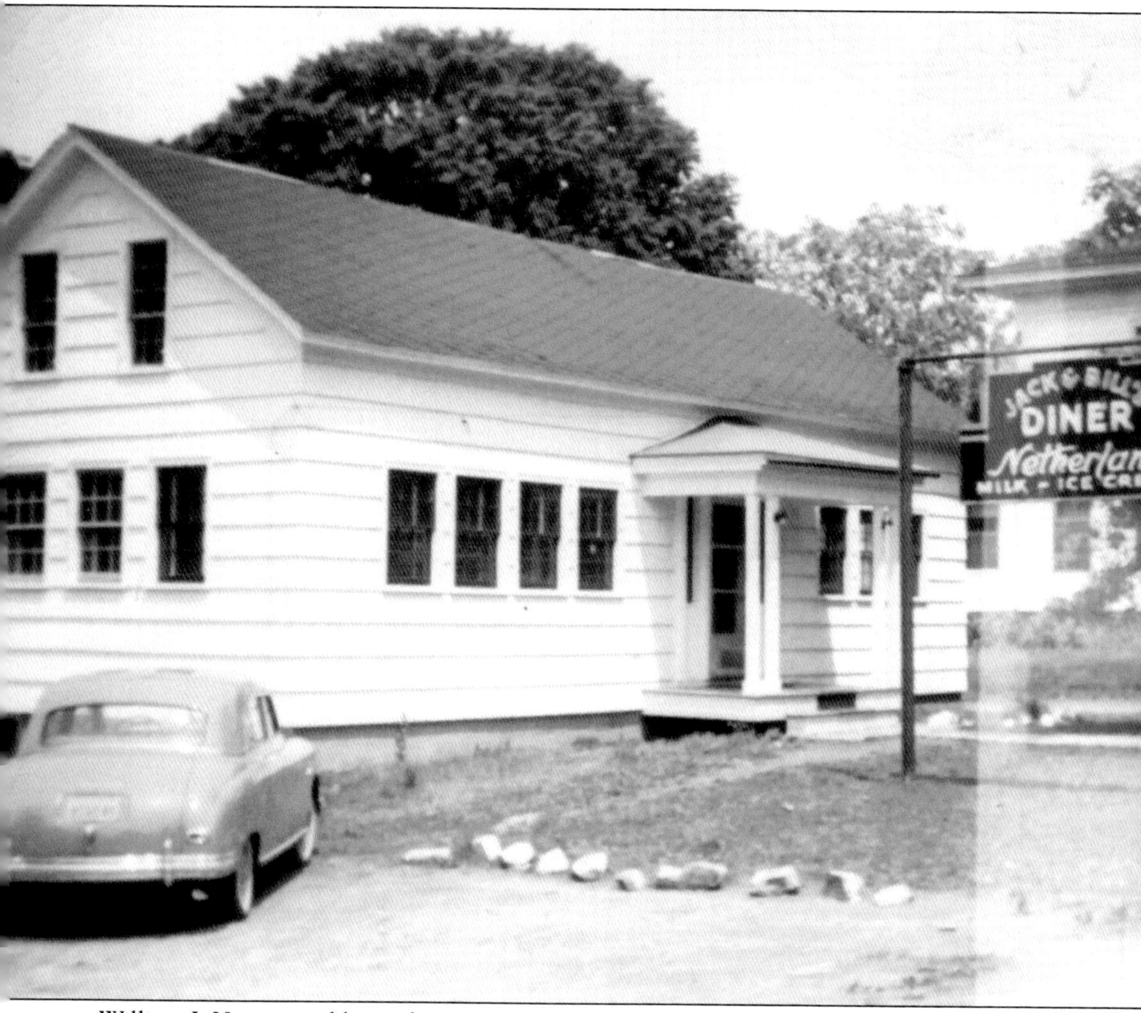

William J. Haynes and his wife Anna Haynes welcomed their two sons, William C. (Bill) and John (Jack) Haynes, into the business when they came home from the service after World War II. The name of the new diner was changed to Jack and Bill's and was soon a popular place; the men stopped for a coffee break in the morning, the young people stopped after school for soda and french fries, and teachers and other staff members stopped for a piece of homemade pie on their way home. The diner had tables under the windows on the west side and booths across the front. Adelma Greenstone purchased the property in 1968 and added a large dining room and a cocktail lounge. Other owners continued the restaurant business until it was destroyed by fire in 1995. This building was on Main Street where Kinney's Drugs is located in 2009. (Courtesy of the Barry Haynes collection.)

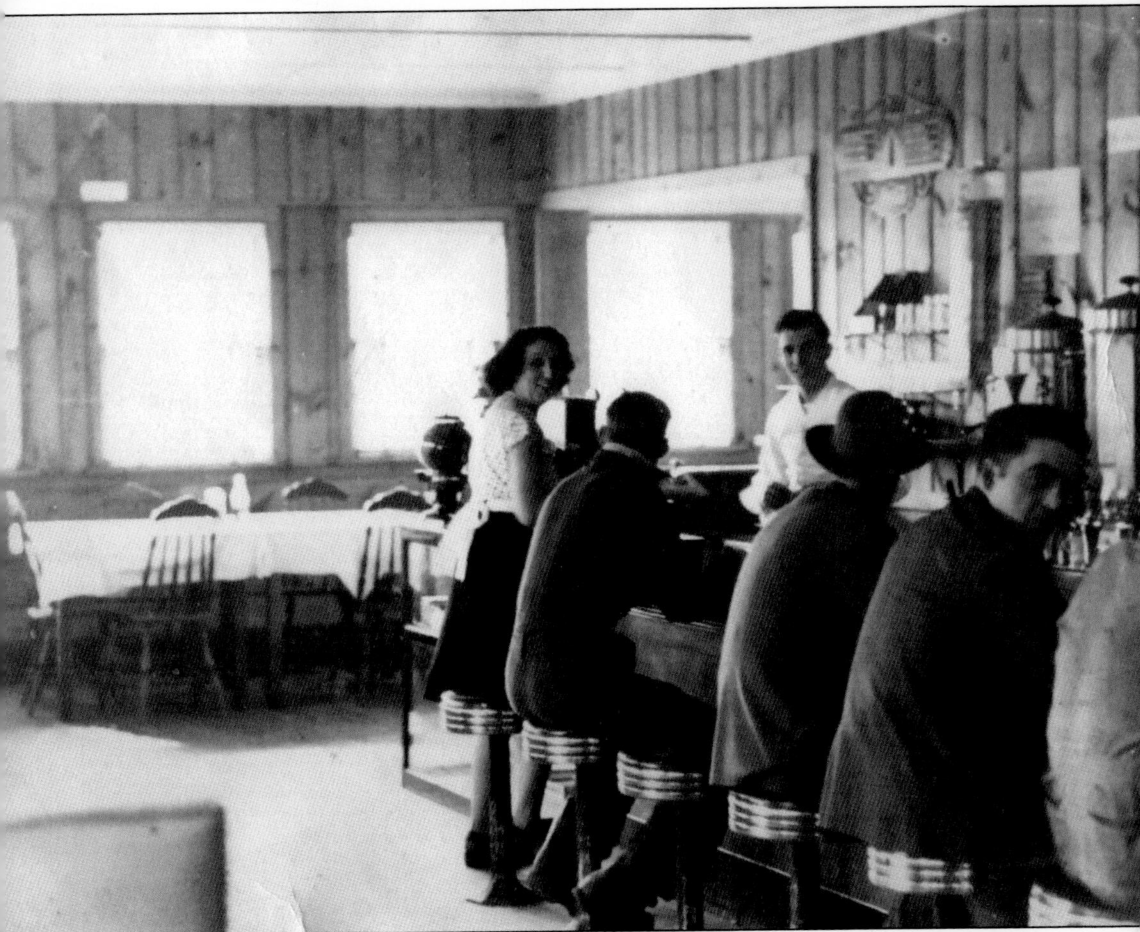

This diner was Jack and Bill's from 1946 to 1967. Standing at the end of the counter is waitress Anna Haynes, mother of Jack and Bill Haynes. Jack Haynes is shown standing behind the counter in this 1946 photograph. Jack Haynes was a volunteer fireman, and this caused confusion at the diner whenever the fire alarm went off. He would immediately leave to run to the fire station a block away, leaving whatever was cooking for other workers to figure out how long food had been frying and who it went to when it was done. Luckily this did not happen too often. The restaurant served meals as well as fast foods, so the family or friends went in for a good supper and topped it off with homemade desserts. Society became more mobile and far-reaching through the years, and the Haynes family decided to sell the business after 20 years of serving Mexico.

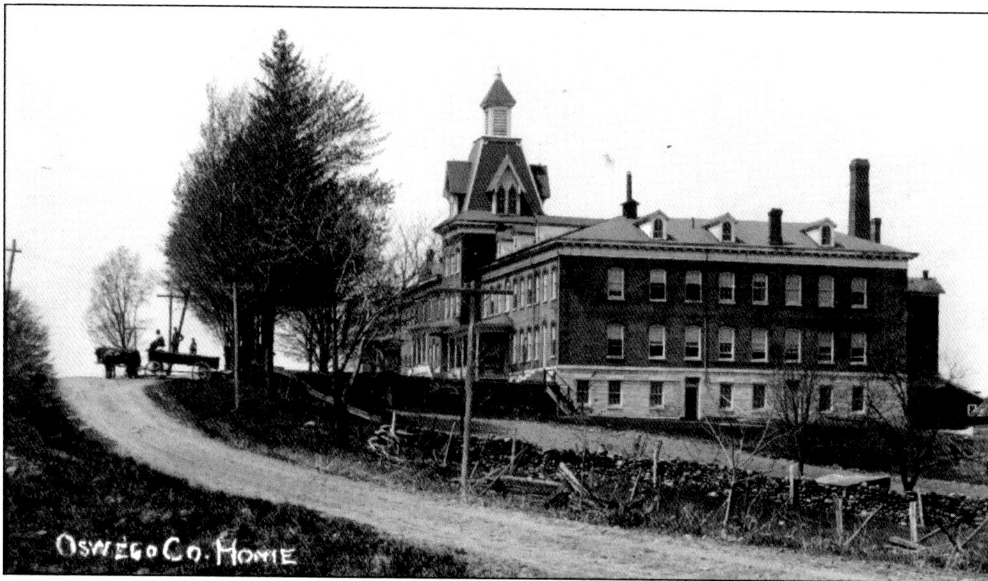

The first Oswego County home for the needy was established in the town of Mexico in 1828 in a small farmhouse on County Route 64. Later a two-story addition was made. In 1860, a brick building was constructed for the care of the insane. A new building to care for all those in need was constructed in 1870. The building included a small hospital section, a men's section, a women's section, rooms for the superintendent and his family, and the dining room and kitchen. The insane were placed in state hospitals in 1890. The smaller building was connected to the large one. In May 1972, the building was deeded to the Oswego County BOCES by the county board of supervisors. The aged had been moved to rest homes throughout the county, and the welfare department was moved to the former Taylor home on Main Street. In June 1972, a wrecker's bucket tore into the aged mortar and limestone walls, and the old bricks turned to dust. Another landmark vanished from the roads of Mexico. (Above, author's collection; below, courtesy of the Barry Haynes collection.)

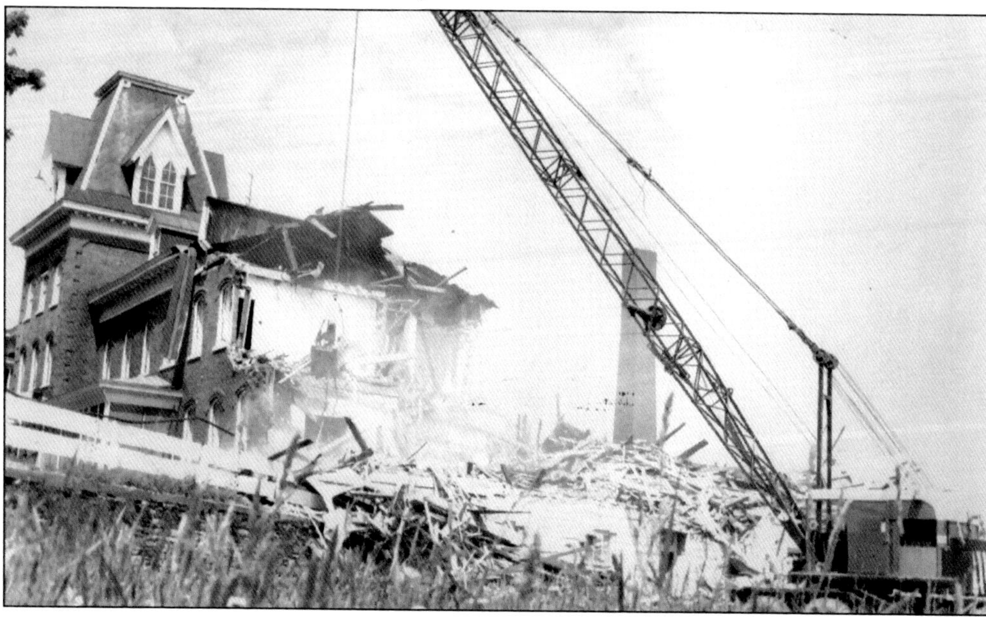

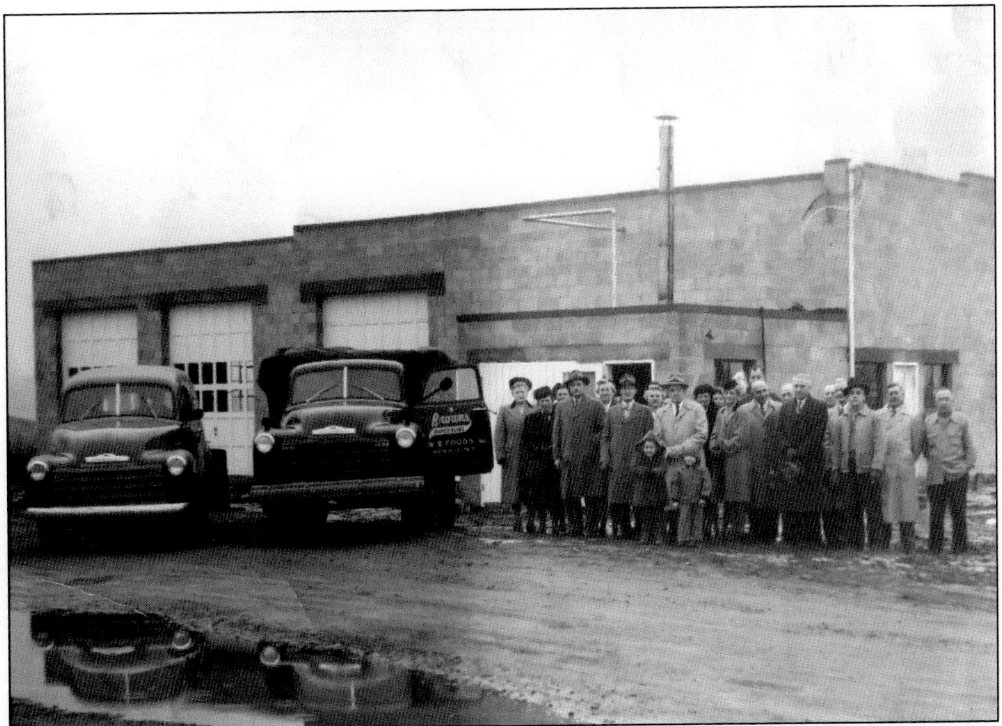

Friends gathered in 1947 when the first section of Brown-Whitney-Brown Foods on Scenic Avenue was completed. Lulu Brown is in the middle of the first row. Robert Brown is at the end of the first row in a jacket and hat. The two little girls are Sandra and Marcia Brown, daughters of Robert and Loretta Brown. Sandra is now president of Grandma Brown's Beans, still made in this plant in Mexico. (Author's collection.)

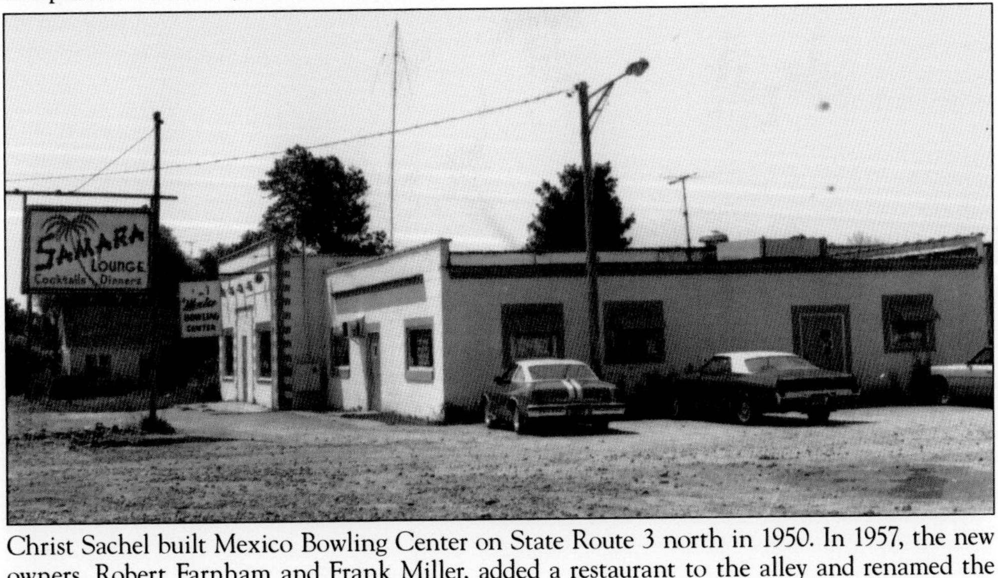

Christ Sachel built Mexico Bowling Center on State Route 3 north in 1950. In 1957, the new owners, Robert Farnham and Frank Miller, added a restaurant to the alley and renamed the business Samara Lounge. The alleys were busy every night with men's, women's, couples', and other groups forming leagues. Weekends were for open bowling, and many families have happy memories of hours spent at the bowling alley.

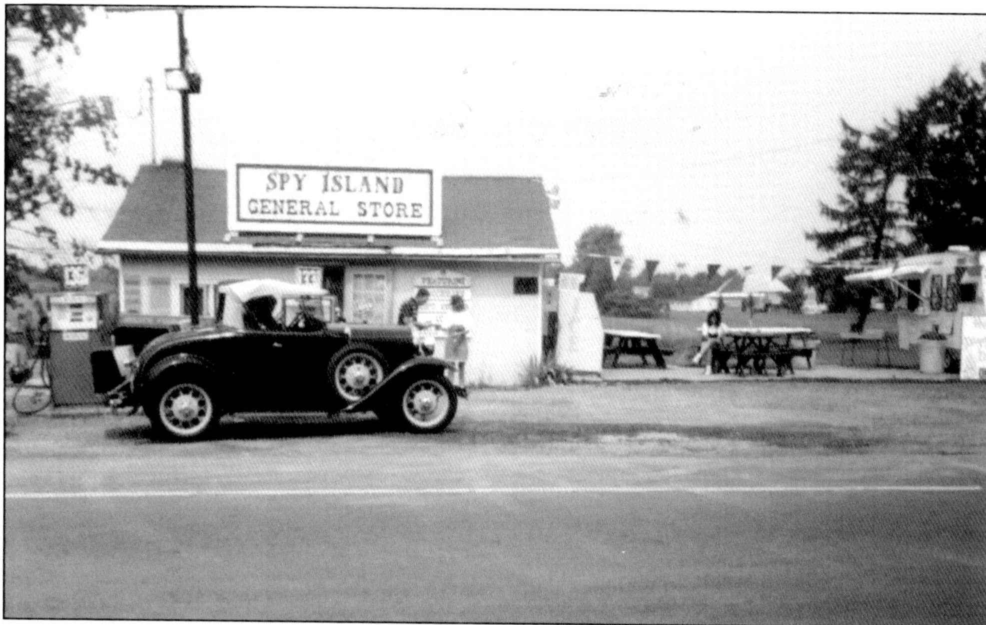

Loran D. Loomis opened a store in the hamlet of Texas in 1846 and continued in business for over 50 years. Various other merchants had similar businesses through the years. One of the others, the Spy Island General Store, opened in 1947 to meet the needs of the local people and the summer residents. Melina and Raymond Rurey bought the store in 1989 and sold it in 1996. The business soon closed. (Courtesy of Melina Rurey.)

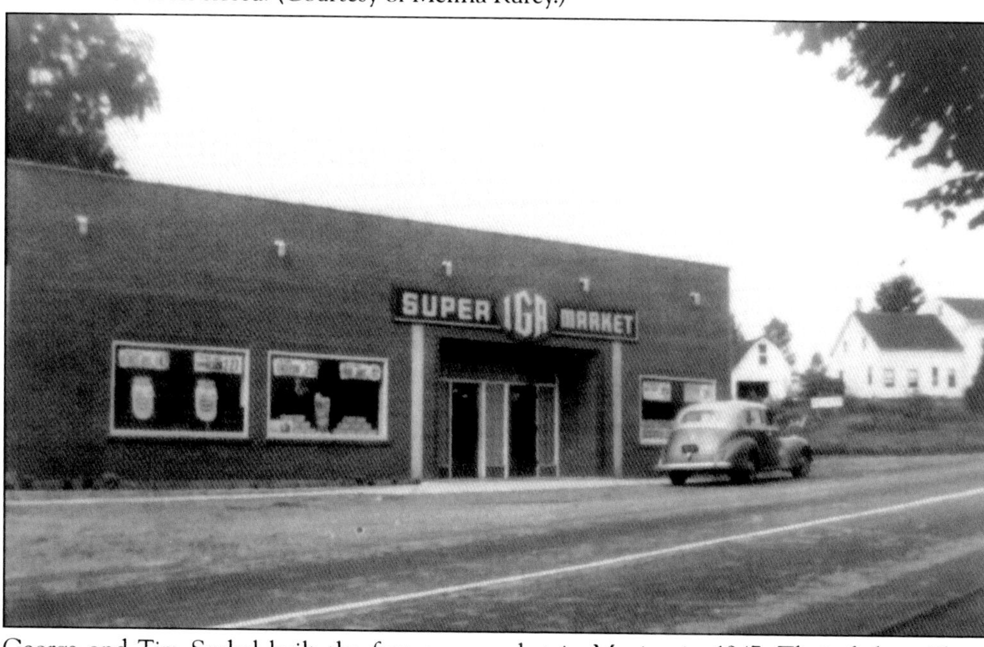

George and Tim Sachel built the first supermarket in Mexico in 1947. Their father, Christ Sachel, bought the property at the forks of the road on West Hill in 1933. The business started with a gasoline station and became a convenience store in 1942. The supermarket was built on the north side of the business. In 1969, Edward and Alice Nykaza bought the IGA supermarket and opened Eddie's Big M, which later moved to Main Street.

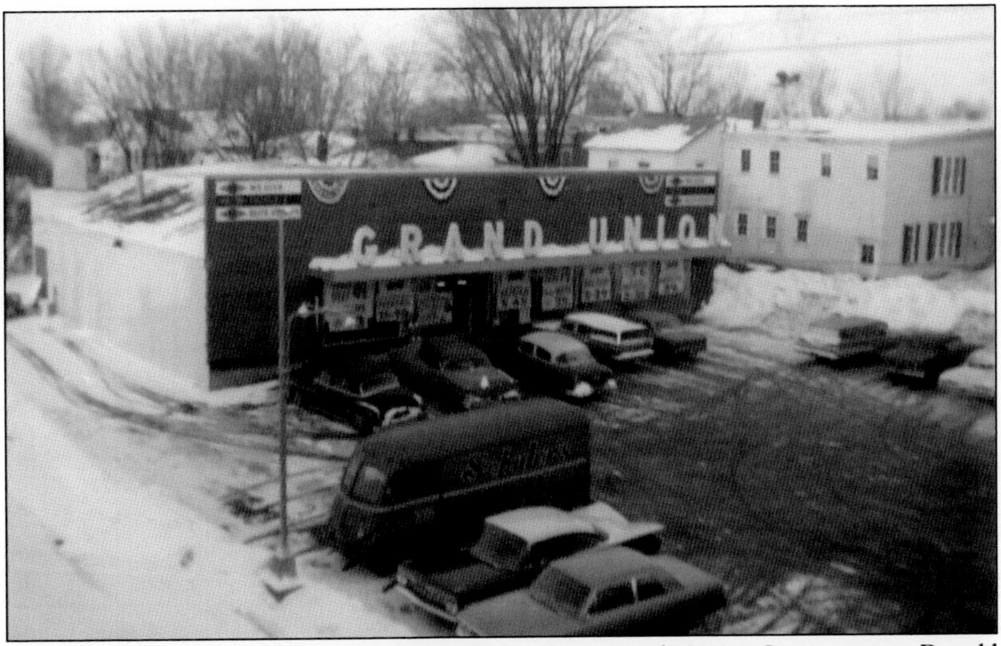

The Grand Union was the second supermarket in the town of Mexico. Store manager Donald Pierce and area supervisor Donald Streeter were both very active in the community and were sorely missed when the store closed in 1975. The Mexico Volunteer Fire Department bought the building and moved the fire equipment there after extensive renovation. (Courtesy of the Barry Haynes collection.)

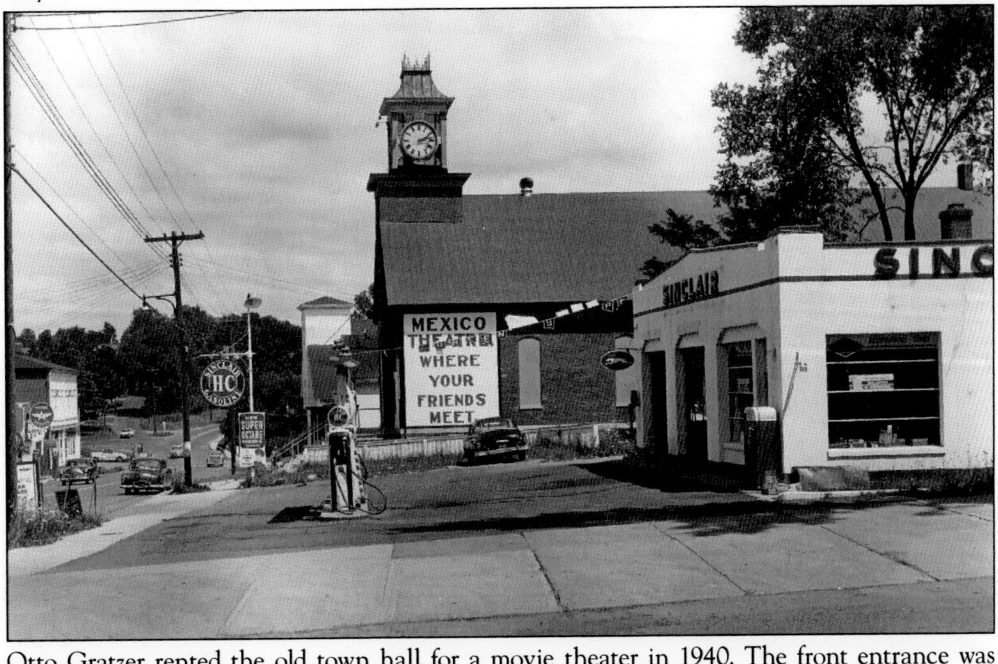

Otto Gratzer rented the old town hall for a movie theater in 1940. The front entrance was moved to the middle, and the two side doors became signboards. The theater was popular with young and old, especially at Christmas when the elementary school students were treated to a free movie. The theater was sold to the Masonic lodge in 1967.

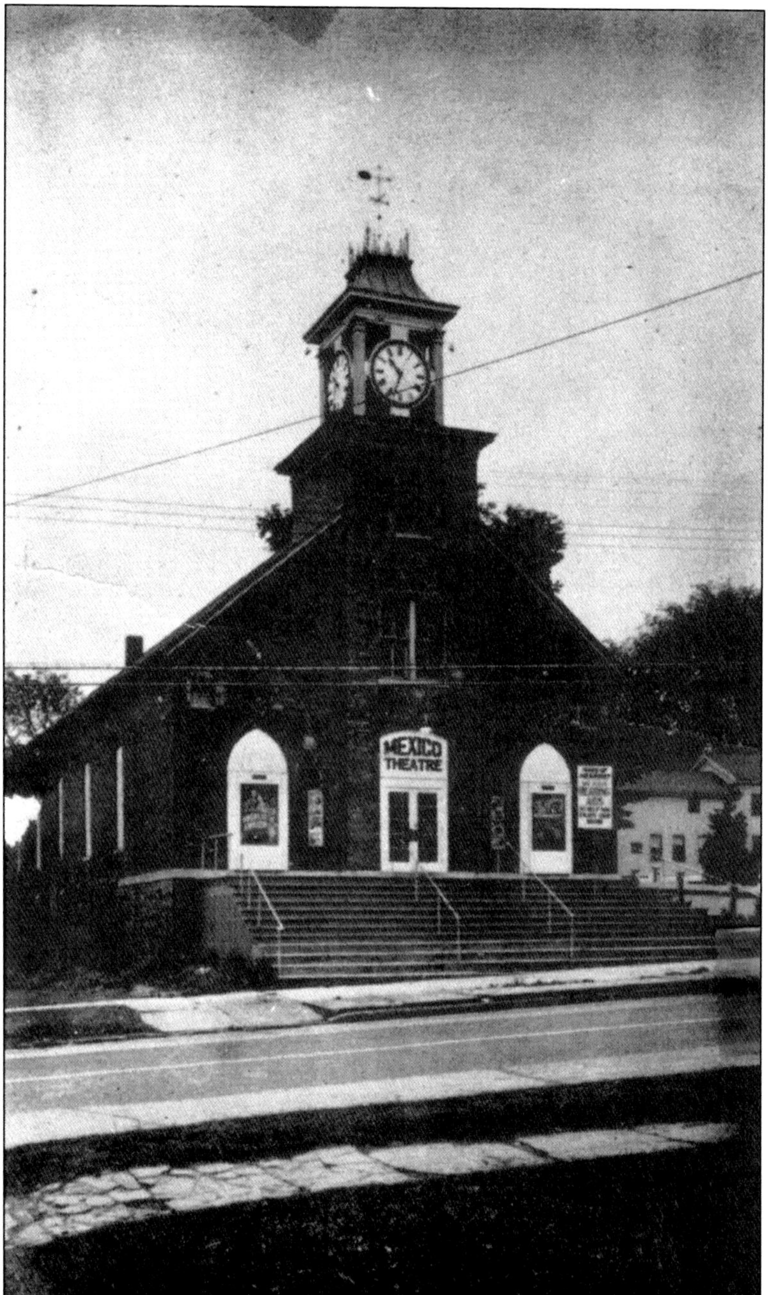

The people of Mexico voted in 1940 to allow a movie theater to open in the town hall. The town hall was built in 1878 and 1879. It was named Washington Hall and was used for the yearly town meetings, lectures, local and traveling theater groups, balls, political meetings, roller-skating, basketball, and even graduation. When Otto Gratzer proposed a movie theater, the people were not sure, even though it was seldom used after 1940. Through the years, the theater was used for war bond drives, and at Christmas the elementary children were treated to a free movie. Times change, and the movie theater closed in 1966. The Masons purchased the building in 1967 and sold it back to the town and village in 2007. (Author's collection.)

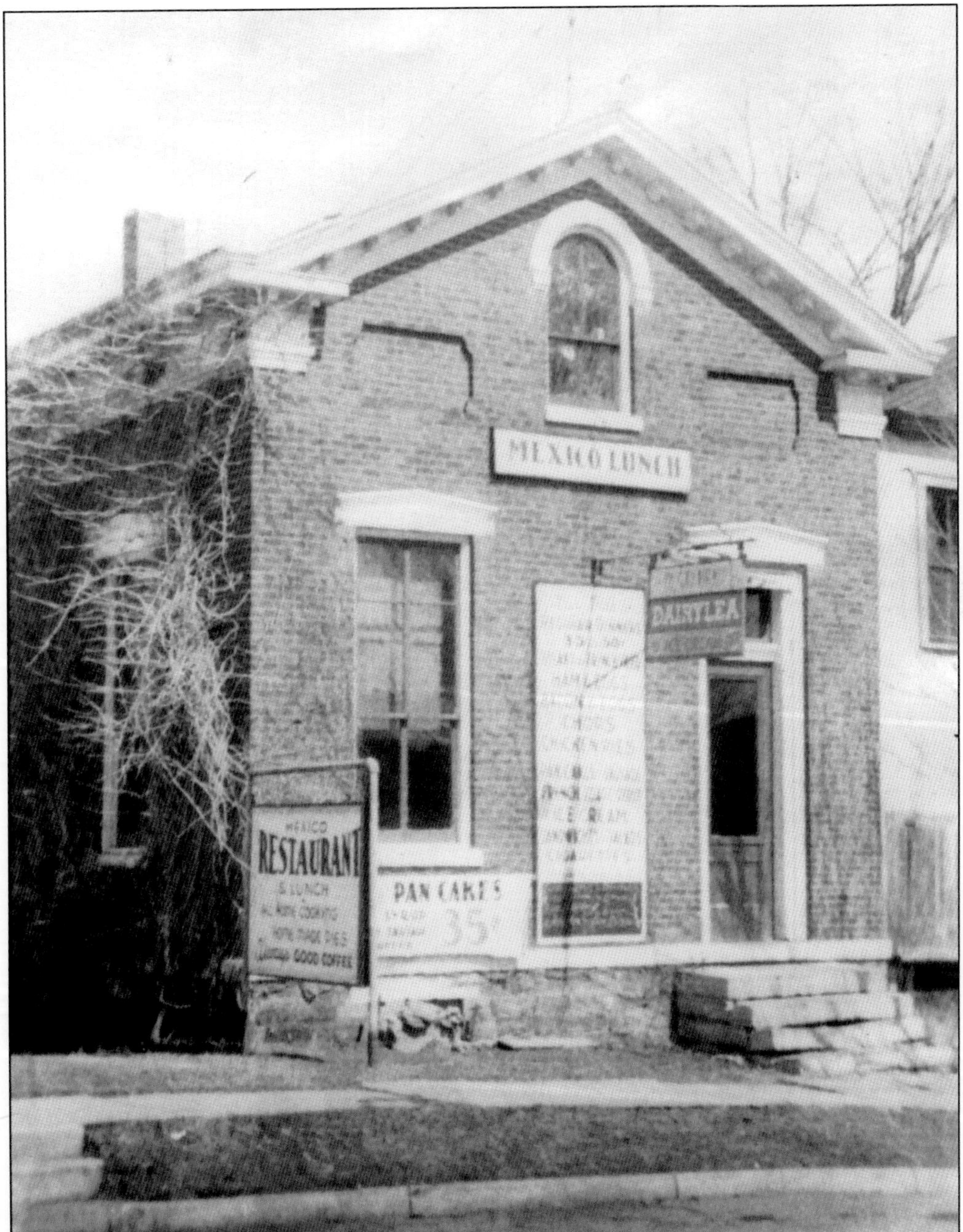

James S. Chandler and Leonard Ames Jr. built the brick bank on Main Street in 1865 across from the present location of the Kwik-fill gasoline station. Ames withdrew from the firm, and Chandler continued until 1867. Other bankers used the building until 1900 when the business was sold to Charles H. Peck, who moved the business to Jefferson Street in 1903. Mexico Lunch Room began in 1934 with $100 and room to seat 14 customers. Seating was increased as the business grew. The building remained unchanged through the years, except for the front window. As the owners changed, the building was used for a bank, a law office, Backus Pedigree, the lunch room, and Farm Production Credit. It was also the village office until 1996.